'A much-appreciated colleague, supervisor, and teacher, and a much-beloved and committed mentor, Dr Claire Bacha has written a suggestive and stimulating study of what group analysts today conceptualise as the tripartite matrix of various kinds of social systems, including societies, organisations, groups and persons. Sensitive to the restraints and constraints of the external world and the development of it, each chapter in this highly accessible book demonstrates the importance of recognising and working with socially unconscious processes'.

Earl Hopper, *PhD, Psychoanalyst, Group Analyst and organisational consultant in private practice in London, Editor of the New International Library of Group Analysis.*

'From despair to hope, Claire Bacha extends Foulkes' dictum that the individual is social to the core by weaving a fascinating story linking "Our Time of Monsters" that is now, to the possibilities of the "Group Dimension" that is our possible future. She explores the contributions that our economic system, evolutionary history and neuropsychology have made to our present state while emphasising the importance of learning to trust the possibilities of dialogue in social settings to change our future. This book suggests new thinking!'

Teresa von Sommaruga Howard, *architect and group analyst; initiator of a series of ongoing Creative Large Group Dialogue workshops*

'Bacha has attempted to do what she wants us all to do – to reflect upon where we have arrived (in Western society at least) and take responsibility as individuals embedded within the social community to eschew polarisations which lead to unending disagreement, inequality and violence and instead work together for the good of all. To embrace economics, sociology, affective neuroscience and the psychodynamic psychotherapies – particularly psychoanalysis and group analysis – within one text is a bold task. You may not agree with all she says but hopefully you will be inspired to think and then act rather than be cowed by the enormity of the forces that seem arrayed against our essential humanity as lived with and through each other.'

Dr John Hook, *Consultant Medical Psychotherapist*

'A clarion call indeed, for greater psycho-social mindedness and a warning of the awful monstrosities we nurture when we ignore/neglect the true intertextuality of our lives.'

Professor Nick Barwick, *Guildhall School of Music and Drama, London*

'Some books are "life projects", even if they did not start out as such – life in the obvious sense of completed over a long stretch of personal time, project in the spirit of an ambitions, integrative contribution, across disciplines. This book has "Claire" written all over it – passionate, committed and unorthodox, in the best sense. I visualise her talking about it, in dialogue with its readers, but sadly her last breath came before she saw it in print. The love of friends and colleagues made sure it sees the light of day.'

Martin Weegmann, *Clinical Psychologist, Group Analyst, author of Novel Connections: Between Literature and Psychotherapy*

The Group Dimension

Capitalism, Group Analysis, and the World Yet to Come

Claire Bacha

LONDON AND NEW YORK

Designed cover image: © Claire Bacha, 'Sylphs'

First published 2025
by Routledge
4 Park Square, Milton Park, Abingdon, Oxon OX14 4RN

and by Routledge
605 Third Avenue, New York, NY 10158

Routledge is an imprint of the Taylor & Francis Group, an informa business

© 2025 Claire Bacha

The right of Claire Bacha to be identified as author of this work has been asserted in accordance with sections 77 and 78 of the Copyright, Designs and Patents Act 1988.

All rights reserved. No part of this book may be reprinted or reproduced or utilised in any form or by any electronic, mechanical, or other means, now known or hereafter invented, including photocopying and recording, or in any information storage or retrieval system, without permission in writing from the publishers.

Trademark notice: Product or corporate names may be trademarks or registered trademarks, and are used only for identification and explanation without intent to infringe.

British Library Cataloguing-in-Publication Data
A catalogue record for this book is available from the British Library

ISBN: 978-103-2-39514-2 (hbk)
ISBN: 978-103-2-39513-5 (pbk)
ISBN: 978-100-3-35008-8 (ebk)

DOI: 10.4324/9781003350088

Typeset in Times New Roman
by codeMantra

Contents

List of illustrations ix
Forewords x
Preface xii
Acknowledgements xv

Introduction: The evolution of capitalism and
the group dimension 1

PART I
Capitalism and the time of monsters 9

1 It was not always like this 11
2 Keynes and Keynesianism 32

PART II
Neoliberalism: Hayek and the Mont Pelerin Society 51

3 Hayek as a response to Keynes 53
4 The strange fruits of neoliberalism 66

PART III
**The story of how humans evolved is the story of the
group dimension** 77

5 Freedom before humans 79
6 Early humans 93

PART IV
The social brain   105

7 Jaak Panksepp and his unique contribution   107

8 The basic feelings: Seeking, Fear, Rage   115

9 The relational feelings: Lust and Care   132

10 Panic/Grief, Play, integration and social homeostasis   145

PART V
Figurations and groups   159

11 Seeking is the foundational feeling of life   161

12 The role of groups in everyday life: Synthesis with Panksepp   180

Index   *193*

Illustrations

Figure 1 'Storm in the markets'　　　　　　　　　　9
Figure 2 'Mountain'　　　　　　　　　　　　　　51
Figure 3 'On our way'　　　　　　　　　　　　　77
Figure 4 'Gobleki Tepe man'　　　　　　　　　　105
Figure 5 'Woman, Life, Freedom'　　　　　　　　159
All photos taken and transformed by Claire Bacha

Forewords

I

Claire Bacha was a maverick. She was an intellectual, an independent-minded person, a non-conformist, an unorthodox, free-spirited, strong powerful rebellious woman, who lived life on her own terms. Claire was born in Chicago, USA and moved to Brazil in her twenties, married Edmar Bacha and completed a Masters in Political Science. She arrived from Brazil in her late twenties to Manchester University to do a PhD in Sociology titled 'The Emergence of Finance Capital in Brazil 1930s to 1970s'. During her years living in Manchester, she was a student, she became a single-parent, a baker and went on to train in psychotherapy and group analysis.

Claire was political throughout her life. In the 1980s, she would hand out the *Socialist Worker* in Chorlton precinct and take part in political demonstrations in Manchester. She would engage people in conversations about politics, economics and sociology wherever she went.

Claire always worked and she worked hard. In the 1980s she began training as a psychotherapist while working at MIND in Ashton-under-Lyne. Claire was passionate about her work and devoted her mind, energy and time to her psychotherapy training, her clinical practice and to Group Analysis. She started her Prestwich-based private practice in the 1990s.

Claire was energetic, fiercely intelligent and strong spirited in everything she did and was always seeking to find interest in the world around her: from understanding humans, to politics, to music, to art. She created her own abstract expressionist photographic art.

Claire's main passion towards the end of her life was writing this book, *The Group Dimension*, and it is her life's work. It is a culmination of conversations, reading and creative thinking about politics, economics, sociology, human evolution, neuroscience, psychotherapy, and Group Analysis.

Karin Bacha, September 2023

II

Claire told us that she had been working bit-by-bit on 'The Group Dimension' for 25 years. She managed to complete it a few weeks before her death, and was greatly reassured that colleagues would see it through to publication. The breadth of its endeavour and the richness of its references are a reflection of the Claire we knew.

Group Analysis North has much to thank Claire for. She was not only there at the beginning, but was instrumental in its conception. She was one of a small group of fellow aspiring group analysts in the North West of England who wanted to continue their group analytic training. This became the IGA block training Qualifying Course in Manchester. In 2019, near to a hundred group analysts, students, ex-students, friends and family gathered together to celebrate it being thirty years since the start of that Qualifying Course training. Claire never wavered in her staunch and robust advocacy of Group Analysis North and the Manchester trainings. You won't find an element of Group Analysis North that Claire wasn't involved in at some stage, being in that first cohort of Qualifying Course trainees, an early member of the Board, and working on the Introductory Course and the Advanced Course. Then later, she was at the heart of the shift from the courses being led by London-trained Group Analysts to being led and developed by homegrown ones. She was Training Group Analyst, Supervisor and Seminar Leader. As well as making history, Claire held and documented much of it. She was a prolific reader and writer, with papers appearing in *Group Analysis* as recently as December 2022.

As well as her commitment and her wisdom, she brought creativity, lightness and playfulness to the work. Her interests were wide and varied and this is evident in *The Group Dimension* where she captures the heart of group analysis with its far-reaching roots in sociology, anthropology, neuroscience, philosophy, economics and politics.

After leaving the courses in 2021 she continued to bring her thinking, experience and determination to other group analytic projects. One of these was the IGA Power, Position and Privilege Working Group. She had a long-standing and compassionate commitment to anti-oppressive and anti-racist practice. She was known and respected for being able to stay with difficult conversations. Claire held her beliefs and her convictions deeply. Amongst many other things, she will be remembered as someone able to hold her position robustly, and bear you holding yours; significantly without retaliation, resentment or being destructive.

Towards the end of *The Group Dimension* Claire says she hopes that each one of her readers will be able to take away something new and important to grow in their internal and external groups, to help them towards 'liberation'. Those of us at Group Analysis North are privileged to have worked and learned alongside Claire. I am glad that, through this book, many more will have the opportunity to experience her intellect, her creativity, her energy, her compassion, her warmth, and her fundamental belief in the group.

Debra Nash, Group Analysis North (Courses Director 2015–2022)

Preface

The Group Dimension carries with it and insists upon the elements in its provocative subtitle. The book is very clearly about capitalism as a political-economic system of exploitation and oppression that seems always to have always been with us but actually, as Claire Bacha shows us, has only existed in the blink of an eye in the complete span of life on this planet. It is sometimes said that it is now, with impending climate disaster and the failure of anti-capitalist movements, that it is easier to imagine the end of the world than the end of capitalism. If we examine the history of life on earth and the development of consciousness and the civilizational accomplishments of human beings we will discover that there are deep obstacles to change, but also deep resources.

Claire Bacha is concerned with our deep biological and evolutionary history not in order confirm that things can never change – as if this very short-lived political-economic system is immutable and universal – but precisely the reverse, to explain how the 'group dimension' provides us with the capacities to learn from history in order not to repeat it, and to learn from each other. That is why, not incidentally, this book is, in some important ways, not only a collective project in the sense that the ideas have been shared and discussed, but also that a number of attempts to explain and find a way out of contemporary modes of being that are so self-destructive are subject to such close study.

This latest twist on capitalism, the neoliberal version now being deliberately implemented or unconsciously endorsed globally, is, for Claire Bacha, qualitatively worse, posing threats that we must grapple with if we are to move on. Neoliberalism ties together three elements in policy and ideology; there is, first the stripping away of social and welfare support (the very context in which group analysis as a therapeutic practice thrived) and there is, second, the isolation of people from each other so they imagine that there are only individual solutions to the social problems we face (the very predicament that group analysis helps us reflect upon and surmount) and there is, third, an intensification of state power in order to enforce obedience (a ramping up of disciplinary procedures that is inimical to the founders and practitioners of group analysis).

This neoliberal nightmare is, Claire Bacha tells us, the 'time of monsters'. These monsters are, in some parts of the world, already active and efficient in crushing hopes as well as practical solidarity, enforcing segregation and separation of each of us from others, sabotaging what group analysis patiently attempts to put in place and, in the process, betraying the 'group dimension' that makes us human. We cannot speak of this neoliberal time of monsters in late capitalism unless we also speak of alternatives, and Claire Bacha conjures this yearning for something better, something that is in tune with the group dimension at the heart of our nature, with the phrase 'the world yet to come'.

And then, contrary to expectations, the book engages with a series of arguments that are not usually included in a book that proclaims its radical stance on the cover. Now we discover, in the course of the patient careful explanation in the five parts of the book of how we have come to this pass, that we need to learn from what has been said from different perspectives about our past and our trajectory, learn from those who are often assumed to have nothing to say. The argument that 'it has not always been like this', an argument that gestures to what is valuable in our collective history, is followed by an exploration of what are sometimes side-stepped as 'reformist' perspectives (and here the work of John Maynard Keynes takes centre-stage) and then, even more surprisingly, a close reading of one of the architects of neoliberalism, Friedrich August von Hayek.

This controversial figure was admired by Margaret Thatcher, as Claire Bacha points out, and taken as warrant for the famous statement that 'there is no such thing as society,' that 'there are only individual men and women and their families.' But you will find buried in F. A. Hayek's work, and Claire is determined to find it and show it to us, that, just as in the work of Adam Smith, the nemesis of Karl Marx, there is a 'social' element presumed in the account. How could this not be the case if the 'group dimension' is an enduring possibility and requisite for building any kind of society whatsoever, even a society that disavows what is social and resolutely focuses only on what is individual about us.

Claire Bacha then embeds this account of what is assumed but hidden in the theories of society that are today so dominant in the popular imagination – ideologically so, she will say – in an even more ambitious project, to read the group dimension into prehistory, into evolutionary history and into our very biology. We are embodied beings, but we need to ask what those bodies afford us; not only competition and the ideologically potent images of nature red in tooth and claw, but also the possibility of relating to each other and supporting each other. That is foundational to what it is to engage in group analysis, but group analysis as a therapeutic practice needs to learn from traditions of research – including neurobiological research – that will enrich it, we could say, enable it to realise itself.

The message repeated over and again in these accounts of our evolutionary heritage and then in the work on wired in affective states that are usually, in ideological common sense and, unfortunately, in some professional psychotherapeutic trainings, this message is reduced to what are, for shorthand, in a mistranslation of Freud's work, to 'instincts', is that we need to read and learn rather than exclude and shun such research. Pride of place, you will read, is given to the work of Jaak Panksepp, and this, you will find, poses some challenges for how we think about what we are as social beings. However, it does not contradict what we might want to hold onto – the thought that we are social beings – but rather confirms it; it is there too that we will find the 'group dimension'.

Then, after this conceptual journey, we are in a position to appreciate and develop what we have, in our trainings perhaps, already learnt about group analysis. Claire Bacha reminds us of what we have learnt, but reframes it in light of the narrative she has been steadily accumulating through the book. These are careful and generous readings of economics, evolution and neuropsychological research that are designed to enable us also to engage thoughtfully with ideas we disagree with. Claire Bacha will not leave those domains of work to those who would close down dialogue, but, instead, she insists on dialogue.

This book is as much about 'dialogue' as it is about the 'group dimension'. Dialogue is intrinsic to the group dimension, and the learning and thinking and reflective appreciation of different arguments that Claire Bacha brings to these many different authors is attentive to contradiction, not in order to disparage and disregard but in order to engage in a dialogue with them. In this sense, the book is about 'dialogue' but it also enacts it in the structure and flow of the book. This is a dialogue that shows us how dialogue might be done, how it must be done in the group dimension and how it might be done in group analysis. There is close involvement with ideas precisely in order to enable considered detachment from them.

This is an extraordinary book by an extraordinary woman. Claire Bacha was someone I knew as a colleague, one of what Freud once referred to as the 'mad horde', those who take transference and resistance seriously in their therapeutic work, and as a comrade in political movements. She was a feminist, bringing that sensibility to the readings she makes of many authors who are not, by any stretch of the imagination, feminist, but she has the imagination to imagine a world in which they too participate in constructive dialogue instead of being mobilised as weapons in favour of racist and hetero-patriarchal capitalism. Most recently we participated together in 'Zero Covid' online meetings that attempted to grapple with what the pandemic was doing to us. She was a practising senior Group Analyst until shortly before she died, but she had a healthy suspicion of the 'psy' professions.

Claire held to her commitment to 'dialogue' while also maintaining a dialogue with those who were suspicious of it, as well as those who were suspicious of the ideas she was busily mining from the books she describes here in this book. For Claire, dialogue included disagreement, and disagreement with this book will be at the heart of her legacy, enabling the 'group dimension' to come to life among us.

Ian Parker, Manchester Psychoanalytic Matrix

Acknowledgements

Claire would have made this list of acknowledgements much longer, and we have not been able to do justice to the many people that Claire discussed iterations of the manuscript with; this because it was a collective project as well as an individual accomplishment. Erica Burman, Suryia Nayak and Ian Parker assembled the final manuscript from an almost complete version that Claire entrusted to us shortly before she died. Claire had asked Ian to write the preface. We have borne in mind comments from colleagues to whom Claire also sent the manuscript including Nick Barwick, Isobel Conlon, Sue Einhorn, Alasdair Forrest, Matthew Rich-Tolsma and Teresa von Sommaruga Howard. Susannah Frearson at Routledge has been a very helpful editor. Many thanks to Karin Bacha for her help in assisting with practical arrangements with the publisher and for providing her mother's images, of which we have included some, as Claire wished, in the book.

Introduction
The evolution of capitalism and the group dimension

My aim in this work is to call attention to a whole dimension of human life that has been obscured by the way that capitalism has evolved, particularly in its present form of neoliberalism. This dimension is not, in itself, new. Groups have been ubiquitous in human life. However, general knowledge of groups has become unconscious, lost and distorted into a dimension that is always there, but discounted and denied. In order to be able to leave neoliberalism and the time of monsters, consciousness and knowledge about the group dimension is an essential ingredient in the battle between different conceptions of the world.

The group dimension is a lens through which to view human life and the products of human work. In this sense, I will contribute only marginally to the critiques of capitalism, colonialism and globalisation. I will also contribute only marginally to the many ideas about how the world to come might look in the future. My focus in this work is on improving general consciousness and understanding of how knowledge, feelings and thoughts in the group dimension come together to realise a potential transformation from the staleness and fear in the time of monsters to the lively creativity needed to lead into the world yet to come. This transformation, from alienation to action, is a necessary ingredient of the ideas that can motivate processes of change from the time of monsters to the world yet to come.

Dialogue, a better democracy and intersectionality

Developing a better democracy is the key. Majority-rule democracy is clearly not good enough to preserve even a democratic facade in the time of monsters. A democracy that can be more diverse and caring of minorities and individuals cannot be born without a sense of being able to disagree and enter into conflict while also remaining in a safe environment. Majority-rule democracy has never left room or developed containment for disagreement and conflict outside the market-driven ideas about negotiation and compromise. The promise of a better democracy is inherent in the group dimension. The group dimension emphasises the need to contain difference and conflict over even seemingly irreconcilable and paradoxical conflicts of interest. The group dimension values the coherence of differences and conflicts over the cohesion of sameness. In the group dimension the processes of coherence of differences and conflicts is called dialogue.

DOI: 10.4324/9781003350088-1

In order to have a better democracy, dialogue in the group dimension requires ever more precise ideas around the questions of who is included in 'we' identities. The questions of who 'we' are and what 'we' want as individuals, nations, cultures and religions are not obvious when 'we', humanity, are losing, or have already lost, the talent for speaking to each other and reaching conclusions together.

Shouting opinions at each other from respective silos and echo chambers is not dialogue. Instead, dialogue requires a deeper sense of interpersonal and transpersonal connections between the people attempting to talk to each other. These connections take time to build. They also require interest and curiosity as to what others think, feel and why they think and feel these things. Dialogue requires the time and effort needed to be able not to know, to see things differently and to think new thoughts. With better and better dialogue, democracy can flourish from the 'grass roots' of the bottom up as opposed to the neoliberal formulations of top-down authority and compliance. Even conflicting 'we's can combine to find the best ways forward from any particular moment in dialogue, given personal depth and time.

The ideas of the group dimension cut across basic capitalist and neoliberal ideologies. If emphasis shifts from structures to processes, then the processes of dialogue open up the possibility that the world yet to come will always have a partially indeterminate future. The importance of the differences between structures like capitalism and socialism, together with the differences between right and left political factions will dim. Instead, political, economic and personal processes will look more like permanent reform and/or permanent revolution. The dialogue processes allow for deeper understandings between self and others which are ever more inclusive. This process is sometimes referred to as the processes of intersectionality. Only through dialogue can economics and politics become inclusive.

Questioning fallacies

In order to approach dialogue as the necessary underlying dimension of individual, social and political life in the world to come, many of the assumptions and thought processes that are taken for granted in the time of monsters must be questioned and revised. This may be thought of as part of a process of internal and external decolonisation. Economics will continue to be important but less important than humanity, for example. The state will be important, but policies will be determined from the bottom up and not from the top down. Freedom and equality can co-exist, indeed, must co-exist. In the group dimension, polarisations created in neoliberalism become reasons for dialogue and not reasons for contempt, conflict or war.

The first fallacy of the time of monsters to be questioned has to do with process and structure. The mantras from the time of monsters include: 'It has always been like this,' and 'Poverty has always been with us'. It has not always been like this. The emphasis on timeless and inevitable structures provides a false sense of strength, security and control. Structures are important. However, in the time of monsters, it is the structures and the processes that hold the structures together that are leading to the destruction of humanity through climate and environmental changes, and technology. 'We', as in humanity, are running out of time. We may already have run out of time. Many people are now feeling this as an emergency and others are turning away in helplessness, alienation, disavowal and denial. Neither of these positions will enable the birth of a world to come from the present time of monsters.

The second fallacy of the time of monsters to be questioned has to with the assumption that feelings must be suppressed in order to think clearly. There is now much evidence that feelings are important in all aspects of life, not only the intimate aspects. Modern economic, political and employment processes are based on 'nudging' peoples' feelings in the desired directions as acts of compliance. The importance of feelings, certainly in regard to creating and maintaining dialogue, may not be quite as obvious. However, feelings are the universal motivator and director of thoughts. Without a conscious basis in feelings, thoughts can go around in circles, ending, again, in denial, polarisation and conflict. When feelings are not sufficiently recognised and reflected upon, they come out in unexpected, always confusing and, usually, destructive, ways. In the time of monsters and without a constant and conscious reflection based on feelings, humans are at the mercy of 'nudging' and manipulation by the mass media, employment and sales techniques.

Further, 'we,' as in humanity, do not feel feelings or have thoughts on our own. The third fallacy that keeps humanity stuck without being able to leave the time of monsters to give birth to the world yet to come is the assumption of individualism. Individualism is a fallacy that assumes that humans exist essentially isolated inside their heads. This assumption obscures the importance of the group dimension in both feelings and thoughts. Individualism also obscures the importance of feelings and the necessity to be in touch with them in the interests of better human interactions, politics and democratic practices in the dialogue process. The fallacy of individualism, linked to a particular concept of freedom, keeps people from being in touch with themselves and with each other. It makes dialogue difficult, if not impossible.

The identification of these three fallacies – structures over processes, thoughts over feelings and individuals over pluralities – emphasises how increased consciousness of the group dimension can make a political difference. In other words, an increased consciousness of the reality of the group dimension of processes, feelings and pluralities is a powerful and necessary ingredient for breaking the hold of the time of monsters, leading to a different, more human, world yet to come.

Decolonising from neoliberalism

The reality of the group dimension becomes clearly present when the stronghold of the fallacies of neoliberal capitalism are broken. In order to start to leave the time of monsters behind it is crucial to have in mind and body some version of a better future. This book on the group dimension aims to support a hopeful vision of the future by encouraging consciousness and knowledge of the group dimension through feelings and dialogue.

The group dimension, in fact, has always been with humans, providing a foundation for all human activities. The group dimension is a level of perception and understanding which lies beneath the cognitive, individual and logical dimensions that constitute 'common sense'. Consciousness of the group dimension comes from a sense of beginning to perceive and understand feelings, thoughts, relationships and actions of self and others that have seemed mysterious or inexplicable in the past. Words that describe the group dimension might include 'weird' or 'uncanny'. This is because the group dimension comes from the deep past, the evolution of human biology and human biologically-intense connection. The group dimension is the antithesis of the lack of connection to others in the time of monsters. Humans do not exist individually and alone. In the time of monsters, 'we', as in humanity, are losing our consciousness of this dimension that defines our humanity above all else. Although there will be much in this book that is new to readers, most of the knowledge here is already known, though, perhaps, not always known in conscious minds.

Because the origins of the group dimension are in deep evolutionary history, the term 'group' takes on a very wide meaning. There are all kinds of groups. Some are large, some are small, some are face to face, some never see each other. The family is a group, but only one kind of group. Looking at history and evolution through the lens of the group as a dimension changes the way that history and evolution are seen, as well as the way that groups are seen. For example, it becomes apparent that the ideas around the evolution of capitalism and colonialism in the group dimension include a sense of how everything is connected to everything else. Both capitalism and colonialism have historical starting points in Britain before moving to reproduce essentially the same capitalism in the rest of the world through the colonial processes and structures. Capitalism cannot be known accurately without its method of reproduction, which is colonialism in all its different forms, including the present form of globalisation.

In the group dimension, beginnings and their particular historical evolutions are important above and beyond the structures and functions of institutions in the present. Racism, misogyny, homophobia, ableism and heteronormative patriarchy are all part of the specific origin and evolution of capitalism through colonialisation. This means that inequality, exclusivity, capitalism and colonialism are inextricably bound up with each other through their specific origin and evolutionary history. This is not always apparent in terms of ahistorical structures, functions and other kinds of historical theories.

In the group dimension, it is apparent that capitalism, with the inequality of capitalists and workers at its heart, cannot be reformed out of the time of monsters through changes in structures and functions by themselves. Permanent reform and permanent revolution to lead out of the time of monsters will only take place when inclusivity and diversity are guaranteed by processes of constant review and dialogue from the grass roots. Only this constant process of dialogue will be able to contain the differences and conflicts from the time of monsters. This containment is needed to produce better forms of democracy than the present forms of majority rule within states and territories.

Decolonising from the neoliberal ideologies is not easy or simple. It has costs as well as gains. Decolonising takes courage, energy and knowledge. In the group dimension, neoliberal capitalism and its consequences live inside everyone. However, it is the colonisation of minds that keeps humanity in danger in the time of monsters. Decolonisation is a necessity, not a choice.

Dialogue in groups creates internal integration

The group dimension is where the individual, social and political dimensions come together. In groups, individual internal relationships between aspects of self are inextricably linked with external relationships with others. Integrated interpersonal dialogues in groups and integrated internal dialogues are, in fact, identical processes. These processes do not happen all the time or in all groups. However, when they do happen, the result is the creation of more integrated individuals at the same time as the creation of stronger groups.

In the time of monsters where groups, even the family, are devalued, the opposite of internal and external integration occurs. Individuals are weakened and driven mad by social phenomena such as the breakdown of extended and nuclear families, illness, poverty, deprivation and fear. In the group dimension, mental ill health and other kinds of madness come from frustration and deprivation of caring relationships, not from inside individuals, chemical imbalances or genetic factors. Mental ill health and madness are treated primarily with chemicals in the time of monsters. However, in the group dimension, it is understood that it is only caring human relationships that can provide real emotional healing. In the time of monsters, this aspect of healing is best known and understood in the knowledge silos of the 'psy' professions of psychotherapy, psychoanalysis and group analysis. In the group dimension, this knowledge of human emotions and relationships must become part of knowledge of self and of other people in everyday life outside the knowledge silos.

Dialogue produces and sustains the sense of internal integration that is crucial to emotional wellbeing. In the time of monsters, the politics of fear and the technologies of social splitting, aggregation and massification promote conflict, violence, emotional breakdown and relationship breakdown in many people. These people are the more sensitive. In the group dimension, the more sensitive people are the ones who feel the emotional costs of social deprivations and faults. In the group dimension, emotional and relationship ill health indicate where the processes that are destructive to humanity lie. These are the voices that need to be heard and amplified, not silenced, invalidated or shut out.

The group dimension, in other words, links the other dimensions and levels of life experiences from the most personal to the most political. These are the links that need to be made, felt and understood in order to decolonise from neoliberalism and to leave the time of monsters. It is only when these links are understood that individual and collective thinking will be clear and the best choices can be made from moment to moment.

These ideas may sound utopian, strange or at least unfamiliar on a cognitive or logical level. However, the group dimension is a reality, as I will show in the chapters that follow. Knowing about the group aspects of reality will help readers to understand and take more effective action in their individual, social, political and historical contexts. This is the hopefulness of this book. If it has not always been like this time of monsters, it need not always be like this. Self-knowledge, understanding, communication and integration bring a sense of being able to belong, to be oneself with others. In dialogue, groups can work out what is best to do next. This is the real freedom.

Chapters and methodologies

The variety of groups is an empirical reality. That the group dimension is also a reality can only be known indirectly. This is one of the challenges of the group dimension. It is known through its consequences in the knowledge, feelings and thoughts that do not make common sense. The group dimension has its own logic, which is knowable. Knowledge of the group dimension cuts across academic disciplines. The aim of this book is to introduce the concept of the group dimension to a general readership.

There are five parts. Each part is a snapshot of an aspect of the group dimension in depth. It is in the combination of the five parts of the book that the unity of the group dimension begins to emerge and to be understood enough to be useful. These parts are not exhaustive. These particular parts are meant to make connections between the story of Keynesian and neoliberal capitalist political economy as a description of the time of monsters with elements of knowledge that will lead to a deeper understanding of how the group dimension works mainly beyond consciousness. Each of the five parts can stand alone. However, in the group dimension each part needs the others to complete the main ideas which are, at the same time, political, social, economic and emotional.

These five parts are:

Part I, 'Capitalism and the Time of Monsters', is an in-depth reading of John Maynard Keynes' *General Theory of Employment, Interest and Money*, in the context of the evolution of capitalism in Britain. Reading Keynes in the group dimension brings out very different aspects of Keynes' thought when compared to the usual, more mathematical, interpretations. This unique understanding of Keynes' political economy includes his 'psychological' factors and why these are so important to understanding how the group dimension underlies economic as well as political action. Keynes and the modern labour movement grew up together. This understanding of Keynes is important to the movement and its recognition of the possibilities of the world yet to come.

Part II, 'Neoliberalism, Hayek and the Mont Pelerin Society', charts the evolution of neoliberalism from Keynes with an in-depth reading of Friedrich Hayek's *The Road to Serfdom* and a review of the political and economic effects of neoliberalism in the UK. Neoliberalism is revealed as a rallying cry to the political economic interests that were side-lined by Keynes and his followers in the creation and management of the large and complex state apparatus. The application of neoliberal ideology to the UK has created increasing levels of inequality and real deprivation and poverty. This stage of capitalist evolution is already spreading to the rest of the world.

Part III, 'The Story of Human Evolution is the Story of the Group Dimension' counters the time of monsters to other, much earlier, human times. It has not always been like this. This reading of human evolution in the group dimension emphasises the importance of groups in human history and the ideas around a human biology based in both groups and individuality. A review of the San in South Africa, sometimes known as the 'first people', links early human evolution with the human hunter-gathering clans and tribes that defined humans for over 200,000 years. Even within the silo of early human deep history, there are controversial findings that create a conflict between those who give the group dimension some importance and those who ignore and deny it.

Part IV, 'The Social Brain' is a reading of affective neuroscientist Jaak Panksepp in the group dimension. Panksepp clearly believed in the social brain. His findings of seven foundational feelings shared between humans and animals are capable of defining new approaches to human emotional life relevant to the 'psy' professions, in particular, as well as to people in general. Panksepp defined a new feeling that he called 'Seeking'. In humans Seeking takes on an added importance when combined with its basis in human evolution and contemporary analytic and group analytic knowledge. This particular neuroscientific knowledge brings the group dimension closer to consciousness.

Part V, 'Figurations and Groups' charts how knowledge from the 'psy' professions, especially from group analysis, can greatly improve understandings of relationships in everyday life. With improved understanding and dialogue, relationships, particularly relationships in groups, encourage individuals to reflect on how power, greed and love can damage and repair self and others. These understandings create situations in which dialogue can and must happen in order to facilitate working together, especially in areas of difference and conflicts. This is important for work in organisations and politics, as well as for other kinds of groups, like schools and families.

Evolution

These five parts are held together by two interweaving factors. One is the theory of evolution and the other is a trio of theorists who recognise and use elements of the group dimension in their writings.

Evolution is a basic element of the group dimension. Evolution is not simply history. Much of history is written as a history of knowledge, in the order that discoveries were made. Other kinds of history are written in themes. Of course, history often refers to the more recent times of written history. Evolutionary thinking emphasises the moment-to-moment changes from the past to the present and from the present to the future. This can be about evolution itself, starting from more remote times. Evolution can also refer to the evolution of ideas, discourses and institutions.

The three theorists who also hold the five parts together are Hannah Arendt, Norbert Elias and S. H. Foulkes. Choosing beginnings and charting the evolution of ideas and actions are an important part of the methodologies of both Hannah Arendt and Norbert Elias. Arendt had a background in philosophy and considered herself a political scientist. Elias termed his use of a similar methodology as 'figuration'. Elias founded the discipline of figurational sociology. Figurations are formed by the interactions of individual and groups together in continuous processes. Foulkes founded group analysis, which is essentially a combination of concepts and techniques of therapy in groups, and worked together with Patrick de Maré to found the Group Analytic Society in London. Arendt, like Elias and Foulkes comes from a similar time and tradition as the Italian Marxist Antonio Gramsci. Although Arendt, Elias and Foulkes come from similar times and traditions, they chose different topics and starting points. Elias focused on the civilising process that accompanied the rise of the absolutist state. Foulkes chose Freudian psychoanalysis. Arendt chose to start her work, *The Human Condition*, with the political ideas of the Greeks and Romans.

Part I

Capitalism and the time of monsters

'the old world is dying and the new world struggles be born: Now is the time of monsters'.
Antonio Gramsci (1929)

Figure 1 'Storm in the markets'

DOI: 10.4324/9781003350088-2

Chapter 1

It was not always like this

Antonio Gramsci (1971) wrote his 'Prison Notebooks' between 1929 and 1935. At that time, it seemed to many people that a new world could be born out of revolution in Russia and potential revolution in Germany. This proved false. Germany was saved from revolution by fascism, the ultimate form of the time of monsters. Soviet Russia was isolated. The unequal relationship of capital and labour in capitalism evolved into neoliberal capitalism. Communism and socialism have not fulfilled their potential for equality and freedom. The birth of a new world outside of capitalism is yet to come.

Gramsci identified an ideological struggle. This ideological struggle, a 'battle between different conceptions of the world', was at the root of the inability of an economic force, labour, to translate itself into a political force that is capable of overturning the old capitalist structures and processes. Capitalism has evolved since Gramsci. The ideas about the world yet to come and the means to bring it about have also evolved. It is now apparent that capitalist inequality has meant increasing costs to life, human potential and environmental balance. It has become apparent, too, that the ideas of democracy and freedom at the basis of modern capitalism are not good enough to sustain humane nations in the social, the political or the economic spheres under the conditions of colonialism and globalisation.

The result is an increased sense of being stuck in a world of monsters, without a clear way into another, more human, world. Feelings of futility and alienation combine with a renewed sense of desperation that the old-world powers continue to profit from old-world ideas in more and more draconian ways. The challenge is to decolonise, move on from the old ideas and to develop ones that can lead the way into a new world. The new world will be without the old-world dominance of the many inequalities inherent in the exploitative relationship between capital and labour and its increasing reliance on coercion and violence.

It is encouraging to remember that neoliberal, globalised capitalism was created historically. Capitalism had a beginning and it has an end. In between, capitalism has shaped the world environment. On the one hand, capitalism has created both wealth and poverty, on the other, capitalism has also created the nation state in the interests of capital-owning classes and class fractions. Ideas about economics stem from ideas about the capitalist nation state. Capitalism created everyone and is part of us. Capitalism has shaped power and powerlessness, as well as all relationships with ourselves and with others.

Humans have created capitalism but capitalism has also created humans. The present form of capitalism was formed by historical and social forces. These forces are no more than the product of people working with and against each other. The present form of capitalism was created by an intellectual and political process that can be traced. It was created by modern humans. What humans collectively do next will help to reproduce this form of capitalism or, alternatively, we (as in humanity), can start to build something different. Understanding how this form of capitalism came to be here will help us to know better what we want to do next. The story of how neoliberal capitalism has come to rule human lives is vital to this understanding.

The seeds of capitalism in work

It is tricky to trace social institutions to their origins. The roots of many accepted ways of being are much further back in history than has been imagined. Work, for example, is part of being biologically human. In fact, work can be thought of as a human superpower. Humans are capable of producing more than they consume. This is part of specific human biology. No other animal is able to do this to the extent that humans can. Producing more than we consume is the power that created human communities, where vulnerable mothers and babies are cared for by the group as a whole. Without these communities, human large brains would not have evolved. Only humans, through the work process, produce a value which is surplus to what we need to reproduce ourselves. What happens to this surplus is at the basis of Karl Marx's ideas about different modes of production. Work was around a long time before capitalism. Work, production and creation are essential aspects of the human condition.

In the capitalist mode of production, a worker sells their labour to someone else for money. As a result of this transaction, the worker becomes one of the factors of capitalist production. The person who buys labour and organises production by providing the other elements needed for production becomes a capitalist. The capitalist extracts the surplus value of the work from the worker, leaving the worker only enough to reproduce their labour, if that. With this transformation, the magic of production appears to pass from the extra power of the worker's work to the capitalist, and then to the capitalist's money, which has come to be called 'capital'. Money is the blood of transactions. The worker's money becomes wages. Work becomes a commodity and the capitalist's money, capital, appears to be the magic transformer of raw materials into useful objects. Capital also appears to be the magic transformer of work into profit, which the capitalist takes as their own. This exploitative and extractive relationship is at the heart of capitalism.

Capitalism had a beginning and a long period of development in the Middle East and then in Western Europe. To give some idea of time scales, life on earth is about 4 billion years old. The last common ancestor of humans with chimpanzees, bonobos and gorillas was 8–6 million years ago. Human ancestors evolved to stand and walk on two legs about 4 million years ago, becoming anatomically modern about 200,000 years ago.

Humans lived as hunter-gatherers for these 200,000 years, starting in Africa. Humans moved from Africa into the rest of the world from 60,000 to 45,000 years ago. In the Middle East, some hunter-gatherer tribes gradually settled and became agricultural peoples, creating the first settled communities and then the first cities. The transition from hunter-gatherer to farmer created private property, walls, privacy, cities and individualism. The beginnings of agriculture were 10,000 to 15,000 years ago. Biblical times are counted from about 7,000 years ago, around the time of the first settled cities in the Middle East. The Greeks and Romans, Arendt's starting point, were dominant in Britain from around 2000 years ago. The capitalist relationship of workers being freed from the land and working for wages began to develop inside feudal agriculture about 800 years ago. Put into context, 800 years is a very short time.

What happened 800 years ago in British agriculture which led to both the poverty and the riches that have formed the modern capitalist nation state? Perhaps it is unsurprising that it turns out that capitalism started with the agricultural workers who were surplus to the land. Capitalism began with increases in agricultural productivity and the poverty consequential to it. It also led to the breakdown of the relationship between the Greek and Roman *polis* and the 'households' of women, children and slaves, described by Arendt. These households, originating in Greek and Roman times, were the basis of agriculture in feudal Britain. The breakdown of these households is part of the transition to capitalism from feudalism.

Capitalism began in Britain 800 years ago

The ideas that accompanied, and helped to form the developments of the capitalist mode of production are in Adam Smith (1776), Marx (1846), the Fabian Society (1920s), Keynes (1936), Hayek (1945) and in the Mont Pelerin Society (1947). Real world actions shaped these ideas. These ideas have, in turn, shaped the actions of people and institutions. Some actions and discourses have led to their opposites, in complex social formations. This is the way that each mode of production has sown the seeds of the mode of production to come.

Around 800 years ago, improvements in the productivity of agricultural work brought about the decline of feudalism. Peasants, who had been previously tied to the land, were dispossessed and offered themselves, or were forced by necessity, to work for wages. This process began in Europe around 1200 to 1300. Feudalism began its decline. Later, the workers who were excess to the land, along with the farmers who were offering to employ them, created the beginning of capitalism as the dominant mode of production.

The arrival of the Black Death in 1346 hastened crucial changes in Britain. Twenty per cent of the population died during the first four-year period. It subsided in 1353, but never disappeared completely. One of the consequences of the enormous tragedy of the Black Death was a shortage of labour. For the first time, high wages were offered to 'poor' workers without land.

The link between the peasant and the feudal lord was broken, as was the link between the peasant and the land. There was a freedom in this. This is the basis for the great value that many people put on concepts of 'freedom' as they appear and reappear in the economic and political narratives. However, this 'freedom' also created poverty, the big, powerful nation state and 'women's work' in the place of slave labour.

The 'Poor Laws' formed the working class and the state

The origins of the creation of the working class can be traced through the development of the English Poor Laws. The first English Poor Law, passed in 1349, was aimed at combatting both 'excessive' wages and idleness. The English Poor Laws were designed to keep the population working while in the midst of death and under the threat of death. The Poor Laws recognised poverty, but were not charitable. These laws were a remedy for the shortages of the workers that production and commerce required. The first Poor Laws both defined and regulated poverty by defining and regulating paid work. The 1349 Poor Law specified wages and prices. It required all those under the age of 60 to work. It prohibited the enticing away of others' servants. It became illegal to give anything to able-bodied beggars 'under the colour of pity or alms'. It regulated how employers used and treated employees.

These laws, that both defined poverty and the poor, also drove the development of the nation state. The poor laws transformed landless peasants into potential providers of work for wages, and required them, by law, to sell their labour. The early laws forced landless peasants into selling their labour. These laws also controlled wage inflation in a situation where workers were scarce and the wages offered were high. In this way, the poor laws were an early development of a state that acted in the combined interests of the dominant classes, under a new form of production. What defined this new form, or mode of production, was a relationship between employers and workers, where the workers sold their labour to the employers who offered wages in money in return. This relationship, though, was characterised by an unequal, exploitative transaction guaranteed by the Poor Laws.

This new mode of production grew up inside the feudal mode of production. In the feudal mode of production, the relationships involved were those of feudal lord to serf, or master to slave. The seeds of the capitalist state in Britain of the 1300s protected all employers, capitalists, feudal landlords and slave masters from a labour force that might have gained some power from its scarcity. The state did not protect the labour force. The state defined and protected the employers.

Nevertheless, the period from the 1350s to the 1450s was a time of relative prosperity created by workers earning wages and spending them. Enclosures, linked to sheep farming, led to a further 'free' population that either worked for wages or became the 'poor'. The 'poor' lived off the land and begged. The Poor Laws sought to limit the 'disorder' caused by poaching, begging and general free living off the land at the edges of society. At the same time, the ruling class became increasingly differentiated into merchants, landlords, farmers and manufacturers. Wealth depended on plentiful and relatively cheap labour. Workers earning wages also entered into production as consumers, giving workers an added importance and power. The creation of wealth depended on work. Wealth created poverty and poverty created wealth for some but not for others.

In the early 1500s, the time of Henry VIII, prices began to inflate and wages began to fall. The gold that came into Europe from South America ended up in India and China. Living standards collapsed. There were fresh generations of dispossessed people. During this time, the poor laws became more and more draconian, with branding, slavery and death as punishments for those who refused to work.

By the time of Elizabeth I, in the second half of the 1500s, outright repression of the poor was no longer tenable and draconian laws were mostly ignored. For the first time, a compulsory poor rate was levied on all owners of property to provide relief for those who could not work. The monasteries were suppressed and there was a transition from slavery to 'free labour'. America had been discovered, initiating the age of colonialism and its subsequent riches for Europe.

By this time, too, the youth had been brought up to work for wages. People took the money economy for granted. This was the point of real cultural change. At this point, the state became responsible for the poor. A working class, created by capitalism as a dominated class was being formed. That the state became responsible for the poor is important in the formation of the working class in British capitalism. The idea of state responsibility for the poor is still the basis of Labour and working-class politics and leads to the kind of state, including the contradictions, that characterises neoliberalism.

The Poor Relief Act of 1601 established a system of relief and parish employment for those unable to attain their own subsistence. This law is crucially important to what comes next. The law gave workers both the right to relief and the right to work. This was different from feudalism. In feudalism, ownership of the land gave certain duties to the owners of the land and to the people who lived on it. In the capitalism that grew up inside feudalism, this social contract was broken. Also, people were given rights instead of duties. The Poor Laws attempted to occupy the excess labour force by limiting people's movements and tying them into apprenticeships. However, they also created people who could look to the state to care for and to support them. People were given rights, whether they were working, or not (Novak, 1988). The poor laws created the working class, and a new kind of politics.

Money and industry

With more and more people inside the money economy, finance was also developing. The year of 1601 saw the first use of banknotes; these were receipts for values deposited with goldsmiths. The first banknotes were thus counters for gold held in storage. The goldsmiths were the country's first bankers. Money, as representative of wealth and power, became the life blood of capitalism. Merchants could use the notes to settle their financial obligations. Finance, commerce, work for wages, poverty and the state, as responsible for the whole population, all developed together and interdependently.

The English Civil War (1642–1651) swept away the remaining barriers to enclosures and to the 'modernisation' of agriculture. At this point poor relief became a local responsibility. Poor relief became the responsibility of the 15,000 separate parishes in Britain. In Puritanism, each individual is responsible for their own destiny. These Puritan ideas were gradually replacing the older ideas about a society fixed by divine order. A rural, property-less proletariat was created. The Poor Laws were overseen by local officials called Justices of the Peace. The poor were set to work; workhouses are often said to be the first places of capitalist production inside walls, the first factories (Novak, 1988).

At the end of the 1600s, the first national banks of England and Scotland were formed by groups of goldsmiths. Money was already being socialised. Gold flowed into Britain from the Brazilian gold mines by way of an advantageous treaty with Portugal. By the early 1700s, the Bank of England was granted a monopoly on issuing notes. The state was taking charge of, and supporting, finance.

When the industrial revolution started in the 1750s, regional and private banks outside of London provided the funding. Industrialisation began in the villages and valleys of the Pennines. Like the ruling classes, the peasantry was also no longer homogenous. Yeomen shared an outlook with gentlemen and merchants rather than with landless labourers. The state was becoming more complex. Work was already yoked to finance before the first economists began to try and understand that which was already taking place.

The economists Adam Smith, Karl Marx, John Maynard Keynes, Friedrich Hayek and the Mont Pelerin Society are the most important ones. It is important to understand how these economists defined the emotional underpinnings of the 'science' of economics. In their writings, they define how to think again about both the emotion and the science of economics as part of human collective activity.

Adam Smith, emotion and economic man

The capitalist mode of production started with the poverty of landless peasants. The discipline of economics started with Adam Smith. Smith was a Scottish philosopher, educated at Oxford. Returning to Scotland, he became a Professor of Logic and then Professor of Moral Philosophy, in Glasgow. In 1759, Smith published his first book, called *The Theory of Moral Sentiments*. Although *The Theory of Moral Sentiments* is on philosophy, it bookended Smith's later work on economics, *The Wealth of Nations* (Smith, 1776 [2009]). In other words, the first edition of *Moral Sentiments* came out before *The Wealth of Nations* in 1756, and the sixth edition of *Moral Sentiments*, much expanded, was also his final book, published in 1790 (Smith, 1790 [2012]). Smith, in effect, split his ideas of rationality from his ideas about emotions into two separate books, and sandwiched the economic rationality in between his emotion studies. In this respect, it is important to recognise the 'moral sentiments' book as an integral part of Adam Smith's thinking.

In essence, *The Theory of Moral Sentiments* is about human emotions, motivations and sociality, including sympathy, self-love, and many of the other emotions that drive human beings. Its considerations include: an appreciation of the demands of rationality, the need for recognising the plurality of human motivations, the connections between ethics and economics, and the co-dependent, rather than free-standing, role of institutions.

Smith has been taken up by the discipline of economics that he founded, as the major promoter of the motivation of capitalism based on self-love. However, this first, and final, book started with the senses of propriety, sympathy and pleasure between men. The second section was about passions, social, unsocial and selfish. Even though *The Theory of Moral Sentiments* was considered radical when it was published, it met with a great deal of approval and was popular. In talking about the emotional human being, Smith put something important about capitalism, and the pre-industrial capitalist moment, into written words. It is this understanding that is at the basis of what we consider to be the 'science' of economics. Adam Smith made the use and exploitation of human work in the capitalist mode of production, based on rationality, into an acceptable, and even admirable, enterprise.

When Adam Smith was writing, industrial production, the development of money, and the accumulation of gold reserves, came together into the industrial revolution in Britain. Smith never used the term 'capitalism'. Instead, he used the term 'political economy'. The political economy had two main tasks: 'first, to provide a plentiful revenue or subsistence for the people, or, more properly, to enable them to provide such a revenue or subsistence for themselves; and secondly, to supply the state or commonwealth with a revenue sufficient for the public services' (Smith, 1790 [2012], p. xiii). Public services were free education and poverty relief. He was in favour of greater freedom for the indigent in place of punitive 'Poor Laws'. Smith's work recognised that the state has a role in caring for the poor. This is important because dependence on work, wages and the money economy is not the same as dependence on land and agriculture. There are no alternatives to employment, other than wealth, property or crime in the money economy.

Smith's work was essentially a book on manners and morals needed for a capitalist economic production. It was, at the same time, individual and social. He linked the need for an internalised moral compass to virtue. He identified this as the conformity to reason. In order to evaluate this reasoning, Smith invoked what he called, an 'impartial spectator', an internal helper to assess 'impartial reasoning'. It was this impartial and reasoning human, whose humanity was based on emotion, and on the social, that Smith appealed to in his work on economics.

Far from being the selfish and self-centred capitalist that Smith is credited with identifying, Smith's ideas about a third, observing, internal position, in order to create 'impartial reasoning', is a sophisticated psychological concept, akin to Freud's superego, Elias's observer of social figurations and Foulkes's internalised role of the conductor in groups. Smith employed this internal observer as a witness to the beginnings of the industrial revolution. By separating out the emotional human from the rational human, Smith laid the basis for the Victorian mode of being, in which the emotional and rational became separated and detached from each other. Smith's writings, at the beginning of economics emphasises that part of the work of overcoming the capitalist mode of production is finding ways of connecting emotion and reason up again by creating a deepened consciousness about human emotional dynamics and human groups.

Adam Smith witnessed the creation of a whole new world. We do not know very much about Smith personally. He never married and was close to his mother. He was a solitary, bumbling man, apparently, who thought that he was only beautiful in his ideas, and not in his looks. The separation between the emotional and the rational that Smith described sounds like a man who struggled, perhaps, to keep his feelings under control.

The Wealth of Nations

James Watt patented the first steam engine in 1769. The first modern industrial factory opened in 1771 in Derbyshire. The first stock exchange opened in 1773, starting the process of the socialisation of money and capital. In 1776, the year that America declared independence from Britain, inspired by the incipient French Revolution, Adam Smith published his classic book on economics, *The Wealth of Nations* (1776 [2009]).

In *The Wealth of Nations*, Smith proposed that labour, rather than land, was the source of wealth. In this way, Smith defined the mode of production that was later to be called 'capitalism' and marked the start of a more conscious struggle for industrial hegemony between classes and class fractions. Classical economics is based on the proposal of the rational and individualised economic man. Smith proposed that, when economic man pursues his self-interest, he also promotes the good of society. A self-interest that promotes the good of society is the bedrock of today's neoliberal economic ideology. Smith observed that each workman had a great quantity of his own work to dispose of beyond what he was enabled to exchange for his own goods. However, for Smith, wealth did not come from the work itself, but from the 'deepening of the division of labour'. By 'deepening the division of labour', Smith meant the deepening separation of roles and power between capitalists and workers. In other words, it was the organisation of production that liberated, not expropriated, the wealth contained in the excess labour. In this way, the organisers of production, the entrepreneurs or the capitalists, benefitted from their contribution to the organisation of the division of labour with profit. Without the organisation of the division of labour, the labourers' excess work does not become productive, according to Smith.

Smith also made a distinction between what he called productive and unproductive capital. He saw unproductive capital as being that which is earned in rents and tithes, part of the income of the feudal landlords. In this sense, Smith championed industry, as contrasted with agriculture and finance. Wealth, in industry, depended on work and on the organisation of production. Work, and the organisation of work, were the elements that gave value to the objects produced, which are the commodities.

Smith wrote economic theory in a way that proposed that industrial interests, as opposed to agricultural, financial and commercial interests, become hegemonic in the state. That is, the proposition was that the interests of finance, commerce and agriculture were best served by serving the interests of industry, where capital was used in production that depended on labour sold for money.

The link between poverty and production became lost for a time at this point. It was assumed that laissez-faire production would eliminate poverty because all workers would come to be employed. Left to itself, laissez-faire capitalism would provide full employment of both capital (money) and labour (work) to the benefit of society as a whole. That was the theory. To this end, Smith advocated both free trade and the non-intervention of the state into the affairs of industry. Industry would take care of itself, and, in the process of taking care of itself, industry would also take care of everyone else. Our present neoliberal capitalism claims to have returned to the theories of Adam Smith of 1776, with some crucial differences.

Men's and women's work

Adam Smith's ideas constituted a perceptive observation of the dynamic processes already produced by the movement of social forces. His ideas gave them shape, purpose and rationalisation, as well as rationality. In effect, the old households of feudalism were smashed. Field work, the work of tied peasants and field slaves, became waged work when employed by productive capital. What became of the work that was done in feudal households by women and household slaves? In creating waged work, the dynamics of capitalism also created, as a consequence, a mass of smaller households where the waged worker was lord of the manor and the work formerly done by slaves in the house was done by women. Household work that became women's work, was not a productive use of capital and continued to be unpaid. This was the ideal only, of course. Women and children were often put to work. Without the waged man to protect and own them, women and children became part of an even lower-waged workforce, but all work defined as women's work was unpaid, underpaid and undervalued.

The same processes that liberated men's work did not liberate women's work. Capitalists who employed male waged workers also gained the added value of the unpaid women's work. This double exploitation of work was only possible when women were kept at home. In effect, feudal households were broken down into smaller groupings. This new grouping, the family, became identified as a basic unit of society along with the individual. The families in feudalism that had existed before were no longer large independent units. With capitalism, families evolved into smaller interdependent units within communities and states.

This aspect of the evolution of capitalism becomes glaringly obvious only under the lens of the group dimension. Hannah Arendt's (1958 [1998]) work, *The Human Condition*, helps to understand why this particular aspect of transition is so important in the capitalism that followed. In *The Human Condition*, Arendt charted how historical modern thinking from the 17th century to the beginning of the 20th century created the modern age that began in 1945 with the first atomic bomb. For Arendt, the major danger of the modern age was the loss of humanity itself. In order to encourage thinking about what comes next, Arendt went back to her starting point, which was the political and existential philosophies of the Greeks and Romans.

Arendt began with the Greeks and Romans as the philosophical basis of contemporary ideas about democracy. How have these ideas about democracy been betrayed by the evolution of capitalism? One of her major starting points was to emphasise the plurality of this democracy and the importance of dialogue, which are also elements of the group dimension. For Arendt, only contemplation is solitary and individual. Contemplation is the only situation where there is complete freedom. Contemplation is neither thinking nor action, which can only be plural.

Thinking and speaking for the Greeks and Romans was in the plural life of the *vita activa*, the life that is active. This was the group dimension for Arendt. Thinking together happened in the polis, which was the arena for politics and action. Arendt also recognised the group dimension when she made the distinction between 'work' and 'labour'. Work occurs in the world and is done by *homo faber*, the man who makes. Work creates the artificial world of things. Work is worldliness. Labour is done in the home, the private sphere, and involves the biological world of the human body and its needs. Labour is life itself (Arendt, 1958/1998, p. 7). The labourer is called *animal laborans*.

The state, the family and Hannah Arendt

Arendt's definitions of terms and their relationships are very close to Smith's. This is because the feudal large houses in Britain were a legacy from the time of the Romans. However, Arendt and Smith both missed an important element in the transition from feudalism to capitalism. This element is that it is only men's work that becomes productive and thus, paid. In the transition from feudal large houses to smaller capitalist family units, work for men became part of the paid economy whereas the work of women became akin to that of animals and slaves, unpaid and unproductive. Also, implicit in the transition is that women were left out of the plurality of politics and action of the polis. Women's work is never completed. Nothing artificial is ever made by women's work.

Arendt did not write about capitalism and feudalism explicitly, although it is difficult to believe that these were not in her thoughts. Even more interestingly, Arendt did not distinguish between men's and women's work. In her writing she used only male pronouns. Did these include females or not? It may well have been in her mind that she was only thinking about men's work. In that case, women are missing entirely.

However, the important element that Arendt missed was that part of the transition from feudalism to capitalism was in the creation of the smaller family groups that continued to carry the culture of the large feudal households. That is, the male worker considers himself the authority and power, the master, of the household, based on his participation in productive work and in the polis. Women and children remain relatively isolated in the smaller households without power or voice. Capitalism has seized on this evolutionary development and made use of the labour power of two people, with the theoretical return of sufficient wages to enable the reproduction of labour power through the family. In this way, it is one of capitalism's basic supports that women and women's work are excluded from the plurality of the polity, of politics.

For Arendt, the transition to capitalism and its further evolution in the modern world threatens humanity at its very roots. For her, the polis has become lost in what she called the 'social'. This was the new realm in the modern age. The tragedy of the social for Arendt was that it was neither public nor private. The social, for Arendt comprised all the other realms. Its form was the nation state. The social obscured politics and turned people and political communities into families with family dynamics. As a result, the political, the polis is no longer a place of plurality of words and action, but an administrative form of a super family (Arendt, 1958 [1998], p. 28).

The modern, capitalist, social sphere included economics for Arendt. Problems of physical survival moved from the family sphere of the private, large feudal households to the public sphere and the realm of the political and thus of the nation. *Homo faber* was taken over by *animal laborans* as economics suppressed politics, discussion and group decisions. The rise of the nation state was also the rise of mass society. In mass society, the few rule the many. The elites rule the masses.

Arendt observed that private households became the nation state. In the group dimension, with this movement to a nation state only preoccupied with economics, large private households have also broken down into smaller versions of themselves. In both arenas, the group, Arendt's heterogenous polis was squeezed out. Heterogenous groups became homogenous. Group dynamics evolved from coherence to cohesion. Difference became relegated to the violence of suppression and silencing. Small differences became large, requiring adherence to patriarchal heteronormativity and promoting racism, sexism misogyny, homophobia, transphobia and ableism. People were expected to behave rather than to act. Purity replaced diversity.

The human senses of individuality and freedom were lost at exactly the same time as these were being presented as the ideal that held the social economy together. These are the contradictions and continuations that Arendt has helped us to understand at the transition from feudalism to capitalism. These characteristics are all inherent in the paternalistic and heteronormative character of capitalism at its inception. They are all part of capitalism, but they are not necessarily part of democracy. The challenge is to reprise the polis as a better democracy, based on dialogue and action in the plurality. This must happen in both the arenas of the state and also in the arenas of the families and communities created by capitalism. The group dimension shows this possibility and how important it is that this happens in order to leave the time of monsters. The group dimension will also suggest ways in which this might happen. Although the forces of capitalism have evolved since

Adam Smith, the forces of capitalism have not yet found ways to think and act that might show the way out in terms of what will be possible in the world yet to come.

Freedom and the first workers' organisations

As Smith published *The Wealth of Nations*, the American War of Independence in 1776, and then the French Revolution in 1789, established an alliance of capitalists and workers in industry. This alliance was based on the dominant ideas of democracy, class conflict and freedom. This was the Enlightenment. The alliance between workers and capitalists has always been ambivalent. Workers' political movements were promoted and then defeated. Workers were protected, and then attacked. Smith's promise of a laissez-faire economy has never been realised, but it has become the bedrock of ideas around the struggle, and the resulting moving and changing hegemony, between capitalist classes and capital class fractions.

The concept of 'freedom', though, has remained critical in the alliance, both ideological and real, between capitalists and workers. In capitalist ideology, workers are 'free' to sell their labour for money. Of course, this freedom can only be realised when there are enough jobs for all, and when workers are organised to protect their collective rights. However, in 1776, the concept of freedom, to sell labour, on the one hand, and to buy and use labour on the other, the laissez-faire element, was a new and exciting concept. The concept of freedom is also highly emotive. The concept of freedom is linked to the foundational feeling of Seeking, as will be shown in Chapter 4 of this work. The concept of freedom was enshrined in the concept of democracy at the beginning of the industrial revolution. The idea of democracy is powerful. The idea of freedom is much more powerful.

In the French Revolution (1789), workers were involved in organising and protesting. In Britain, in 1799, one of the reactions to the French and American Revolutions was the passage of the Combination Acts. As with the Poor Laws, the Combination Acts recognised the working class in the act of attempting to control it. The Combination Acts of 1799 and 1800 prohibited the formation of trade unions and made strike action illegal in Britain. Punishments were three months in jail or two months' hard labour. With the Combination Acts, as with the Poor Acts, the state intervened in industrial production in the interests of the industrial capitalist class and to the detriment of the industrial workers. This intervention disenfranchised and punished the workers, and their incipient organisations. The intervention also recognised them. The industrial working class, was created and recognised, at this point, by capitalism itself. These processes led to new kinds of groups and a displacement of the polis.

In 1801, the London Stock Exchange, as the socialiser of money capital, became a state-regulated organisation. The industrial revolution was dependent on investment in coal mining for energy sources, in railways, for creating the demand for energy, and in commerce. The stock exchange enabled people to buy and sell stocks and to move capital to where it would be most productive of commodities and of more capital. The state progressively took control of the responsibilities of developing and containing the workers. The state also took control of organising the socialisation of the market between money and goods. In reality, laissez-faire capitalism has never lacked an active state and an active state bureaucracy. The reality and the ideology are completely at odds with each other.

The first workers' organisations began to appear, because, or in spite of, the Combination Acts. In 1811, the Luddite movement was formed. In 1815, in Manchester, a peaceful meeting of workers was violently attacked by agents of the state. This 'Peterloo' revealed a new stage of conflict between workers and capitalists. In another about turn, the Combination Acts were repealed in 1824.

Industrial hegemony

At this point, the state responded to workers, and the poor, in the newly socialised interests of industrial hegemony. Another watershed moment occurred in 1830. Amid widespread unrest, a Royal Commission was appointed to investigate the Poor Law. This year also marked the starting point of the cooperative movement. In 1832, the Reform Act was passed. The Reform Act extended the right to vote to all male holders of property, owned or rented, worth £10 and over. This extended the voting franchise to industrialists, landowners, tenant farmers and shopkeepers, but not to most workers and certainly not to women. The Act explicitly banned women from voting. It was something, but not enough.

In 1833, the first Factory Act was passed to regulate conditions in manufacturing. Children under nine years old were banned from the factory and working was limited to 12 hours a day for workers under the age of 18. There were government inspections prescribed to enforce the Act. Although the government inspection team was small, it led the way to the state expanding its responsibility for the people who worked in factories. In 1834, a law requiring national supervision of poor relief was passed. No one will starve. The poor have a right to relief. There was, theoretically, a society of support to subsistence that was not the same as punishment for workers.

The Factory Acts of 1833, however, also individualised the responsibility of the workers for themselves. Workers were required to sell their labour and to take the blame individually, if they failed to do so. The state represented, at this point, a certain set of social relationships, as well as an economic force in itself. The paradoxical and contradictory unity of the state as carer and liberator, as contrasted with the state as the facilitator of exploitation, is obvious. The capitalist state, with democracy, proposed to be both carer and exploiter, thus its resilience, and this reinforced the power of the 'democratic state' ideology.

Striking though these advances were, they were also destructive. The middle classes had advanced their cause by selling out the working classes, with partial male suffrage. The Factory Acts of 1834 made poverty the responsibility of the individual and pushed the outdoor relief to inside the workhouses, which increased oppression. These laws were not repealed until 1948. In emotional terms, the reforms of the 1830s emphasised the importance of fairness as a political concept. The bourgeoisie, or middle class, was taken into the political institutions by changes in representative democracy and the working class was left outside.

The Chartists

By 1838, the Chartist Movement had been formed, with the aim of promoting universal male suffrage. The People's Charter called for six reforms to make the political system more democratic: A vote for every man 21 years of age, of sound mind, and not undergoing punishment for a crime; the secret ballot to protect the elector in the exercise of his vote; no property qualification for Members of Parliament in order to allow the constituencies to return the man of their choice; payment of members, enabling tradesmen, working men, or other persons of modest means to leave or interrupt their livelihood to attend to the interests of the nation; equal constituencies, securing the same amount of representation for the same number of electors, instead of allowing less populous constituencies to have as much or more weight than larger ones; annual parliamentary elections, thus presenting the most effectual check to bribery and intimidation, since no purse could buy a constituency under a system of universal manhood suffrage in each twelve-month period.

The Reform Acts and the Chartist Movement in the 1830s set the scene for the first phase of the industrial revolution. They established a state, a working class and a political process that were to last more than 200 years. It is glaring that women were left out of these movements, when they might have been included. This further underlines the importance of the patriarchy to the capitalism whose formation was already well under way. Men and women became involved in capitalism in very different ways, even if both were exploited. Because of this, the unity of the working classes in capitalism was compromised from the very beginning. The conflicts between capitalist class fractions, between capitalists and workers and between male and female workers, between those in paid work and those in unpaid work, mediated by a limited, unequal, democracy and an incipient welfare state, were all in place.

At the same time, the Bank of England became the only authorised issuer of banknotes and created a gold standard for British currency. The state took finance also as its ultimate responsibility in order to enhance and make industrial capital more productive. The gold standard provided a guaranteed and secure form of exchange of commodities for work and work for commodities.

Karl Marx and Friedrich Engels

The first workers' movements predated Marx and Engels. Friedrich Engels published *The Condition of the Working Class in England*, in German, in 1845. In this book Engels described the appalling working and living conditions of the working class in Manchester. Engels observed that laissez-faire capitalism, in fact, far from eliminating poverty, created more and more of it. Engels predicted that the conditions that were prevalent in Britain would spread to Europe. *The Condition of the Working Class in England* became the basis of Engels' lifelong collaboration with Marx.

It took very special men and women to want to investigate the human suffering involved in the beginning of the industrial revolution in England, and to write about it. Marx and Engels both lived their lives around the urgency of their ideas. It was vital to Marx and Engels to put their ideas on paper, to have them published, and to have them discussed in various kinds of political organisations. For this, they suffered greatly, Marx perhaps more than Engels. They would have been very different without each other.

Marx and Engels, writing between the 1840s and the 1890s, created the counter-discourse to Adam Smith's *The Wealth of Nations*. Working together, they produced both the theory and the theoretical bases of the actions that have enabled a perspective on capitalism that does not only belong to the capitalist classes.

Neither Marx nor Engels were working class by birth. They were both Victorian gentlemen and Marx came from the new Jewish professional classes. These new classes were opened up to Jewish people by the Western Enlightenment. Engels came from a mixture of aristocracy and the new industrial bourgeoisie. They were both born in Germany, in the midst of the transition between the old social order and the new world of the American and French revolutions. They were born into the aftermath of the second French revolution, but lived their lives in the conflict between the new world and the old one, the old world being personified by the Prussians. They were both the children of their fathers' early enlightenment in terms of freedom and democracy.

While we do not know a lot about the origins and personality of Adam Smith, we do know quite a lot about both Marx and Engels. They both had authoritarian fathers, for example. Marx's father was descended from a family of rabbis. His early manhood was spent becoming a lawyer under a new emancipation for the Jewish people which allowed a wider variety of professions. However, the short window of emancipation closed. Karl's father converted to Protestantism in order to continue in his profession, eventually baptising all his children and his wife. Marx's father hid the conversions from his wife's Jewish family. Karl was the eldest living son of nine children. He had one older brother who died less than six months before Karl was born. Karl had one older sister. Marx's mother had nine children in 11 years.

It can only be surmised how Karl experienced his brother's death and his mother's mourning. Much of Karl Marx's adult life was plagued by financial difficulties and conflict with his mother, who withheld his inheritance. He was close to his father, however. He carried a picture of his father and spoke of him often. Until he was 12, Karl was educated at home. Marx's father died of tuberculosis when Karl was 20, seriously compromising Karl's financial future.

Karl Marx was a passionate man from the beginning. He became engaged to Jenny von Westphalen, the daughter of a good friend and colleague of his father. She was four years older than he was. They had played together as children. He was 18 at the time of their engagement, which lasted for seven years until they married. In the meantime, Karl went to study away from home. He caroused and brawled all through university, while also reading extensively. He was nearly involved in three duels throughout his life, and too many skirmishes with political opponents and colleagues to count.

Intellectually, Karl Marx fell in love with the German philosopher Hegel, and remained a Hegelian for all of his life. It was the dialectic from Hegel and the materialism, possibly from Engels, Adam Smith and the other economists, that motivated the personal sacrifice involved in maintaining his political struggles and in writing *Capital* (1867).

The dialectic

The dialectic refers to a process by which knowledge, of self, an idea or an object, can be found by recognising and resolving conflicts. This is sometimes referred to the simplified form of thesis-antithesis-synthesis. The dialectic is often countered with the empiricism of cause-effect appearances that have become the modern dominant logical mode. Marx is credited with preserving the dialectic, which originated with Hegel. However, dialectic logic is also found in many forms of thought, such as psychoanalysis, evolution, biology and other human sciences in the form of modern complexity theory. Simple cause and effect empiricism is not rich enough to comprehend reality.

Marx set about trying to make a life in the dialectic, but ran into political difficulties with the ever more repressive Prussian regime in Europe. He turned from philosophy to journalism. Marx became, in effect, a worker as a freelance journalist and activist. Karl and Jenny's married life was a constant movement between Paris, Cologne, and Brussels, finally ending in London.

Marx and Engels met in Paris in 1844. Engels came from Nordic ancestry. His father was an industrialist. His father was also a member of a Protestant religious minority, called the Awakening. Engels broke with his father on matters of religious faith and spent some time in the army. He also became a Communist around this time. After army service, Engel's father sent him to a thread-making mill in Salford, England. Engel's father wanted Friedrich away from his Communist friends. Instead, Engels met a working-class woman named Mary Burns, who showed him around Manchester. This shocking experience led him to write *The Condition of the Working Class in England* (1845).

Engels ended up working in Manchester for his father, at a job that he hated, so that he could share his wages with Marx and his family, who were in London while Marx was writing *Capital*. Engels lived with Mary Burns, and her sister Lizzie, until their deaths. Engels led a dual life of bourgeois factory owner and free lover of working-class women. He kept these relationships separate from each other. There was also his secret financial division of labour with Marx. However, the money that he gave Marx was never enough.

Karl Marx also led a double life of sorts. Jenny Marx became pregnant seven times. Her two eldest girls, born in Paris and Brussels lived to adulthood, but two boys and one girl died as children in London where Karl and Jenny lived in appalling conditions while begging for money from family and friends. Marx withdrew to spend his days in the library of the British Museum and to write *Capital* from

1850 to 1857. Volume One of *Capital*, the only one that Marx actually wrote and finished, was published German in 1867 and later in English, in 1887.

The years of writing *Capital* were difficult for Karl and Jenny Marx. Three of their children died, and there was one stillbirth. There were two healthy births in this time, their youngest daughter, Eleanor, and Frederick, who was the child of their housekeeper, Helene Demuth, with Karl. It is probably no accident that the emotional theme of *Capital* is alienation. *Capital* was written with a cold angry passion and with the intention of dissecting capitalism to discover the contradictions that would overthrow it. In writing *Capital*, Marx turned the helpless dependency of the working classes in capitalism into the most powerful and determining force of the mode of production. This force was labour.

Marx's economics did not go much beyond what the classical economists observed about capitalism. What he added is a sense of historical process, a different viewpoint, emphasising the political element of economics and dialectical thinking. In bringing these politics and dialectics to economics, and with his political activism, Marx changed the world.

Capital

Marx's major work of economics, *Capital*, had the subtitle 'A Critique of Political Economy'. The subtitle 'Critique' suggests that Marx wanted to emphasise that he was making a criticism of accepted economic thought, derived mainly from Adam Smith. In his critique, Marx showed how the dialectical conflicts inside capitalism would lead to its destruction. These dialectical conflicts were those between capitalists and workers. Like Smith, Marx thought that the division of labour was a key feature of capitalism. Unlike Smith, however, he saw the division of labour as being the basis of wealth for some, while bringing poverty and suffering for others.

Marx did not specify what was to come after the capitalist mode of production. He had been schooled in socialism as a youth, but he did not speak of a socialist mode of production. He was dedicated, though, to human freedom. Like Smith, Marx wanted a world that was rational and transparent, where humans would be liberated from the control of external forces. Marx emphasised the emotional content of the experience of work. While Smith took the point of view of the capitalist, Marx took the point of view of the worker. In Marx's view, the product of the worker becomes fractured by the processes of the division of labour in capitalist production. Consequently, the worker becomes alienated from the product of his time and effort. Alienation is at the basis of the emotional experience of being a worker in capitalism.

Expressed most vividly in an earlier form of *Capital*, in notes published much later as the *Economic and Philosophic Manuscripts of 1844* (Marx, 1844), the alienation of the worker comprises three layers. In the first layer, the worker is emptied out into his product. Workers produce commodities and capital, neither of which will belong to them. In the second layer, the process of work is also alienated and not under the workers' control. This alienation of the process of work is a loss of the workers' self-expression and control over their bodies and, thus, of the workers' self. The third layer is the alienation resulting from the consequences for humanity of the capitalist political economy. This is the alienation of the human species, or species 'essence'.

Adam Smith wrote for the owners of capital. Karl Marx and Friedrich Engels wrote for the workers. Their goal was to make it possible for workers to see the value of their labour beyond the value of their wages. Alienation is the emotional symptom of the workers' exploitation.

For Marx, all value in the product comes from the work that is put into it. Profit and interest come from the exploitation of that work in the capitalist relationship. Progress, in terms of the growth of the productivity of labour, comes from the dialectical conflict between labour and capital in the process of production. The means of production develops but with progressively less live labour involved. Ultimately, the surplus value of the product, sometimes termed profit, tends to zero, as machinery takes over from live workers. Machines do not produce more than they consume. In this process, the rate of profit tends to zero and capitalism enters into crisis. The crises of capitalism become the points at which revolution is most likely to happen. If revolution succeeds, capitalism fails and something new is created. Part of Marx's vision of the future after capitalism included the withering away of the state as it would no longer be needed. In Marx's dialectic, the seeds of the destruction of capitalism and the creation of something new are inherent in its processes.

The group dimension in capitalism

Capitalism has, however, lasted longer than Marx and Engels thought possible. Until now, the conflicts, contradictions and developments of capitalism have not led to its demise. Capital has adapted to its crises, primarily through the power of monopoly and the concentration of power in the state. Capitalists can produce profits that are no longer only dependent on live labour. These profits come from innovations in technology, the role of the worker as consumer and on the extraction of profits from workers through monopoly pricing practices, from colonies and from the environment.

In Adam Smith's classical economics, humans act exclusively in their own self-interest and are driven by their one desire, which is a desire to acquire material goods. This is what we have come to understand as economic man. Economic man is guided by an 'invisible hand', which is the outcome of all independent and individual self-interested and acquisitional acts.

Arendt's critique of Marx began with what she saw as Marx's 'socialised man'. For Arendt, Marx's socialised man was constructed from the conflict of two major interests: those of the capitalist and those of the workers. Instead of individual and isolated men making decisions in their own interests, Marx saw classes and class interests as moving history. Marx proposed a conflict of classes, rather than

Smith's invisible hand guiding the outcome of many individual actions. However, for Arendt, Marx's socialised man was not an active being but a passive member of a class. In a class, behaviour becomes more important than individual action. The class is a kind of group based on mass and cohesion, not on dialogue and coherence. For Arendt, this meant that politics, the polis, also become impossible. For the group dimension, the difference is that, in groups which are capable of dialogue, conflict is contained. The social forces involved in classes push the conflicts to outside the groups, causing conflict between groups and fractions of groups which are only resolved by coercion and violence. The division of labour between capitalists and workers is an example of this process and this is one of the reasons that it is difficult to find a way out of the time of monsters.

When action gives way to behaviour in classes, for Arendt (1958 [1998], p. 45), the state becomes a bureaucracy, where no one is in charge. Humans become a conditioned animal. 'Society devours political, private and intimate', she wrote. From this, Arendt painted a bleak picture of a future where humans as social animals 'reign supreme'. The survival of the species can be secured, but humanity is threatened with extinction. Ultimately, now, the survival of the species is also threatened.

All modern communities, she wrote, become societies of labourers and jobholders. All community members consider that whatever they do, it is always a way of sustaining their own lives and those of their families, alone. Further, by promising an end to labour at a time when everyone has become a labourer, leaves an immense void. The work void becomes filled with consumption, rather than self-realisation. In order to survive the modern world, humans, in Arendt's eyes, will have to be different and more active in our complex webs of interdependence. A real consciousness of the human group and its dynamics enables us to do this more active political work.

What Arendt described and explained so articulately is how capitalism has developed, how capitalist development is reflected in economic theories and why it is so difficult to think beyond the neoliberal capitalism that we have formed for ourselves. For Arendt, it is because the life process itself has been channelled into the public realm. An important corollary is that we humans are in danger of losing the capacity to talk and think together in the groups from which we might create our day-to-day political, alive, world.

Whatever we do next, thinking beyond the economic theories and also beyond Arendt entails a consideration of the Group Dimension. Arendt's classical distinction rested on the identification of issues of survival of the individual and of the species. The idea of *animal laborans* rests on the oneness of human kind, as she wrote: It is the 'mass society where man as social animal rules supreme' that threatens humanity with extinction (Arendt, 1958 [1998], p. 46). However, Arendt also said that the one-ness of human mind is a fact. In this, she has left room for something else that distinguishes humans from animals. This something else, captured by Arendt in the concept of the *vita activa*, can also be viewed as the interdependence of individuals and groups from Norbert Elias (1987), combined with the interdependence of humans in groups, in the group matrix, as described by S. H. Foulkes (1948).

Certainly, Marx and Engels, their ideas and their dedication to their ideas, were produced by dialogue in small groups: workers associations, coffee houses and publications. These were a species of the polis. Interestingly, the women were still performing the role of *animal laborans* at home, trying to cope with consumption, the survival of their children and the dependence of their men. It is part of Arendt's ideas that *animal laborans* is wordless, but longs for abundance, whereas *homo faber*, the maker of the world, longs for permanence, stability and durability. Whatever else happens in the group dimension, it is the dialogue that questions the sexual division of labour and its emotional consequences that capitalism has inherited from feudalism that is most crucial. The silence around this dialogue lies at the heart of all other forms of discrimination and exploitation.

Responses to Marx's Capital

It is a testament to the strength and durability of Marxism, but also to its detriment as a theory, that the publication of *Capital* in English was almost immediately followed by a counter-discourse. In 1898, Eugen von Böhm-Bawerk published his major work, *Karl Marx and the Close of his System*. This work is at the basis of all subsequent criticism of the Marxist theory of value. Böhm-Bawerk set out to transform Marx's dialectic into logico-positivism in order to destroy it. The term 'value' was identified with the empirical concept of price. In this way, the term 'value' lost its dialectic power, which came from its character as an abstract, and thus essential, concept.

The most devastating attack on Marxism from classical economics was that the rate of profit did not tend to zero, empirically. This criticism has become more and more debatable. In globalisation, capital looks increasingly frantic in its search for profit worldwide. Britain, for example, where capitalism originated, is rapidly losing its standing as a wealthy and developed nation. From Böhm-Bawerk onwards, a major motivation of 'scientific' economics was the refutation and negation of Marxism along with the refutation and negation of the essentially emotional nature of the human.

While Marx was writing in London, the British working classes were making progress as well as losses. In 1867, the same year *Capital* was first published in Germany, urban working men in Britain were given the vote. In 1868, the British Trades Union Congress was formed. Trade unions were officially recognised by the state in 1871. Also, in 1871, local government boards took over responsibility for the Poor Law. They ended the hated indoor workhouses that separated families and stigmatised the poor and unemployed. The Paris Commune, a revolutionary government was established in 1871 until 1795. For Marx, only the workers could end capitalism and create Communism. The Paris Commune proved that this was possible, if only for a very short period.

In the period between 1870 and 1913, London became the economic hub of the world, based on the pound sterling and its gold standard. Britain became the first industrial nation. Consumer goods, wool and textiles, along with heavy, capital goods such as iron and steel and coal-mining shaped a world of industrial production, commerce and trade. The British working class also grew in influence under the Chartists. Marx's writings were the basis of what was to be a successful revolution fomenting in Russia, and, later, an unsuccessful revolution in Germany. The Fabians in London were founded on anti-Marxist, but socialist, principles.

References

Arendt, H. (1958 [1998]) *The Human Condition*, 2nd edition. Chicago, IL: University of Chicago Press.
Böhm-Bawerk, E. (1898) *Karl Marx and the Close of His System*, https://www.marxists.org/subject/economy/authors/bohm/
Elias, N. (1987) *Involvement and Detachment*. Oxford: Blackwell.
Engels, F. (1845) *Condition of the Working Class in England*, https://www.marxists.org/archive/marx/works/download/pdf/condition-working-class-england.pdf
Foulkes, S. H. (1948) *Introduction to Group-analytic Psychotherapy: Studies in the Social Integration of Individuals and Groups*. London: Maresfield Reprints.
Gramsci, A. (1971) *Selections from the Prison Notebooks*. London: Lawrence & Wishart.
Marx, K. (1844) *Economic and Philosophic Manuscripts of 1844*, https://www.marxists.org/archive/marx/works/1844/manuscripts/preface.htm
Marx, K. (1867) *Capital: A Critique of Political Economy*, https://www.marxists.org/archive/marx/works/1867-c1
Novak, T. (1988) *Poverty and the State*. Buckingham: Open University Press.
Smith, A. (1776 [2009]) *The Wealth of Nations*. Harmondsworth: Penguin.
Smith, A. (1790 [2012]) *The Theory of Moral Sentiments*. Cambridge: Cambridge University Press.

Chapter 2

Keynes and Keynesianism

The changes in relationships of the elements of production, capital and labour were chronologically in advance of the theories that described them. The changes were also in advance of the institutions that contained them. In the foundation of the Mont Pelerin Society, which spoke for present neoliberal capitalism, Hayek said that he wanted to emulate the Fabian Society, and the way that they captured the machinery of the state. Hayek might have been referring to one of the founding principles of the Fabians as recounted in a Fabian Society pamphlet: 'For the right moment, you must wait, as Fabius did most patiently … but when the time comes, you must strike hard, as Fabius did, or your waiting will be in vain.' Fabius was a Roman commander who won battles by delaying confrontation.

When Karl Marx died in London in 1883, he was relatively unknown. The Fabian Society was founded in London in 1884. It consisted of a small group of intellectuals who were seeking a non-violent end to a divisive system in society. George Bernard Shaw was a member, as were Sidney and Beatrice Webb. One of their founding principles was to advance democratic socialism through gradualist and reformist effort, rather than by revolutionary overthrow.

The Fabians proposed alternative cooperative economics that they wanted to apply to ownership of capital, as well as to land. They sought a capitalist welfare state, with a national minimum wage, slum clearances and a health service. The Fabian Society founded the London School of Economics in 1895. In 1900, The Fabians participated in the formation of the Labour Party. The Trade Unions Council left the Liberals and joined the Labour Party at the point of its formation.

So, by 1900, all of the present currents of political economics were in place. Free market individualistic economics and the theories of the value of labour of Adam Smith contrasted with the counter-discourse of the theory of class conflict of Karl Marx and Friedrich Engels. The welfare economy and cooperatives were envisaged by the Fabians, the Trade Unions and the Labour Party. These theories and institutions were all created by social forces and conflicts that centred on employment, unemployment and capital. Marxist political economy continued to be developed in Europe, primarily in Germany and Russia.

John Maynard Keynes

This was the world into which John Maynard Keynes came of age. Keynes was born in 1883, at virtually the same time as the foundation of the Fabian Society. By the early 1900s, just after the formation of the Labour Party, Keynes was a Fellow at King's College. Cambridge. Keynes' importance to the group dimension lies in his conception of the nation state and his understanding of the centrality of emotion in his economics.

Keynes' essentially non-political and technocratic understanding illustrates Arendt's fears of the end of politics in a state that only looks after survival and values behaviour more than action. In formulating and describing how economics work within this state, however, Keynes laid the theoretical basis for much of the controversy between 'left' and 'right' as to how the power of this state should be used. Keynes' understanding of the state is also an important element in thinking about how the world to come might appear. However, neither this understanding nor the controversies around this state are capable of ending the time of monsters because they are limited democratically. None of the present controversies is capable of restoring the *polis*.

Keynes's father, Neville, was an academic and his mother, too, was intellectual; she became, at one point, the first female mayor of Cambridge (Wapshott, 2012). Keynes had a privileged education at Eton and then studied mathematics at King's College, Cambridge. There, he was intellectually adopted by his father's mentor, Alfred Marshall. Alfred Marshall had written the English textbook on classical economics. Keynes subsequently became an economist.

Keynes was neither a Fabian nor a Marxist. He supported the Liberal Party for most of his life. For all his individual brilliance, Keynes was definitely a product of group dialogue. The formative social group for Keynes was the Bloomsbury Group that included E. M. Forster, Lytton Strachey and Virginia Woolf. The Bloomsbury group continued in dialogue with one another throughout their lives. As a group Bloomsbury was inclusive of women, as well as accepting a variety of sexualities.

Like Marx and Engels of 50 years before, Keynes was a Victorian, and lived a divided and contradictory life. On the one hand, he was promiscuous and openly gay, in full revolt against the stuffiness of the Victorian morals that separated thought from feeling. On the other hand, his expertise and knowledge in economics put him in great demand from the governments that were to face two world wars during his working life. Keynes objected to forced conscription and applied for status as a conscientious objector but his work at the Treasury exempted him from military service. Keynes thought that war was immoral, yet he continued to work for governments during both wars. He was not afraid of contradictions. He speculated on the stock market while recognising it as 'the casino'. With this term, Keynes expressed his thoughts about the economic and social destructive potential of the stock markets. He donated a portion of his market winnings to his friends who lacked money.

Fundamentally, Keynes was able to contain his own contradictions because he was passionately interested in the application of economics as a means of improving the lives of others. Keynes was *homo faber*, Arendt's 'man who makes'. He wanted to leave the world a better place. From the time of the First World War, Keynes saw the potential power of the formation of economic policy by the state. He also saw the positive and negative results of the application of this power, both economically and politically. These contradictions honed Keynes' thoughts. Marx's practice came from theory honed by practice. Keynes' theory originated in practice.

Mass production and mass destruction

By 1906, while Keynes was still at Cambridge, the world had rapidly evolved. The Labour Party, newly formed, achieved the election of 29 members of parliament although the government was a progressive Liberal one. There were some welfare reforms, along with hunger marches in the 1930s, in London. The secret ballot was introduced realising a Chartist demand.

A new, consumer, middle class was being formed. In 1908, The Model T Ford, for example, went on sale in America, motivated by this new class. In 1913, Henry Ford introduced the assembly line form of manufacture which increased labour productivity by speeding up production. Ford also increased his workers' wages and reduced their working hours to 8 hours a day, 5 days a week. Ford argued that workers must be paid enough in order to be able to buy mass-produced goods and have enough free time to enjoy them. Mass production needed a mass market. Mass capitalism was in the ascendence.

Perhaps 'mass' is the operative word here. The nature of modern life in terms of masses, rather than groups, motivated Arendt to write about the primacy of *animal laborans* in Marxism and in the modern state to the detriment of homo faber, who works to produce the durability of the human artifice and stability. The man who invented the assembly line and mass production, Henry Ford, became virulently antisemitic after the First World War. He went on to be one of the original funders of Adolf Hitler's National Socialists in Germany.

The First World War changed everything. European national boundaries were reformed. Death, like transport, was mechanised and mass produced. A whole generation of young men was lost, with profound social consequences. These consequences included the rise of antisemitism and racism as a feature of the politics of the masses. Again, cohesion was created by externalising conflicts from human groups to intergroup conflict by elites and leaders.

The end of the First World War brought revolutionary movements in Europe such as the Bolshevik revolution in Russia in 1917 and the German Revolution of 1918–1919, led by Rosa Luxemburg. Although the German revolution failed, the ideas of Marx and Engels were coming alive in reality nevertheless. This had profound effects in Britain.

Britain after the First World War

In 1918, the Labour Party adopted Clause IV which proposed that the state promote common ownership of the means of production, distribution and exchange. Full male suffrage was passed into law while women were again left out of the settlement. The demands of the suffragettes, who had been active before the war and who had ceased protest in order to participate in the war effort, were ignored. Again, a distinction was made between males who were allowed to participate in politics (homo faber), and females who were not (animal laborans). By this time, though, many women no longer accepted the role of the wordless producer of life and survival. In the real world, women always divided their time between labour and work, and, indeed were increasingly required to do so, even among the new middle classes.

In 1919, Keynes attended the Paris Peace Conference as Treasury representative and advisor to Prime Minister Lloyd George. Keynes argued against the exacting of punitive reparations by the defeated nations in the interests of future prosperity and to counter Marxist revolutionary threat. Against his arguments, the Peace Conference imposed responsibility for reparations on Germany and Austria. Keynes resigned in protest. Keynes wrote an analysis of, and attack on, these decisions, and that year *The Economic Consequences of the Peace* (Keynes, 1919 [2007]) was published. This book took his case against the Treaty of Versailles from closed meeting rooms to the reading public. It was the start of his public life. Reparations imposed after the First World War were disastrous in ways that could not be imagined in 1918.

The Keynesian revolution

Keynes' ideas were revolutionary. His theories changed the way that we think about work and about state intervention today. Keynes' ideas were influenced and reinforced by workers' needs and demands, but they were not of those demands. Keynes was looking for a better world within capitalism, and not outside of it. Keynes' economics were a product of class conflict, but, like the Fabians, sought to resolve, or dissolve, class conflict within the capitalist relationship with the buffer of an active state.

Within capitalism, though, Keynes defended the interests of the workers by making employment his central focus. Most importantly, Keynes has forever blurred the lines between capitalism, socialism and communism with his theories that privileged full employment and an active state.

1926 brought Britain's first general strike. Labour was returned to power in June 1929. The US stock market crashed in October. The American stock market crash of 1929 ushered in 12 years of depression and mass unemployment.

In 1931, the British pound sterling was unhitched from the gold standard. Keynesianism became the standard economic theory of government. The world financial solution to the economic crisis was that only the dollar could be converted to gold. This solution lasted until 1971. Finance was controlled for the first time. Public money was invested in public works, supporting the capitalist economy by providing employment.

After the stock market crash of 1929, Keynes offered a glimmer of hope amid the gloom. In 1933, Franklin D. Roosevelt was inaugurated President of the United States and the New Deal began. This was also the beginning of the 'Keynesian revolution'. A world economic conference was held in London in 1933, heralding international cooperation.

In the US, the Glass–Steagall Act of 1933 regulated commercial and investment banking by separating money used for trade as opposed to money used for speculation. In the same year, Hitler was appointed Chancellor in Germany. State direct investment in the economy was also the dominant economic policy in Germany. In Germany, Hitler used state funds for a massive rearmament. As a consequence, unemployment fell for the first time since the First World War. In Britain, in the following year, 1934, Unemployment Assistance Boards were established as centralised relief for the unemployed. The importance of these boards is that poverty relief was no longer the responsibility of the community, but was the responsibility of the state. The 1935 Banking Act was passed, barely, further regulating the activities of the banks by the state.

Turning classical theory on its head

In 1936, John Maynard Keynes published *The General Theory of Employment, Interest and Money* (Keynes, 1936 [2017]). The 'General Theory' book turned 'classical' economics on its head, in order to explain and manage the thorny economic problems of cyclical crises and unemployment. In effect, Maynard Keynes foreshadowed Hannah Arendt's more political and philosophical concerns with labour, work and the *vita activa*. In writing *The General Theory*, Keynes laid down the conditions for a kind of capitalism that could perhaps perform the task of Arendt's human work, which is to 'offer mortals a dwelling place more permanent and more stable than themselves' (Arendt, 1958 [1998], p. 152).

Arendt does not mention Keynes in her writing. However, she may have been thinking about Keynes when she described animal laborans as those who labour with neither beginning nor end and contrasted this image of workers with homo faber where fabrication has a definite beginning and a definite end. The work of homo faber provides self-assurance and satisfaction. The labour of animal laborans brings about abundance, according to Arendt.

Keynes proposed an economics of a nation state run like a machine on technological lines to provide stability above abundance, within what Arendt would see as a consumers' and labourers' society. For Arendt, this was the end of politics, of the polis. For Arendt, happiness was achieved through life processes of exhaustion and regeneration of pain and release from pain with a balance between the two. For Keynes, economics was about bringing stability from economic crises.

When Keynes (1936 [2017]) wrote *The General Theory of Employment, Interest and Money*, it was an act. He was acting into his web of interrelationships, and has continued to do so.

The General Theory is the work of a mature economist. Keynes published it in the later part of his life revealing the wealth of his experience and learning in state and private finance. Keynes proposed the general theory as a third way, between capitalism and socialism. Keynes' general theory is a consciously anti-Marxist economic theory. A Fabian future (Clause IV), according to Keynes, was no longer the most desirable solution to political economy, because the power of the state could be used to support and rescue, rather than to replace, capitalism. On the other hand, liberal economics was no longer sufficient because it did not relate to the real world.

Thinking in the aggregate and process over structure

Keynes's general theory changed the face of the 'science' of economics. He created the new economic discipline of macroeconomics. Macroeconomics emphasised the role of aggregation and the state over and above the actions of individual capitalists, or 'entrepreneurs', as Keynes called them. State economics, according to Keynes, had different possibilities and dynamics. Thinking economically in the aggregate is a powerful tool that can be used to solve the problems of the 'real' economy, especially those caused by changes located in aggregates of individuals, which are beyond individual direct control.

Some of the problems of what Keynes considered the real economy were also problems for Adam Smith and Karl Marx. One of these was the problem of cycles, or economic crises. It is an underlying assumption in economics that economies (and social structures in general) reach equilibrium and rest until something disturbs them. This assumption of static equilibrium is nothing like what happens in reality.

In economics, the classical position is that the economy will come to rest when there is full employment. This means that employment is not a problem in classical economics. It is a given. In classical economics, work becomes abstracted as one element among others in the process of production. Wages are abstracted as a cost to the capitalist employer. In classical economics, capital is at the heart of wealth production, as we have seen. Capital is the arrangement of exploitation where the worker sells their labour to the capitalist and the capitalist produces wealth.

What Keynes argued, in the general theory, is similar to Marx. These economists put work, employment, at the heart of economics. The crucial economic problem then becomes how to create and foster employment, not capital. In Keynes, as in Marx, capital became the tool and employment once again became the element that produced wealth.

Workers are consumers as well as producers

Keynes turned classical economics on its head, and allied the worker with the state, but within capitalism. In other words, Keynes identified work as the central concern for economists, as well as for the politicians of the 1920s and 1930s. Keynes, however, also followed Henry Ford by showing that workers are not only central to capitalism as cost, they are also central to capitalism as demand. Workers are consumers as well as producers. So, according to Keynes, when there is a crisis in demand, the state must step in and support employment in order to support the economy. It is employment that must be maximised in order to create an effective economy, on the demand side, as well as on the supply side. The existence of two sides of the economy, capital and labour, create an irresolvable internal conflict and the impossibility of a static equilibrium. In other words, there are no static structures, there are only processes. According to Keynes' general theory, economic processes that give dynamism to the economy for both entrepreneurs and workers can be controlled under certain conditions. It is this combined dynamism that produces 'joy', but perhaps not wealth, for both entrepreneurs and workers.

Further to putting work in the centre of economics, however, Keynes also emphasised the importance of emotion or feelings, 'the psychology', as he called it. Unlike Marx yet like Smith, Keynes viewed economics from the point of view of the capitalist entrepreneur and from the point of view of the state under the control, or hegemony, of this capitalist entrepreneur. An understanding of Keynes helps us to understand more about the capitalist mode of production and will also help to think about what we might want to do next. For this reason, it is important to understand Keynes as he wrote himself.

Keynes was in poor health for most of the ten years he lived after writing *The General Theory* and died prematurely. Like Marx's (1867) *Capital*, Keynes' (1936 [2017]) *The General Theory* was very quickly reinterpreted and the dialectic removed. I give a summary of *The General Theory* here because I think that it lays down a challenge to thinking about how the polis, politics, dialogue and groups coexist with the large and powerful state. It is important to understand the opportunities and the dangers.

Summary of the 'General Theory'

Keynes remarked, at one point, that the General Theory was written for economists. It is difficult to read with more modern eyes, but it is not exceedingly technical. However, in much of what Keynes wrote, he defined his own terms. Underlying these new terms was an understanding of social processes as time-oriented and conflictual. That is, Keynes was actually looking at, and defining processes, rather than trying to describe structures that are essentially static. When he moved economic understanding from static to dynamic, Keynes changed the order of the economic factors and terms. In doing this, he captured a more real sense of how the process of production in capitalism moves through time.

Because Keynes developed his own language, Keynes' general theory is not easy to follow. It is important to understand it, though, as it was written, rather than as it was later interpreted. An accurate understanding of Keynes may well be an important piece of making the world yet to come. It is a somewhat difficult task, but a task worth undertaking. This task includes the understanding of what Keynes called his 'psychological' factors. Economics cannot be 'scientific' without its psychological variables.

Keynes started his theory by defining the entrepreneur's income in the time order by which the entrepreneur organises production. The entrepreneur must first decide his capital outlay and how many workers he is going to employ. The entrepreneur spends his money on the factors of production because he expects a certain profit at the end. The profit, for Keynes, is what the entrepreneur seeks to maximise by employing a certain number of workers. The profit, in other words, is the proceeds of the employment over and above the costs. In this way, Keynes put work at the centre of the process of production from the viewpoint of the individual entrepreneur.

The employment will only happen if the entrepreneur has a positive expectation of the future. Employment, at an aggregate level, thus depends on a social psychological variable, which Keynes called 'expectation'. All investment depends on a positive expectation of the future. This concept echoes the Seeking feeling that will be described in Part IV of this book.

Work as production cost and basis of demand

Keynes observed that both demand and supply, on the aggregate, depend on the level of employment. The level of employment enters the process of production as the supply of work, which is a cost to the entrepreneur, and as the demand for commodities. The demand for commodities determines price and profit. This dual function of employment and the level of wages is not apparent to the individual entrepreneur. It only became apparent when Keynes started to think about the economy as an aggregate process.

The simple, and obvious fact, that workers enter into the production process as cost and as demand is one of Keynes' most important insights. With this insight, Keynes disproved the classical economics rule that 'supply creates its own demand'. In other words, Keynes showed that people will only buy what is made if they have earned the money to do so by selling their labour. Rather than supply creating demand, in fact, employment (demand) creates the products (supply) when the variable of time is taken into account in the process of production. 'Expectation', the social psychological, emotional, variable is what turns a theoretical value into an actual value.

Demand and supply, Keynes continued, are not always related to each other in the same way. Different communities, or classes, consume different proportions of their incomes. In fact, poorer communities and classes consume proportionately more of their incomes than wealthier communities. As communities become relatively wealthier, a gap appears between incomes and consumption. The gap between income and consumption that appears over time, must be made up by the entrepreneur, in the form of new investment, in order to maintain the same level of employment.

The community's propensity to consume and the volume of employment determine the level of wages. As real wages increase, the propensity to consume decreases and employment also decreases at the same level of new investment. This explains the real world paradox of 'poverty in the midst of plenty'. Capitalism creates poverty as well as wealth, as we have seen above. 'For the mere existence of an insufficiency of effective demand may, and often will, bring the increase of employment to a standstill before a level of full employment is reached' (Keynes, 1936 [2017], p. 31). This dynamic, again, is not apparent to the individual entrepreneur, and is only available when the economy is viewed as an aggregate and over time.

The interdependent economy

Keynes (1936 [2017], p. 53) wrote that only he and Karl Marx have 'paid enough attention to aggregate demand'. Only Keynes and Marx, as noted above, put work in the centre of their theories. Only Keynes and Marx considered the movements of the whole interdependent and emotionally-oriented economy, as opposed to the classical view of the individual, isolated and rational economic man, guided by an invisible hand.

While wealth comes from individual rational enterprises, Keynes proposed that the reason for the unexplained cyclical nature of capitalism is because the aggregate of the individual decisions will inevitably lead to economic stagnation. In the real world economy, in other words, booms lead to busts, but busts do not always lead to booms. Thinking about the aggregate, or the common good, is necessary for the process of production to run smoothly. In Keynes' world, everyone needs to think about the aggregate, which is also the common good, for the tendency to stagnate to be controlled or reversed. For Keynes' theories to work, long term class conflict between workers and capitalists needs to end. It is questionable that this can happen within capitalism without a better form of democracy, dialogue and an understanding of the group dimension.

Marx proposed something similar when he proposed that the rate of profit tends towards zero. For Marx, the rate of profit tended to zero as the means of production developed and constant, or dead capital, replaced wages, or live capital. The two theories are very similar in this respect, although Marx also predicted that the crises of capitalism would lead to its destruction and the creation of something new. For Marx, the idea that everyone could think together about the common good could not happen because the interests of the capitalists, Keynes' entrepreneurs, and the interests of the workers could never coincide. Keynes was trying to create a world in which capitalism could survive, but, effectively and fairly, under the hegemony of work, if not the hegemony of the workers. This aspect of Keynes' theory was the downfall of political Keynesianism in the 1970s and the rise of neoliberalism and the time of monsters.

Keynes proposed a remedy for the economic cycles of boom and bust. For Keynes, consumption was the sole end and object of all economic activity, not profit. As prosperity grows and poorer communities become wealthier, the proportion of income that is consumed, on aggregate, goes down and the demand for capital diminishes with the demand for consumption. Consequently, new capital investment must always outrun capital disinvestment sufficiently to fill the gap between income and consumption. This is the boom. When new capital investment can no longer outrun the capital disinvestment, a positive expectation turns into a negative expectation, and the boom turns into a bust. This is the dynamic of the cycles.

State intervention as a remedy for economic cycles

Keynes' proposal was that, when private capitalists, the entrepreneurs, falter, the state must step in to provide new capital through the provision of work as jobs. In other words, the Keynesian state must be prepared to become an intermittent employer. This was Keynes' remedy for the economic cycles. For Keynes, the level of employment and the level of wages are the key determinants of the level of investment in the economy. For maximum collective wealth, the level of wages must be low and the level of employment must be high. Savings, the gap between wages and the amount consumed, are a brake on investment. When wages go up, the investment gap widens. When employment falls, the investment gap widens. The Keynesian state, which looks after the greater good, can step in with state-financed works at the moments when investment fails.

What makes the difference between the state employment and the individual employment of workers is what Keynes calls 'the multiplier'. This is a concept contained in Keynes' General Theory.

Once again, the state, representing the interests of the aggregate, the 'common good', can move in the opposite direction from the individuals that make up the aggregate. The multiplier means that 'increased employment for investment must necessarily stimulate the industries producing for consumption and this leads to a total increase of employment which is a multiple of the primary employment required by the investment itself' (Keynes, 1936 [2017], p. 103). When the state invests, the effect is some multiple of the original investment, since the increased employment increases consumption which, in turn, increases investment, which increases employment and so on.

Most importantly, for aspects of globalisation, in an open system with foreign-trade relations, some part of the multiplier of the increased investment will accrue to the benefit of employment in foreign countries. Of course, the greater the propensity to consume, the greater the multiple, and hence the greater the addition to employment corresponding to a given change in investment. The paradoxical conclusion is that a poor community, in which saving is a very small proportion of the income, will be more subject to violent fluctuations (or cycles) than a wealthy community where saving is a larger proportion of income and the 'multiplier' will be smaller (Keynes, 1936 [2017], p. 109). This is Keynes' idea about colonialism and what later became known as globalisation. Liquid investment, finance, can cross national borders and employ workers of other countries. When these countries are less wealthy, the investment is more productive of live employment, and thus of profit.

The employment of a given number of men and women on public works will have a much larger effect on aggregate employment at a time when there is severe unemployment. Thus, public works of even doubtful utility may pay for themselves over and over again at a time of severe unemployment, if only from the diminished cost of relief expenditure.

Here Keynes clearly departed from Marxist and Fabian economics. In some Marxist and Fabian economics the state is the permanent owner of the means of production. The Keynesian incentives are not actively applied at all times. The power of Keynesian economics is that the state provides a balance to private investment that can be instituted when times are hard, when workers are unemployed, or underemployed, and then taken away again when times are better. The state works against what is happening in the private sector and improves the relations between the classes under capitalism because it is working in concert with the owners of private property.

Glitches, flaws and contradictions

If the state is the permanent owner of the means of production, the temperature-like balancing that brings stability may not be possible. By providing employment in public works, and then withdrawing the employment, the state can make small balancing manoeuvres, like a temperature gauge or a homeostatic biological process. For Keynes, it is the change in employment that is the crucial issue for the multiplier, and not the quality of the task at which the workers are employed. However, it is also true that, in capitalism, where capitalists and workers see their interests as conflicting, giving state employment to workers is much easier than taking it away. This 'glitch' or 'fatal flaw' laid the basis for the political change from Keynesian economics to neoliberalism in the 1970s.

There are a great many contradictions in Keynes' thinking. Keynes left blanks and gaps. For example, the greatest efficiency for a capitalist state will occur when wages are low, so most of the workers' incomes are consumed, and not saved, and very little in the way of new investment is needed. However, in the real economy, when nearing full employment, wages will rise and more new investment will be needed in order to employ those who are not employed. At some point, if no new investment is forthcoming from the private entrepreneur, investment will cease or go abroad. This creates a new crash and a new economic cycle. When the casino, otherwise known as the 'financial markets', is dominant, the investment often goes abroad. This did not become a major part of Keynes' thinking. This is a flaw in terms of today's real world economics. However, the importance and potential destructiveness of the national and international financial markets in the national economy are still important theoretically when thinking about a world yet to come.

Keynes's solution was the management of the economy, through state employment in public works, financed by borrowing and other fiscal measures. The Keynesian state technocrat must thus be able to calculate and control the rise and fall of investment and employment in order for the strategy of economic management to work. In order to do this, the state technocrat must understand how and when to induce the entrepreneur to invest. This presupposes the existence of an autonomous technocratic bureaucracy, unaffected by class interests and politics, which, of course, borders on socialism and is also unrealistic in human political and emotional terms. The only way to have such a state technocrat is to have a democracy that allows people to think, decide and act together in dialogue across different and sometimes conflicting interests. In the neoliberal time of monsters, the state technocrat reflects the very narrow interests of a very small part of the population.

Keynes, capitalism and socialism

Keynes hoped that his fellow economists would be advising the politicians who govern the capitalist state. He recommended that the state provide incentives to entrepreneurs or capitalists to invest. Keynes believed that the manipulation of interest rates was not very useful as an incentive to investment. He also believed that the introduction of financial markets constituted a disincentive for long term investment. He called the financial markets 'the casino'.

This was his argument: the capitalist will only decide to invest when he has the expectation that his investment will return as much, or more, to him at the market rate than he would receive if he did not invest. What he receives when he does not invest is the market rate of interest. However, the rate of interest is a current phenomenon. The rate of interest is happening in the moving present. The marginal efficiency of capital, the variable that will induce the capitalist to invest, is an expectation of the future, an aggregate, psychological or social phenomenon. In Keynes' world, the capitalist invests in employment by hiring workers and investing in durable equipment in the present for an uncertain future. The point that Keynes made was that interest rates have little effect in the real world if the capitalist does not believe that there is a better future ahead.

What is needed for investment to occur in the real world, Keynes said, is an expectation of long-term gain. In this sense, the facts of the present situation enter disproportionately into how the entrepreneur or capitalist expects that future to be. Keynes referred to this psychological factor as the 'state of confidence', again, not just an individual state of mind but a social one. The 'state of confidence' is a powerful factor in determining the marginal efficiency of capital, which is based on a calculation of what will happen in the next five or ten years.

The point that Keynes wanted to make was that the world has changed since the classical economists were writing, even if only 50 years before. The businessman is no longer someone who is motivated by a desire to create a factory, a mine or a farm. 'There might not be much investment merely as a result of cold calculation', Keynes said. Ownership and management in the past were in the same person. Decisions to invest were largely irrevocable (Keynes, 1936 [2017], p. 130).

The casino and the group dimension

The present differs from the past in that ownership and management have become separated with the development of organised investment markets. In other words, the virtual world of the investment markets has become separated from the real world of investments and expectations over the long term. '... all sorts of considerations enter into the market valuation which are in no way relevant to the prospective yield. [...] Investments, which are "fixed" for the community in the real world, are "liquid" for the individual financial investor' (Keynes, 1936 [2017], p. 132).

The underlying ideology, which gives the appearance of stability and unity between the real world and the investment market, is that the existing state of affairs will continue indefinitely. This is the static equilibrium mentioned above. However, Keynes realised that the ideology is nowhere near reality. Once again, he recognised the importance of time and psychology in the management of economic decisions. The ideology is 'precarious', as Keynes put it. And the precariousness of the ideology creates a large part of the problem of securing sufficient investment. The busts will not always lead to booms.

The day-to-day fluctuations of the investment market, in the end, have to do with day-to-day fluctuations of the 'weather'. The 'weather', in this context, is the mass psychology of a large number of people in the group dimension, often influenced by the mass media. The professional investors, it seems, spend much more time anticipating changes in the news than in noticing how the enterprises in which they invest are run. Investment is no longer based on long-term expectation. And, most recently, since Keynes wrote, investment is almost always done by algorithms and machines. 'The actual, private object of the most skilled investment today is to "beat the gun", or "outwit the crowd"' (Keynes, 1936 [2017], p. 134). More recently, 'outwitting the crowd' depends on having the most advanced technology in order to follow events instantly with investments and disinvestments.

This means that what capitalists have been doing (and were doing in 1936, and before) is, in effect, socialising capital. Global capitalism as a whole is the owner and manager of the processes of production. The processes of production, in other words, no longer depend upon the investments of individual entrepreneurs. Most investment funds, in fact, are owned by committees, boards or banks. None of these are interested in long-term growth of enterprises within any particular nation state. Socialised capital is not a fixed asset in a community, but a liquid asset that can be invested, disinvested, held in place or moved from community to community. Keynes termed the activity of forecasting the psychology of the market as 'speculation'. He termed the activity of forecasting the prospective yield of assets over their whole lifetime of use as 'enterprise'.

In Keynes' eyes, the community is the loser in this tendency to liquidity. The community in this context is the nation. He wrote about he called 'animal spirits'. In spite of all the calculations, Keynes said, the entrepreneur with 'animal spirits' will have hopes that stretch into the future, and benefit the community as a whole (Keynes, 1936 [2017], p. 139). To be an entrepreneur, 'the healthy man must put aside the expectation of death'. If the 'animal spirits' are lost, enterprise will fade and die. The idea of 'animal spirits' was optimistic. Underneath this optimism was a feeling of pessimism that the death of the entrepreneur was already imminent in Keynes' time. It may be that, in the world yet to come, most entrepreneurs will be those that invest their own capital in their own work, thus unifying the interests of capital and labour in self-employment or cooperative enterprise. If this comes to pass, Keynes will be a relevant resource to enable productive thinking as both worker and investor. In cooperatives and in politics, this will mean thinking together in groups that are capable of dialogue.

Keynes wanted the state to take care of the national capitalists, the entrepreneurs with 'animal spirits'. These are the people who gain from an active state, like the New Deal in the 1930s or the Labour Government in the 1940s. Keynes (1936 [2017], p. 139) described this state as a state that will care for the 'delicate balance of spontaneous optimism'.

Keynes concluded that a monetary policy directed towards influencing the rate of interest would not work. This point is important, because this was the Keynes who, in turn, was turned on his head by the neoliberal economists from the 1970s onwards. The neoliberals abandoned the project of full employment, and of employment in general, in favour of the project of protecting money values from inflation through interest rates.

On the whole, in the world today, enterprise has yielded to the speculation that Keynes feared: 'When the capital development of a country becomes a by-product of the activities of a casino, the job is likely to be ill-done' (Keynes, 1936 [2017], p. 136). We now know that the state that Keynes envisioned has not been possible under the political capitalist regime, and Keynes has explained why. Keynes hoped for a state that would organise investment, but not production, and this was his difference with what we think of as socialism. As we will see, the political limitations of the capitalist state have precluded Keynes' approach and turned it into something other than what he imagined. The political limitations of the capitalist state have led us to neoliberalism and the age of monsters. Keynes would not have been surprised in his gloomiest moments.

However, in his more optimistic moments, Keynes thought that the end of the 'functionless investor', the banker, was close in Great Britain. It would be merely a gradual continuance of what was present when he was writing, and would not need a revolution. The functionless investor could then be harnessed to the 'service of the community on reasonable terms of reward'.

Capitalism and socialism

Keynes did not agree with the idea of a state that assumes the ownership of the means of production. He believed that private, individual and cooperative ownership could bring the rewards of ownership and be contained by an active state. For Keynes, central controls were necessary to ensure full employment, but not to direct the use of that employment. Thus, Keynes supposed that traditional values of individualism could still hold good, even with a strong and active state.

For Keynes, individualism, was best for the exercise of personal choice. Also, individualism, for Keynes, was the best option for the safeguard of personal liberty. The authoritarian state systems solve the problem of underemployment at the expense of efficiency and of freedom, Keynes thought.

Right at the end of the *General Theory of Employment, Interest and Money*, Keynes observed that the ideas of civil servants, politicians and agitators are not the newest, but 'soon or late, it is ideas, not vested interests, which are dangerous for good or evil.' Nearly 100 years on from when Keynes was writing, is it time for his ideas, for good or evil, to reveal their potency?

Certainly, the war years after the publication of *General Theory* interrupted both the problems and the solutions for the unemployment caused by the economic crash of 1929. The young economists in America, though, adopted Keynesianism. By 1936, American national production had returned to its 1929 level.

The act, activism and the group: Opportunities and dangers

Much of what we think about as neoliberalism is a response to Keynes. *The General Theory of Employment, Interest and Money* was an act of creative thinking that has brought about crucial consequences. Arendt wrote a critical response that was aimed at Marx, but was also relevant to Keynes. She wrote a critique of the social, by which she meant a consumers' and labourers' society, concerned only with survival, much as Keynes was describing. Here, Arendt again brought the distinction between labour and work. Arendt used the activity of making art as the benchmark for what she considered work that is different from labour. The only workers left in this society, she said, are artists. With increasing automation of labour, it becomes a problem to provide enough daily exertion to keep the capacity for consumption alive. An ever-recurrent life cycle, perceived to be without pain and effort, is produced when all human activity is sucked into an intensified life process. In this situation, there is no longer any true public realm. There are only private certainties displayed in the open (Arendt, 1958 [1998], p. 133).

Work, on the other hand, best personified by art, according to Arendt, is involved in creating the durability of the world. Work creates the things of the world that have the function of stabilising human life. For Arendt, work brings happiness through life processes of exhaustion and regeneration. This includes a life of pain and release from pain in a homeostatic balance. Work provides self-assurance and satisfaction. Fabrication, she said, has a definite beginning and a definite end. Labour has neither beginning nor end. The Modern Age, Arendt said, creates animal laborans for whom social life is wordless and herdlike. Animal laborans is incapable of building or inhabiting a public realm of their own. Homo faber, on the other hand, has a realm of their own, which is the market place where they shows the product of their hands and receive esteem. This is what the modern world is missing.

The end of homo faber came with the rise of labour and the labour society and, particularly, with pride in conspicuous consumption privileged over pride in esteemed production. The most serious consequence of these processes is that the polis and homo faber are overwhelmed by what Arendt called the social and animal laborans, in wordless labour. I think that this helps us to understand why it is so difficult to move from an increasingly brutal neoliberal capitalism into something else, the world yet to come. Arendt's ideas, along with Keynes, Elias and Foulkes, help to think about how this world yet to come might look and feel. It is important that the people yet to come have ways of making that world.

Recouping the polis and the human condition through making

First, though, we need to find and recoup the polis and the human condition as worker and controller of work. This entails having better democratic processes. The artist, as worker, makes things and shows them as their achievements. Works of art demonstrate durability that lasts through the ages. Art transforms people through feeling and thought, Arendt said; 'Thought is related to feeling and transforms its mute and inarticulate despondency, as exchange transforms the naked greed of desire and usage transforms the desperate longing of needs – until they are fit to enter the world and to be transformed into things ...' (Arendt, 1958 [1998], p. 168). Art comes from thought, but thought itself does not produce the art. Art must become a tangible thing. Artists become homo faber in the making of works that have meaning for themselves and others. This materialisation of thought is something that can be available to all, not only to men or to elites. This is what Arendt saw as fabrication. This is what she believed was lost in the world of job-holders and labourers.

Further, thought is related to action. Speaking and acting, Arendt said, have a common, basic condition. This condition is human plurality. Humans cannot do either of these two things alone. Speaking and acting have a twofold character, of equality and distinction: 'Human plurality is the paradoxical plurality of distinct beings' (Arendt, 1958 [1998], p. 176). We are all the same and we are all different from each other. Speech and action reveal this unique distinctness, which also rests on initiative. This is the group dimension in Arendt. In 'working' groups, we are able to find ourselves as distinct and unique beings among equals.

Most acts are performed as speech. Arendt distinguished what she meant by speech from 'mere talk'. Mere talk happens when people use violence in order to achieve certain outcomes for their own sakes. This happens in wars, she says, or when people are speaking against their enemies. This is not true speech because the words reveal nothing and disclosure comes only from the deed itself (Arendt, 1958 [1998], p. 180).

'We exist primarily as acting and speaking things ... Interests lie between people and binds them together' (Arendt 1958 [1998], p. 182) argued. 'This in-between space is no less real than the world of things that we have in common. We call this reality the 'web' of human relationships, indicating by the metaphor its somewhat intangible quality'. When people act and speak, a new beginning is created through action. This new beginning always falls into an already existing web where the immediate consequences of speech and action are felt. The act and the web together start a new process that never existed before. Every reaction becomes a chain reaction and every process is the cause of new processes. Human interrelatedness is boundaryless.

The political realm arises out of the sharing of the word and deed

Boundaries are thus of great importance to human affairs. Boundaries are important precisely because they are needed to contain the power of the act and its inherent unpredictability. Boundaries create and maintain the polis, the arenas where politics take place, among many other capacities. This is the group.

Real stories have no author, says Arendt. 'Although everyone started his life inserting himself into the world, nobody is the author or producer of their own life story ... The actor is not merely the doer, but always and at the same time the sufferer' (Arendt, 1958 [1998], p. 188). Here, Arendt came very close to ideas about individuals and groups from Norbert Elias (1987) and S. H. Foulkes (1948) to whom we will return later.

The political realm arises directly out of acting together, the sharing of word and deed. The polis is the organisation of people as it arises out of acting and speaking together; 'Without a space of appearance and without trusting in action and speech as a mode of being together, neither the reality of oneself, one's identity, nor the reality of the surrounding world can be established beyond doubt' (Arendt, 1958 [1998], p. 208). The polis is truly a crucial in-between space for humans to create themselves and their acts in the world.

However, it is not the actor, but the storyteller who perceives and makes the story, Arendt says. As storytellers, Smith, Marx and Keynes described a world without a polis. This is a world that where individuals labour together as though they are one with a consequent loss of individuality and identity. This is what Arendt (1958 [1998], p. 215) called the 'social'. It is not equality, but sameness, and is antipolitical. So, although, Smith, Marx and Keynes have helped us to understand various aspects of the world that we live in, they have told the story of interdependent actions that have historically led to processes where we are collectively destroying both our environment and our humanity in the neoliberal world. Arendt, in noting the lack of polis in the political, has called attention to a possible clue as to how we can act, individually and collectively, to gain back both our oneness with our environment and our oneness with each other. This is through speaking and acting in groups, not masses or echo chambers. The processes that create masses without groups lead to totalitarianism; 'When citizens are banished from the public realm, there is only the ruler to attend to public affairs' (Arendt, 1958 [1998], p. 221).

Action produces complexity

Although action is often meant to resolve or simplify, action always produces complexity. Arendt expressed this idea as a threefold frustration with action. First, the outcomes of any action are unpredictable. Second, not only are the outcomes of actions unpredictable, they are also irreversible. Actions never end. Third, the authors of any action very soon become anonymous. These objections, Arendt said, often appear as arguments against democracy. However, they are also arguments against the essentials of politics. At this point in her writing, Arendt identified the human condition of plurality with polis and the public realm. To do away with one is to do away with the other. In this way, Arendt defined human freedom as the human capacity to act into the web of human relationships, with the consequence of having to accept that freedom entails uncertainty as the decisive factor in human affairs. In this view, democracy is that which provides a space for the polis and a guarantee of the capacity to speak and act within it.

Arendt perceived that this space is under threat of being irrevocably destroyed. The accounts of Adam Smith, Karl Marx and Maynard Keynes have been actions that have had unpredictable consequences in creating a social without a polis. In this, they have given us ways of understanding human processes without respecting the human condition of group life, where individuals need groups in order to find and be themselves. These groups still exist in some areas of the social, for now. In some ways, one of the unpredicted consequences of reaching for human equality is that groups are being formed where women, children and former slaves from the world of animal laborans are finding their voices, with disturbing consequences for the status quo. These are the liberation movements of all kinds. It is this new space for a polis that I will write about in the following chapters. Smith created the story of capitalism and of the capitalist entrepreneur. Marx created the story of the class and the conflictual nature of social change and resistance to change. Keynes wrote the story of the nation state and how it might work to provide a caring space for collective survival. Arendt has written the story of the human condition that helps to understand why the world yet to come is so difficult to birth even under the ever most threatening conditions of planetary and human destructive processes.

The 'General Theory' as action

I have thought it worthwhile to include the details of Keynes' theory as he wrote it with understandings coming from the group dimension. The General Theory was certainly not what I had expected it to be from the available critiques and commentaries. These critiques and commentaries are not informed by the group dimension. Much of what Keynes wrote was aimed at finance and financiers, and it was devastating. Much of what Keynes wrote, avowedly anti-Marxist, but with a high content of Marxist thought, was challenging to the economic vested interests at the time. It was challenging to the economic vested interests, but also far-seeing for politicians, who had no remedies for economic crashes and wars. It was both a ray of hope and a devastating destruction of the hegemony of the interests of finance and money. Keynes' ideas were influential in the controls on finance that were instituted after the economic crash in 1929 and the depression that followed. Finance was not released from these controls until the 1970s. This is the subtext to the General Theory and its contribution to the actions that came afterwards.

After Keynes published his general theory, the laissez-faire economists were silent (Wapshott, p. 133). Keynes had silenced his critics, temporarily. However, the fear of state intervention, the consequent loss of control of finance, and Keynes' threatened 'euthanasia of the rentier' opened the way for the counter-discourse to Keynesianism, called neoliberalism. Walter Lippmann told Harvard academics in 1934 that 'laissez-faire is dead and the modern state has become responsible for the modern economy' (Wapshott, 2012, p. 163). The economic interests expressed in classical economics had to have a response that would include a state that was ultimately responsible for production. This modern state was not going to go away.

Keynesian economists in America were concerned that they would be facing a socialist revolution in the 1930s if they did not take care of the unemployed. These were the economists who were in charge of the American Federal Bank, when the banks were regulated more tightly in the 1935 Banking Act. This was the Keynesian Revolution.

Rearmament and the Second World War were great tests of Keynesian ideas about economic activity that can be promoted by an active and investing state, both in democracies and in fascist totalitarian states. Before his death, in 1946, Keynes helped to shape the post-Second World War Bretton Woods Agreement around a revived gold standard. He also helped to found the International Monetary Fund and the World Bank, thus creating the superstate, international capital stores that he had described in the General Theory.

In Britain, foreign exchange controls were in place from 1939 until Margaret Thatcher removed them in 1979. Neville Chamberlain financed the Second World War by public borrowing rather than by taxation. And, in the Beveridge Report of 1942, a welfare state was proposed with family allowances, maternity benefits and the creation of a National Health Service. The NHS was, even at its inception, an enormous state enterprise. It was financed in part by the mass savings plan of National Insurance. There was full employment in 1942, public accounting became more accurate and public planning more predictable. Keynes had, indeed, changed the world.

References

Arendt, H. (1958 [1998]) *The Human Condition, 2nd edition.* Chicago, IL: University of Chicago Press.

Elias, N. (1987) *Involvement and Detachment.* Oxford: Blackwell.

Foulkes, S. H. (1948) *Introduction to Group-analytic Psychotherapy: Studies in the Social Integration of Individuals and Groups.* London: Maresfield Reprints.

Keynes, J. M. (1919 [2007]) *The Economic Consequences of the Peace.* New York: Skyhorse Publishing.

Keynes, J. M. (1936 [2017]) *The General Theory of Employment, Interest and Money.* Stansted: Wordsworth Editions.

Marx, K. (1867) *Capital: A Critique of Political Economy,* https://www.marxists.org/archive/marx/works/1867-c1

Wapshott, N. (2012) *Keynes Hayek: The Clash That Defined Modern Economics.* New York: W. W. Norton & Co.

Part II

Neoliberalism
Hayek and the Mont Pelerin Society

'The philosophers have only interpreted the world, in various ways; the point is to change it'.

Karl Marx (1845)

Figure 2 'Mountain'

DOI: 10.4324/9781003350088-5

Chapter 3

Hayek as a response to Keynes

The classical economists' response to Keynes began with an Austrian-born economist called Friedrich Hayek. Keynes had changed the world. Part of this change was the inevitable reaction, the counter-discourse, to Keynes' powerful ideas about the large and active state. Hayek and the Mont Pelerin Society were the outcome of this reaction. They created an ideology for the world of monsters. The world of monsters is heading for climate and technological disaster. How did this come about and what is needed in order to leave the world of monsters and to give birth to the world yet to come? Hayek, his writings and the writings of those influenced by him are important elements of understanding humanity's present situation and what is needed to change it. At the moment, there is no effective counter-discourse to neoliberalism. A consciousness of the group dimension is proposed as an element of a possible counter-discourse.

Hayek and Keynes had known each other before, and during, the Second World War. They fiercely debated economic theories and philosophies. Hayek had been invited to England, to the London School of Economics, by an adversary of Keynes, called Lionel Robbins, presumably to provide a counter-balance to Keynes. The irony is that the distinctly anti-Marxist Hayek was employed at the university which had been founded by the Webbs, who were also founders of the Fabians and of the Labour Party.

When Hayek read Keynes' (1936 [2017]) *The General Theory of Employment, Interest and Money* written by his rival, in 1936, however, he was silent, along with the others. Keynes had written the anti-Marxist guide to using the power of the centralised state in order to increase consumer spending, cure mass unemployment and modulate economic crises. Moreover, Keynes' theories already had enough political support to inform government policies. Hayek and his theories, resting on the microeconomic level of individual decisions, had no initial response to Keynes, despite their previous passionate debates.

Keynes' general theory proved popular. It also received support from politicians and capitalists. Lived experiences provided support for Keynes' ideas. For example, when American President, Franklin D. Roosevelt, ignored Keynes and made spending cuts as the Second World War began, the American economy immediately went into recession. Industrial production fell and unemployment rose

DOI: 10.4324/9781003350088-6

in 1938. When Roosevelt backtracked on these policies, and promoted state investment in jobs, a Keynesian policy, the American economy immediately recovered. Keynes was proven right. Keynes' ideas were proving useful to the politicians.

In the meantime, Hayek continued to write and lecture. Hayek had a different approach to aggregation from Keynes.

> Economic decisions in real life are made by individuals based on partial knowledge of current conditions coupled with their best guess of what might happen. Each individual comes to a different (and often contradictory) judgment about what those conditions might be. Some get the decision right, some wrong. But, together, these decisions combine to form a moving picture of the market in operation.
>
> (Wapshott, 2012, p. 180)

Classical economics is based on money

In Hayek's economics, individuals come together in the market place. Changes in the market are expressed through price changes. Price changes are the result of the interactions between supply and demand. Anything that interferes with the mechanisms that determine the setting of prices by supply and demand, like state intervention, keeps these mechanisms from working correctly. Thus, state intervention, according to Hayek, is unhelpful. Besides being unhelpful, the 'totalitarian' decision-making involved in state intervention threatens the free expression of individuals by upsetting the mechanisms that the economy needs to guide itself. This is a version of Adam Smith's invisible hand. The invisible hand must be allowed to function freely without the influence of the state.

Hayek had other disagreements with Keynes that seemed to harken back to Adam Smith, but not quite. Hayek doubted that the demand for commodities was the same as the demand for labour. He thus broke the crucial connection that Keynes had made about how jobs and wages enter the production process in two places, as cost and as demand. Hayek again separated them, asserting that money, not work and jobs, was the source of demand. In doing this, he opened up the possibility of an ideology that looked to be egalitarian and to apply to everyone, but was, fact, only responsive to those with money.

Hayek was against state intervention and in favour of the ideological hegemony of money. Employment, as in pre-Keynesian classical economics, was not important. Employment would reach its 'natural level' by means of the smooth workings of the market's invisible hand. Thus, Hayek's economics took employment out of the centre of economics and put money into the centre instead. Controlling inflation was the most important task of the state, not the maintenance of consumption through employment. Controlling inflation guarantees that money keeps its value. It protects those who hold and handle money for profit.

It is easy to forget how important this conflict of theories was in the political economy of the 1930s in Europe and in the US. Inflation, unemployment, and depression threatened the stability of nations, particularly in Germany. In Germany, Hitler, totalitarianism and antisemitism were gaining power in their opposition to Marxism, socialism and communism.

The 'Road to Serfdom'

Keynes had published his 'General Theory' on the eve of the Second World War in Europe. Hayek published his best-known work just at the end of the war, in 1944. Although he barely mentioned Keynes, the whole of his book, *The Road to Serfdom* (Hayek, 1944 [2001]), can be read as the response to Keynes that Hayek did not provide in 1936, when Keynes' general theory was published. In his book, Hayek argued that whenever market forces are replaced with state planning, individual liberties are lost. The result is totalitarian government. By 1944, Hayek had experienced the real-world examples of authoritarian states in both Russia and Germany and the real fear that they produced in the democratic west.

The Road to Serfdom is at the heart of the neoliberal movement. Like Keynes, Hayek acted into his web of interdependencies. Hayek had almost made a return to the liberalism of Adam Smith. The power of a Keynesian active state was too big and too real to be ignored. Hayek's problem was how to make an adjustment in liberal economic theory that also recognised and accepted the power of the state. In this sense, *The Road to Serfdom* is a kind of 'yes, but' to Keynes' *The General Theory of Employment, Interest and Money*.

Hayek was more ambivalent about state planning and intervention than Adam Smith (1776 [2009]). For Hayek, it was acceptable to plan in order to create the conditions under which the knowledge, initiative and decision-making of individuals was best supported. Planning with central direction and organisation of all activities according to consciously constructed blueprints was not acceptable to Hayek. The socialists of all parties, Hayek said, have appropriated the term 'planning' for planning of this unacceptable kind.

Hayek went on to explain that the new liberal argument is not the same as the old laissez-faire argument. The liberal wants to make the best use of competition as a means of coordinating human efforts. This is different from wanting to leave the efforts of individuals to their own devices. Competition needs a legal framework and a legal framework needs a powerful state.

The contradictory elements of neoliberalism are very apparent. The neoliberal theoretical and the practical do not match. In essence, when Hayek later allowed himself to be interpreted by his followers and associated politicians, this ambiguity about planning became the necessity to plan and control when it suited neoliberals and their backers. This is a crucial difference between neoliberals and the original liberals. For the neoliberals, planning is fine in itself, but it depends on who is doing it and why they are doing it. In fact, Hayek's theories were eventually all turned against themselves. A strong state planning was eventually declared necessary to create and preserve 'markets' for individuals with money, particularly the money markets.

Keynes underestimated the opposition

Keynes understood Hayek's ambiguity about planning from his first reading. Keynes failed, though, to take Hayek's book seriously when he read it in 1944. Keynes was on his way to the Bretton Woods Conference in America, where he would contribute to the settlement of the Second World War. He wrote to Hayek saying that he agreed with him!

Keynes wrote to Hayek: 'You admit here and there that it is a question of knowing where to draw the line. You agree that the line has to be drawn somewhere; and the logical extreme is not possible', and continued, 'as soon as you admit that the extreme is not possible, and that a line has to be drawn, you are, on you own argument, done for, since you are trying to persuade us that so soon as one moves an inch in the planned direction, you are necessarily launched on the slippery path which will lead you in due course over the precipice' (quoted in Wapshott, 2012, p. 200). What Keynes missed was that the 'inch of planning' was not at issue. The difference was about who and what the 'planning' was for.

Keynes took Hayek's economic contribution lightly. Perhaps too lightly, since he missed the constant undermining of his own ideas. Keynes thought that Hayek's ideas were not practical in the US and that they would not get noticed. It was, in fact, difficult to find a publisher for *The Road to Serfdom*. When it was published, though, Keynes was proven wrong about its popularity. *Readers' Digest* published an abridged version and *Look* magazine published a cartoon version (Wapshott, 2012). Hayek had captured the American spirit of individualism, competition, fear and hatred of socialism.

In Britain, there was a more negative response to Hayek's book. The radical author George Orwell pointed out that 'free competition means for the great mass of people a tyranny probably worse, because more irresponsible, than that of the state.' Orwell also said that the vast majority of people would rather have state regimentation than slumps and unemployment (quoted in Wapshott, 2012, p. 202). When Conservative party leader in the UK, Winston Churchill, warned that socialist planning could lead to tyranny at the start of his election campaign in 1945, he was defeated by a Labour landslide. Voters feared a return of the pre-war, high unemployment presided over by the Conservative government in the UK.

At this point, the US and the UK became divided. The UK went down the more Keynesian and socialist route of the National Health Service and the US did not.

The legacy of Fabius

Hayek's book was both popular and controversial. It then went on to become the basis of the neoliberal movement that has now touched the lives of practically everyone in the world. Hayek and others formed organisations that worked consistently and logically, waiting patiently over the years for a political opportunity to pounce. They worked, and waited, from 1947 to 1979. What is in this book that provided such ideological and organisational power? The answer to this question is fear.

It is easy to underestimate how important it is to understand neoliberalism in its own terms. These terms are its greatest strength. On the eve of Keynesianism's triumphs, following the Second World War, Hayek did not argue with Keynes' economics. Hayek, instead, argued with the politics of Keynes' whole project of state intervention into the economy. Planning means socialism and socialism means slavery, according to Hayek. Implicit in this formulation is the hidden meaning that economics is not about consumption for all, but only about consumption for some. Money must be protected, not jobs or wages. Hayek's state is a state for those who have money and not for the Keynesian economy of workers and communities, except insofar as they offer opportunities to the market. Opportunities in the market involve having money.

Hayek did not meet Keynes head on. He ignored Keynes' greatest creations: macroeconomics and aggregate statistics of economic performance. Hayek also ignored the thorniest problem of classical economics which was the problem of boom-and-bust cycles, for which Keynes had a solution.

Hayek's contribution was to provide a neoliberal response to Keynes' general theory of the power of the state. To this end, he began his book with the attitude of the liberal towards society. The attitude of the liberal towards society, Hayek said, is one of a gardener trying to create the best conditions for growth. So, Hayek set about building a theory of the powerful state that would enhance the power of choice of the individual over that of society.

Hayek said that he was not advocating the laissez-faire attitude of just leaving things as they were. He supported planning in certain circumstances. In one of these circumstances, he saw planning as a way of helping to make the best use of individualised competition. Planning is necessary for coordination of individuals, he said. Planning is also necessary where it is needed to form legal frameworks. Planning is needed to create social welfare. For Hayek, social welfare was a legitimate state enterprise, but providing work was not. The state that gives money to people creates markets but the state that provides work deforms the market by interfering with individual competition. Providing work and directing its use deprives competition of its power. Price changes (wages, in this case) are then no longer a reliable guide for the individual action of individual entrepreneurs.

State intervention was needed to control monopolies. Hayek spoke of the monopolist action of capitalists and workers in the best organised industries. The original neoliberal call for planning to control monopolies eventually, though, was applied only to labour and to the control of labour union closed shops. The parallel idea of control of monopolies in industry and finance withered away from neoliberalism with time. The lack of control of monopolies by the neoliberal state, eventually, dealt the fatal blow to Hayek's economics. However, this blow did not impede the progress of the ideology of neoliberalism, with tragic effect in the creation of the world of monsters, which has seen steep rises in inequality of power world-wide.

Hayek had several arguments for competition, democracy, private property and money. For example, competition by price conceals conflict, Hayek said. Each individual producer must adapt to price changes because he cannot control them.

The adoption of social planning for different needs brings out the concealed conflict between their aims. Hayek believed that, if the conflict becomes apparent, and is not hidden in these impersonal forces, the people would, inevitably, turn against each other and against the state. When conflict appears to be the product of impersonal forces the state is protected. Fear of socialism and avoidance of conflict are thus two of the basic emotional states expressed in Hayek's writings. These two fears are a denial of anything like the group dimension, where conflicts can occur and be resolved without fear or coercion.

Planning, democracy and equality

Planned democracies defeat themselves, according to Hayek. Democratic assemblies which are trying to plan to carry out the mandates of the people inevitably create dissatisfaction. When it is agreed that planning is necessary, and democratic assemblies are unable to produce a plan, then the people turn to a single person to act. Hayek's model for this assertion was fascism in Germany between the First and Second World Wars.

Hayek believed in democracy. Democracy is the most effective device for safeguarding internal peace and individual freedom, he said, and he feared that in socialism, what he called 'collectivist greed' and the dictatorship of the proletariat, would need to direct the economic system through the ownership of the means of production, which would destroy personal freedom (Hayek, 1944 [2001]). With democracy as the ultimate source of power, expressing the will of the majority, power is limited and prevented from being arbitrary. And, although the dictatorship of the proletariat is actually a long way from what Keynes was proposing, Hayek also stated that planning leads to dictatorship because coercion and the enforcement of ideals is essential if central planning on a large scale is to be possible.

Hayek also believed in money. Money is the symbol of opportunities. Money is an instrument of freedom. Money means being able to choose our rewards and our losses. Hayek thought that planning to secure a more just and equitable distribution of wealth was impossible. It was impossible because 'If we want to decide who is to have what, we must plan the whole economic system and this will bring disagreement, discontent and oppression' (Hayek, 1944 [2001]); there must be someone to blame.

Despite recognising the extreme interdependence of individuals on each other, Hayek thought that the collective satisfaction of needs inevitably leads to totalitarianism. The economic freedom of the socialists is freedom from economic care, Hayek said. The freedom of the socialists also relieves the individual from the necessity and the power of choice. According to Hayek, in the matter of who is responsible for satisfaction of needs, Hayek chose the individual, while Keynes and the socialists chose the state.

Impersonal forces

Hayek contrasted the socialists' freedom with the freedom derived from free enterprise. Unlike under socialism, in free enterprise, chances are not equal. Both private property and inheritance create differences in opportunities between individuals. However, these differences are the consequence of what Hayek (1944 [2001], p. 108) called 'impersonal forces'. While there are differences under free enterprise, there are also no absolute impediments. No one possesses the power of the state in a competitive society. The control of the means of production is divided among many people and no one has complete power over individuals.

There are other advantages, according to Hayek. Inequality, he said, is more readily borne if it is determined by these 'impersonal forces', than when it is due to design. Even mass unemployment is less degrading if it is by misfortune and not deliberately imposed by state-determined austerity. Further, Hayek said, it is mostly the unscrupulous and uninhibited who are likely to be more successful in a society tending towards totalitarianism. In totalitarian societies, he said, there is a general demand for quick and determined government action which is 'strong'. Democracy is slow and cumbersome, by contrast. Ruthlessness is required in a new type of party organised on military lines. In a planned society, it is not the majority of the people who have the power, but the largest group whose number agree sufficiently to make a unified decision possible. These will be the worst elements.

The potential dictator, Hayek continued, proclaims loudly and frequently with passions and emotions. These passions and emotions lead the docile and passive to a totalitarian party. It is easier for people to agree on a negative programme, on hatred of an enemy or on the envy of those better off, than on a positive task. 'The enemy whether he be internal, like the "Jew" or the "kulak," or external, seems to be an indispensable requisite in the armoury of a totalitarian leader' (Hayek, 1944 [2001]).

Here it is obvious that Hayek was referring to Germany and Russia. In Germany, Jewish people were the target of anticapitalist sentiment. German antisemitism and anticapitalism sprang from the same root, Hayek said. It is a universal tendency of collectivism to become nationalistic. Capital cannot belong to humanity in general, but it can belong to a nation. Liberal socialism, said Hayek, is purely theoretical. In practice, socialism becomes nationalistic, as proven in Germany and Russia.

Collectivism thus creates the most concentrated power possible. This power has never been known before. 'In a competitive society, there is nobody who can exercise even a fraction of the power which the social planning board would possess' (Hayek, 1944 [2001], p. 149). Of course, this is only true if there are no monopolies. This was the glaring weakness in Hayek's arguments. If there are monopolies and boards of directors that act together, then that would be the end of competition and the creation of a planned economy. Economic power in the hands of private individuals, though, is never as exclusive or complete as when it is centralised politically, according to Hayek, but he was wrong.

The existence and power of monopolies was a real problem in Hayek's thinking, and one about which he was both ambivalent and ambiguous. Hayek was against monopolies in principle and this is clear. However, he said, even actions against monopolies help to bolster monopolies, and serve to strengthen their power. To the public, monopolies justify themselves by giving higher pay. It might make sense to put monopolies in government hands, except that it is better to have a few owners than only one state owner.

Without a response to the necessity of planning and the desirability of controlling monopolies, Hayek presented an ideal state, almost of innocence, based on individualism and competition, forsaking Keynes' concern about employment. He proposed this as an alternative to Keynes' ideas out of fear of a totalitarian future, it seems. This fear of totalitarianism is what attracted the American public and is the cornerstone of neoliberalism. It is an emotional cornerstone, and one that Keynes neglected to adequately take into account.

Hayek's legacy: Fear and denial

Hayek's liberalism consisted of a partial truth. This truth was that society is made up of individual actions of interdependent individuals and groups. What he missed was the interdependence. What he offered was a state of mind that did not have the limits imposed on the individual by others. He created an individualism without society, and an individual without a web of relationships. Each isolated individual, for Hayek, had a different weight in the world. This weight was the amount of money that the individual has to be able to use in the free flow of buying and selling. Preserving the legal protection for this impossible individualism is the basis of neoliberalism. The neoliberal wants us to believe that, if we take care of individuals with money, we will be taking care of everyone. Neoliberalism is, at its core, the hegemony of money, the stock market and the financiers.

The fear of the future, for Hayek, was a fear of power that is greater than, and limits, the individual. This appears to be egalitarian, but is not, as long as value, of people as well as commodities, is measured in prices. People are paid less because they are worth less, for example. In a world where the frustration of being restrained by society is ideologically promised to end, this frustration turns into a fear of the future and a fear of people who have less destroying those who have more. To maintain this point of view in reality involves much denial.

It was this fear shared, first in America and later in Europe, that made Hayek's book both popular and classic. It is an ideology with a grain of truth. As he neared the end of the book, the roots of the fear became more apparent. Hayek thought that he was watching the end of the 'economic man' of classical economics, in the same way that Keynes feared that the men of 'animal spirits' were about to disappear.

Hayek went on to explain. Individuals are always adjusting themselves to changes whose causes and natures they cannot understand. No single mind, in fact, can grasp them. Each individual is bound up in complex interrelationships which are beyond individual comprehension. These are the impersonal forces of the market. Hayek believed that the growth of civilisation was based on man's submission to these impersonal forces. His view was that there is a stark choice: to return to the fantasy of perfect competition or to submit to the arbitrary power of other men. War gave a single purpose to the political economy. There was a sacrifice of freedom in order to make freedom more secure in the future. This means, and this strikes directly at Keynes, unemployment should not dominate us to the exclusion of everything else.

Hayek added that the single-minded idealist is likely to do the greatest harm. Was this aimed at Keynes? Unemployment is the price that we must pay for a higher general level of wealth, Hayek said. In his conclusion, Hayek suggested that we can make a new start to build a better world. Rather than return to the ideals of the 19th century, we can instead take the opportunity to realise its ideals. The policy of freedom for the individual is the only true progressive policy. Margaret Thatcher later restated Hayek's thought as 'There is no such thing as society'.

Massification and aggregation

Hayek published *The Road to Serfdom* in 1944. In 1945, Labour won a landslide election on the platform of a planned economy, based on a National Health Service and National Insurance. Hayek's book was hugely divisive between left and right, ideologically and politically. Ironically, both Hayek's ideas and Keynes' ideas have been grossly reinterpreted by their followers. In the case of *The General Theory of Employment, Interest and Money*, Keynes' followers and students immediately started to mathematise his principles, thus removing the dialectic that is at the centre of Keynes' thought, but putting Keynes' thought at the centre of economic education. In the case of *The Road to Serfdom*, Hayek himself almost immediately began to build a neoliberal movement in both intellectual and political circles. It was not a case of just writing a book for Hayek.

In the end, in *The Road to Serfdom*, Hayek responded to Keynes on a completely different level from Keynes' 'General Theory'. This is interesting because it looked like he had nothing to counter Keynes' economics. So, while Keynes wrote about real economic processes taking place in real time, Hayek wrote about mass movements and expressed his fear of them. While Keynes wrote about how the state can move in the opposite direction from individual entrepreneurs, thus smoothing over capitalist booms and busts, Hayek saw the state as threatening democratic capitalism. While Keynes perceived that the aggregate sum of individual movements of entrepreneurs leads to stagnation and poverty, Hayek extolled the individual movements of entrepreneurs as the only way to preserve freedom and democracy.

For Keynes, booms and busts were the centre of what he was trying to remedy. In doing this, he discovered that booms always lead to busts, but that busts often do not lead to booms. Hayek did not write about economic cycles, or about real capitalists or workers. Hayek massified his economic actors instead of aggregating them in the way that Keynes suggested. In doing this, he ignored the differences in interests in the economy and the contradictions between workers and capitalists. Hayek broke the identification that Keynes had made between workers as providing value to products and workers as consumers of commodities, thus entering into two parts of the capitalist economic process. Instead, Hayek chose to attack the Keynes project as planning and, as such, inevitably leading to totalitarian, right or left wing, anti-democratic states, with the threats of Nazi Germany and Communist Russia still hanging heavily over Europe.

Hayek did notice, however, Keynes' threats to liberal capitalism. One of Keynes' threats was his underlying conviction that continuous economic growth is not possible without great social costs and also not desirable for most people. Keynes believed that capitalism will run out of steam, so to speak. This mirrored Karl Marx's assertion that the rate of profit will tend towards zero. The second of Keynes' threats to liberal monetary capitalism was that there is no need for interest rates in the modern world and that the stock market is basically a casino that destroys long-term investment and thus employment and wealth, except for the wealthiest. This was an immediate threat to the world's financial interests, and Keynes' forecasts have turned out to be accurate, as we will see.

Arendt would have agreed with Hayek in some senses. She shared his fear of the totalitarian. Keynes and Hayek were both searching for anti-Marxist theories. Arendt could be called a critical Marxist. In theory, Hayek did away with Arendt's *polis* entirely. For Hayek, the state should also act in such a way as to ensure that conflict occurs between humans rather than between the mass and the state. However, these conflicts can never be resolved because there is no political space with any power or authority. There is no dialogue because there is no plurality in Hayek's theories, which are based in ideas of individuals and masses.

There are several aspects of Hayek's theory and ideology that are destructive and inhumane. The most obvious is his concept of freedom, which can only be had in a state of complete isolation from other humans. The attraction of this concept of freedom is its suggestion that humans can exist without any limits. This state of freedom is only possible in contemplative isolation, as Arendt points out. In reality, freedom can only be had when individuals are free to be themselves with others and to act into the web of human relationships.

Norbert Elias (1987) and S. H. Foulkes (1948) formulated this idea in an even more radical way. For Elias and Foulkes, the individual is inseparable from the social. The individual is the singular and the social is the plural. In this view, the neoliberal state that refuses to accept responsibility for people, but instead turns people against each other, is in danger of creating a chaotic and violent society of scarcity for some and the fear of this society for others. In the reality of Hayek's individualistic world, no one wins.

However, the real power brought about by Hayek's book was that it was swept up into anti-Communist and anti-Keynesian movements by those interested in maintaining their freedom from state intervention, namely monopoly industrial and financial globalising interests. These are the neoliberals. The neoliberal movement combined the power of persuasion of concentrated mass media with more intimate and intellectual dialogues between journalists, academics, students and politicians. The formation of these echo chambers was the basis of neoliberalism.

The Mont Pelerin Society

Hayek's book, while not a great economic theoretical work, became the bible of the neoliberal movement. Hayek provided the impetus. On the basis of the popular success of his book in the US, Hayek was asked to do a speaking tour. He was not a natural speaker or showman. The tour did not lead to anything immediately. However, he did meet liberals like himself who believed in orthodox economics and who felt as isolated as he did (Wapshott, 2012). After the Second World War (and the death of Keynes in 1946), Hayek began to build on the movement started in 1938 at a meeting called the 'Colloque Walter Lippmann' in Paris. This meeting had brought together an international group of liberal economists to highlight the threat to liberty inherent in planned societies such as Soviet Russia and Nazi Germany. Walter Lippmann had written a book called *An Inquiry into the Principles of The Good Society* (Lippmann, 1938). At the Colloque Walter Lippmann, liberal economists discussed 'the crisis of liberalism'.

In 1938, between 20 and 25 liberal economists attended the Colloque Walter Lippmann. In 1947, Hayek invited about 60 economists, intellectuals and businessmen, promising all expenses paid, to the Hotel du Parc on the top of Mont Pelèrin, overlooking Lake Geneva in Switzerland. This was going to be a well-funded project right from the start. It brought together people from both sides of the Atlantic. The initial funders included a Swiss bank, a Swiss watch manufacturer, an American think tank and an American industrial capital fund. The far-reaching network that grew out of this meeting was to be called the Mont Pelerin Society. The Mont Pelerin Society has met yearly since 1949 (Wapshott, 2012).

The original Mont Pelerin Society founders came from Paris, Austria, Switzerland, Germany, Manchester, London and Chicago. The task was monumental. Hayek wished to emulate the Fabian Society. The Fabian Society developed social policy in the UK through books, universities and the infiltration of government and other social institutions with an educated elite of public servants. Hayek also envisioned the role of what he called 'second-hand dealers in ideas'. These were the people who read and commented on texts and current affairs, mostly journalists. It is through journalists that the mass of people learns about what is going on in the world and experiments with different ways of thinking about it (Jones, 2012).

The Mont Pelerin Society (MPS) was an international organisation. There were many nations involved but the transatlantic axis between the US and Britain was the major one. Along with policies concerning the 'second-hand dealers in ideas', the neoliberals developed a new type of intellectual and political organisation called the 'think tank'. There was a first wave in the 1940s and a second wave in the 1970s. The individuals who ran these policy institutes were the ideological entrepreneurs who made neoliberal thought accessible to politicians and to the general public (Jones, 2012).

Think tanks

The think tanks turned neoliberal thought into a neoliberal political programme, making the link between the intellectuals, who had expertise, and the politicians, who made policy. They also made the links between intellectual thought and the thinking public. When the economic crises of the 1970s forced politicians and public servants to look around for new ideas, the transatlantic neoliberal network was well established to provide them. The American think tanks, in particular, were supported by business, often American household corporate names such as Du Pont Chemicals, General Electric and Coors Brewing Company (Jones, 2012, p. 153).

The strategy of American business was to fund think tanks and organise campaigns on behalf of free enterprise and against the strenuous regulation of employment practices which involved trade unions, particularly the closed shop. This was an anti-New Deal coalition formed in the 1930s and 1940s. The anti-New Deal coalition became the nucleus of the postwar corporate-driven 'free market' resurgence (Jones, 2012, p. 153). These interests made good use of the ideas about the constrictions of employment and wages in Hayek's thinking. Anti-labour ideas were at the basis of what the neoliberals had to offer to big business and financial interests.

The first think tanks were established before Hayek's book, though, which suggests that these social forces were at work before the theories were developed and published. The first major think tanks in the US were the American Enterprise Institute (AEI), founded in 1943, and the Foundation for Economic Education (FEE), which was set up in 1946. The AEI came out of the American Enterprise Association (AEA), a key anti-New Deal business group that had been established in New York City in 1938. The AEA was disturbed by the prospect of the continuation of price controls. Price controls were the key legislation needed to the control monopolies in peacetime once the war was won. The growing size and power of the American Federal Government would have certainly been a factor in the creation of this new kind of institution.

The FEE was established in 1946 and was directly linked to the Mont Pelerin Society and to Hayek. The FEE, like the AEI, was funded by big business. One of the first FEE publications was called 'Roofs or Ceilings' and was about the 'follies' of rent control. The FEE was trying to roll back postwar working-class gains in property ownership, as well as in employment. Processes like these are good examples of how the dominant economic interests of big business made themselves felt to governments, particularly when governments became big and powerful. Think tanks were not only making policy about wages. Think tanks were also working in favour of the landlords and other property-owning interests.

The 'Chicago School' of economics

A second early development, stemming more directly than the think tanks from Hayek's thought and organisation, was the restatement of the quantity theory of money by Milton Friedman (2002) and the Chicago School of Economics. Hayek had met Harold Luhnow, the president of the Volker Fund on his American tour. Luhnow offered to provide financial support for Hayek, since he was searching for intellectual weapons to curb the power of government in the postwar era.

Hayek went on to provide the pivotal role in the organisation of the Chicago School of Economics in the autumn of 1946. Chicago and Mont Pelèrin became a dual centre for neoliberal thought. Hayek, along with several others, was present at both founding meetings. Luhnow was one of the major funders for both ventures. The ultimate purpose of both the Mont Pelerin Society and the Chicago School was not so much to revive a dormant classical liberalism as it was to forge a neoliberalism better suited to modern conditions. The founding word was 'liberty'. The founding principle was an alliance between capitalist big business and financial interests in order to dispossess working class gains implicit in Keynesianism (Hayek, 1944 [2001]).

However, the doctrine of neoliberalism, as it was being founded and institutionalised, was not exactly as Hayek had envisioned. The founding participants agreed that neoliberalism would not come about naturally. It had to be constructed. Thus, neoliberalism was first and foremost a theory of how to reengineer the state in order to guarantee the hegemony of the market, particularly of the financial market. Its 'most important' participants were the modern corporations, particularly financial interests. They accepted that they must organise politically to guarantee a strong government around their own interests (Hayek, 1944 [2001]).

References

Elias, N. (1987) *Involvement and Detachment*. Oxford: Blackwell.
Foulkes, S.H. (1948) *Introduction to Group-analytic Psychotherapy: Studies in the Social Integration of Individuals and Groups*. London: Maresfield Reprints.
Friedman, M. (2002) *Capitalism and Freedom*. Chicago, IL: Chicago University Press.
Hayek, F. (1944 [2001]) *The Road to Serfdom*. London: Routledge.
Jones, D. S. (2012) *Masters of the Universe: Hayek, Friedman, and the Birth of Neoliberal Politics*. Princeton, NJ: Princeton University Press.
Keynes, J. M. (1936 [2017]) *The General Theory of Employment, Interest and Money*. Stansted: Wordsworth Editions.
Lippmann, W. (1938) *An Inquiry into the Principles of The Good Society*. Boston: Little, Brown & Co.
Smith, A. (1776 [2009]) *The Wealth of Nations*. Harmondsworth: Penguin.
Wapshott, N. (2012) *Keynes Hayek: The Clash That Defined Modern Economics*. New York: W. W. Norton & Co.

Chapter 4

The strange fruits of neoliberalism

It was the Chicago School that innovated the idea that much of politics could be understood as if it were a market process, and therefore amenable to formalisation through neoclassical theory. This idea is part of the strong current of inequality in neoliberalism.

Corporations were characterised as passive responders to outside forces. The only market actors accused of misusing power were the trade unions. Corporation monopoly practices were treated as harmless and temporary, or as the outcome of Keynesian state policy. In reality, neoliberalism is based on monopoly power.

Hayek went on to teach in Chicago in 1950, in a chair funded by Harold Luhnow and the Volker Fund. Had the Chair not been funded especially for him, Chicago would not have chosen Hayek. There were disagreements and conflicts. The issues of agreement were that prices hold the key to understanding the economy and that free-market ideas should prevail over ideas about intervention. The issues of difference were around Milton Friedman's (2002) Keynesian ideas about observing the economy as a whole (the macro level), and using statistics to determine the cause and effect of economic changes (Wapshott, 2012). Milton Friedman, a University of Chicago economist thus brought Keynes back into Hayek's thinking, and reinstated macroeconomics with a financial twist.

From 1950 to 1960, Hayek chaired the Mont Pelerin Society, worked in America and wrote his second book. However, times had changed. Even liberalism had become Keynesian. There were also problems in the Mont Pelerin Society and Hayek resigned as Chair in 1960 and did not attend the meeting in 1961 (Wapshott, 2012, p. 223).

Hayek and the Mont Pelerin Society had to work against a tide of Keynesianism. Keynesianism in public policy included the Bretton Woods Agreement which had fixed the world's exchange rates to the dollar and fixed the value of the dollar to gold. The International Monetary Fund and the World Bank were created. Europe was reconstructed after the war. It was thought that the ups and downs of the business cycle were over. State policies included controlling finance. It was in opposition to this control of finance, as well as to the largely imagined threat of the power of labour, that the Mont Pelerin Society was created and funded; it did not want the state controls of finance that Keynesian economists instituted after the Second World War.

In the UK, Labour was elected in 1945 with the largest majority in parliamentary history. The welfare state was created along with the NHS. The Bank of England was nationalised. In the US, President Truman signed the Employment Act, which gave the government the responsibility to provide maximum employment. The Truman Administration took over the right to manage the economy beyond the constitutional duties to control money and trade.

In the meantime, financial capital continued to develop. Although the welfare state was created in Britain on the basis of National Insurance contributions, poverty and inequality still lay underneath. In 1950, credit cards were first introduced. State money was spent on defence. The Korean War with America lasted until 1953 and defence spending continued after that. The Eurodollar market was created. The first multinational corporations were tasked with rebuilding Europe. Capital became international, based on the dollar and on American gold, but also expanding with increasingly easy credit. The Vietnam War started in 1955. The boom spending involved in the Vietnam War contributed to the end of Keynesianism and to the shift to neoliberalism before American president Richard Nixon ended the war 20 years later in 1975.

The first neoliberals in politics and the collapse of Keynesianism

Milton Friedman participated even more directly in politics than Hayek did. He took part in the post-Kennedy 1964 presidential campaign of the conservative libertarian Arizona Senator Barry Goldwater (Wapshott, 2012). Goldwater believed that taxation should be regressive. Each individual should give the same percentage of his wealth, and no more, in taxes. Friedman told Goldwater that, if Goldwater were president, he could support full employment and stable prices through monetary policy alone. These views were outlandishly exotic at the time and Goldwater lost to the Democrat and Kennedy vice-president, Lyndon Johnson, by a landslide.

The mantle of right-wing Republicanism passed from Goldwater to Ronald Reagan, and so did the services of Milton Friedman. This was in 1967, when Reagan was Governor of California. Together they set out to reduce the size of the California state government. Friedman was passed to Nixon when he was nominated as the Republican presidential candidate, ahead of Reagan.

Economics had already entered politics through Keynes. The idea of fine-tuning the economy led to the attempts of politicians to coordinate booms and busts with the electoral cycles in the US. Although this strategy seemed like it might work in the 1940s, it began to break down in the 1960s and the 1970s. In the 1960s and 1970s, the Keynesian economic strategy of boom control was becoming more and more constrained by the fixed exchange rate system. The economic strategy of boom control was further challenged by ever stronger workers' economic and political organisations. When these factors came together in an out-of-control inflation, neoliberalism was ready with a monetarist policy that was made to combat inflation and a political policy of ending the power of organised labour.

The beginning of the end of the 'Keynesian Revolution' was in the 1960s. The Cold War and the political power of the Soviet Union, the Kennedy–Johnson tax cuts, the War on Poverty, the Great Society in America and the war in Vietnam were all feeding inflation in America by creating a scarcity of money resources. Inflation caused the haemorrhage of gold from Fort Knox. There was not enough gold and dollars to go around all the world demands for money. Raising taxes could no longer be used to fight inflation, since the unions were powerful and would ask for higher wage increases to compensate for reductions in take-home pay. Reducing tax to stimulate the economy would also only ratchet up prices.

The crunch came when the US short-term debt came to exceed its gold reserves. Nixon was forced to suspend dollar convertibility into gold and to float the dollar in relation to other currencies in 1971. Britain followed America's lead and floated the pound in 1972. This was when the Bretton Woods system of monetary control collapsed. Inflation was let loose without the guarantee of gold reserves, and the long boom ended (Jones, 2012). The values of currencies were allowed to fluctuate in relation to each other.

As a result, the reputation of the Keynesian intellectual elite also collapsed. The neoliberal movement was prepared for the stumble of Keynesianism on both sides of the Atlantic. The consequence was the breakthrough of transatlantic neoliberal politics in the UK and the US.

In the UK, the oil price shocks of 1973 and 1979 combined with the International Monetary Fund (IMF) loan of 1976 caused the collapse of British industrial relations based on Keynes. The state turned against the powerful trade unions which were rooted in state enterprise and the welfare state. The failure of the state prices and incomes policies that were supposed to fight inflation created a policy vacuum. Workers fought hard to keep their gains and the state was caught between workers' demands and rising prices. Neoliberal ideas flowed into the vacuum because Keynesianism had no response to this essentially political situation. The major idea of the initial neoliberal policies was to abandon state support for strong trade unions and full employment. Instead state support for full employment, neoliberal economic ideas, privileged the fight against inflation aimed at preserving the value of money.

In the UK, the labour unions proved the bigger obstacle to fighting inflation by the means of unemployment and lower wages required by Keynesian policies. Conservative Prime Minister, Edward Heath, confronted the unions and was answered by a wave of strikes and a three-day week. Heath and the Conservatives were defeated by Labour in 1974. A Labour government was elected under Harold Wilson. Wilson's Labour government was going to try and fashion a social contract between the trade unions and the government. This, too, failed. Wilson's difficulties led to the election of Margaret Thatcher in 1975 as leader of the Conservative Party. Thatcher and her closest colleagues, established the Centre for Policy Studies, a Hayekian think tank. This signalled their intention to develop a new economic policy programme. Their primary focus was to be the trade union 'problem' (Jones 2012). Both Hayek and Friedman were regular visitors to Margaret Thatcher in 10 Downing Street after her election as Prime Minister in 1979 (Wapshott, 2012).

Margaret Thatcher and 'handbag economics'

It is ironic that the decisive turn from Keynes to Hayek was made by a Labour government in the UK and by a Democratic government in the US. In the UK, it was Labour Prime Minister James Callaghan who first confronted the unions. It is also a testament to the strategy employed by Hayek and his corporate and financial backers to defeat Keynesianism in both economic and ideological terms. The neoliberal economists were present in meetings, in politics and in the media. They pursued their ideas and solutions at all levels of state and civic society, including in the bureaucracy of government. The argument of freedom versus totalitarianism was just under the surface of both the party of the right and the party of the left in the UK government.

When organised labour resisted the controls proposed to them by the Labour Party, there ensued a series of public sector strikes and industrial actions across the country. UK Prime Minister James Callaghan was forced to call an election, and neoliberalism entered, by the front door this time, in the person of Margaret Thatcher in 1979.

Thatcher was the prime political neoliberal ideologue and pioneer (Wapshott, 2012). Thatcher and her team had prepared well for government. They started with a philosophy based on the individual and the free market. Inflation was the most pressing issue facing the country. Monetarism, public sector pay restraint, and tight finance were the necessary prescriptions according to this philosophy. Greater independence was also proposed for the Bank of England (Jones, 2012). One of Thatcher's greatest accomplishments was to convince the public that state finances were just like household and business finances. This was just what Keynes (1936 [2017]) had so elegantly disproved in *The General Theory of Employment, Interest and Money* and elsewhere. Thatcher carried her handbag everywhere, as if all ideas about finance could be contained within the domestic budget.

In the process of defeating the unions, Thatcher brought in a whole new political, economic, social and psychological culture dominated by the term 'free market'. The long triumph of the market and the progressive destruction of the public sphere were not inevitable. The triumph of the market and the destruction of the public sphere were chosen by successive policymakers, beginning in the 1970s. These choices continued to be made and remade in the agendas of the Labour Party in the UK and the Democratic Party in the US, as well as by the UK Conservatives and the US Republicans.

In the UK, Thatcher wanted to bring working-class unity to an end. To do this, she radically changed housing policy. The Thatcher housing policy was meant to counter what the neoliberals called 'the culture of dependency' that had been created by the welfare state. This was a big ideological change from the gradual assumption of state responsibility for its people from the 1600s.

Historically, as capitalism created poverty, so the amelioration of poverty also became the responsibility of the capitalist state (as related in Part I of this book). This basic social contract was abandoned by the Thatcher government and the governments following, both Conservative and Labour. Individualism became the social target and the growing interdependence of social people was increasingly denied in the ideology. In Arendt's terms, and as she predicted, one of the consequences of this denial has produced a society of jobholders, many of whom are without jobs or any other legal alternative for personal survival outside of state provision. The culture of dependency that was produced by the welfare state was now being repudiated with the result that poverty was again blamed on the poor, and not on the government. This is the time of monsters.

The devastating effects of neoliberalism in the UK

The economic and social consequences of neoliberalism in the UK have been devastating. Neoliberalism has not led to prosperity and peace. Nowhere is the lack of prosperity, peace, justice and equality produced by neoliberalism better expressed than in the 2018 report for the Institute of Public Policy Research (IPPR) called 'Prosperity and Justice'. The IPPR is a left-of-centre think tank, often referred to in the Labour Party. *Prosperity and Justice: A Plan for a New Economy* was the final report of the IPPR Commission on Economic Justice. The IPPR Report put out a series of policies for use by the Labour campaigns. It also made a complete and shocking analysis of the UK economy from the 1970s up to the time of its writing. The report leaves the impression that something has gone radically wrong. If this is where neoliberal capitalism has brought us, then reforming the economy in the way that the Report itself suggests looks very weak. In order to meet the challenges that neoliberalism has left for the future, economics itself needs to be revised and rewritten with humans in mind in order to serve in a world that is capable of maintaining humanity.

In *Prosperity and Justice: A Plan for a New Economy*, the economic symptoms were severe and the prognosis was bleak. It was particularly clear in the UK that financialisation and globalisation of the economy were impoverishing the people who live and work in the UK with the complicity of the government. It was also clear that impoverishment will continue while UK governments accept and inform their policies with neoliberal capitalism.

The IPPR report chronicles various indicators of change from the Keynesianism of the 1970s to the neoliberalism of 2018, well after the financial crash of 2008, but just before the health crisis of COVID-19 a year after the report was published. The clearly neoliberal handling of the pandemic by the Conservative government of Prime Minister Boris Johnson and other Conservatives clearly come out of the same ideas as these statistics. During the COVID-19 crisis, we were constantly reminded that we had to choose the economy before our health. Although it is as yet unclear what the economic consequences of the pandemic will be, the IPPR Report gives a fair idea of the nature of the economy that we were asked to choose, how it works and who it benefits. In short, with the workers' organisations defeated, the processes of the economy have impoverished and indebted UK workers and enriched UK money and property owners to the point that working no longer lifts a family above the poverty line. The whole economy has become deindustrialised, and generally weakened. Although rates of growth looked reasonable, they were almost totally dependent on debt. Although unemployment looked low, the figures were based on widespread underemployment.

Work without adequate pay

Part of the ideological appeal of capitalism has been that, although capitalists are enriched, they also facilitate a process by which the workers, too, become wealthier over time. This became known as the 'trickle-down effect'. What is good for the capitalists is also good for the workers. This is the basis of the capitalist hegemony that is generally accepted by the UK population. What happened, though, since the 1970s, was quite the opposite to what might have been predicted by the 'trickle-down effect'. If the 'trickle-down effect' ever existed, it no longer worked as part of the production process in the UK. Between 1979 and 2012 only 10 per cent of overall national growth, measured by the Gross Domestic Product (GDP), went to the bottom 50 per cent of the income distribution. At the same time, the richest 10 per cent took almost 40 per cent of the total growth (Institute of Public Policy Research, 2018, p. 13). Further, since 1986, although the economy continued to grow, wages did not grow with it. The majority of workers, the job holders, were not the beneficiaries of the neoliberal economic processes.

The labour share of the national income was nearly 70 per cent in the 1970s, before neoliberalism and under Keynesianism. In 2018, the labour share of the national income had reduced from 70 per cent to 55 per cent. On the other side of the coin, the rising share of income going to the owners of capital, as the returns on financial and real estate assets, consistently outpaced the rate of economic growth (Institute of Public Policy Research, 2018, p. 14). This meant that owners of capital, finance and property, were receiving most of the benefit of economic growth, as compared to those who sell their labour for wages. In sum, the UK economy was financialised between 1970 and 2018.

The 'trickle-down effect' has become more like a 'hoover-up' effect. Neoliberalism has created absolute, as well as relative, poverty for those with jobs, as well as for those without jobs. Having a job is no longer seen as a way out of poverty as it has been in the past. Although the number of people employed for wages was high in 2018, 8 per cent of the workforce said that they would have wanted to work more hours. This 8 per cent of workers considered themselves to be underemployed, even though they were not unemployed.

The structure of work has also changed. Without collective and powerful union representation, new forms of employment have bypassed the guarantees won by unionised workers. In 2018, almost a million workers were on 'zero hours contracts'. These contracts, without specified hours, provided little or no job security. Zero hours contracts caused an epidemic of stress and ill health, including mental ill health. In terms of families, both parents were working for wages as a rule. However, 22 per cent of the population were still on incomes below the poverty line after housing costs. This included four million children, or nearly one in three, and this number has risen since 2018. Life has become increasingly hard for a very large number of people. This was especially worrying as one in three UK children were struggling for economic survival with their families. Poverty and deprivation in childhood creates health and emotional damage, the consequences of which often only become apparent in later life (Institute of Public Policy Research, 2018, p. 16).

Increasingly poor payment for work has formed an economy based on debt. Government policies have aimed to keep wages down but maximise consumption at the same time. The result is that 90 per cent of the entire growth of the economy is coming from household debt. The whole economy is based on people spending more than they are earning.

Money inequality

Under neoliberalism, the power of the state in the economy has been replaced by the power of the shareholders, the owners of money. Like the demise of union membership and the lack of working-class power, the structure and use of UK capital has been shaped by conscious legislation on the neoliberal model. In the UK, the current system of corporate governance, the rules and structures by which a company is directed and controlled, gives overwhelming primacy to the rights and interests of a company's shareholders. Only shareholders have voting rights to appoint the board of directors and to make other strategic decisions. The legal duties of directors are explicitly focused on promoting shareholder interests. This is one of the factors that explains low UK rates of investment and productivity, high rates of pay inequality and low levels of public trust in large businesses.

Between 1990 and 2016, the proportion of discretionary cash flow returned to shareholders from UK, non-financial corporations, increased from 39 per cent to 55 per cent. Further, since the 2008 financial crisis, dividend payments remained relatively constant, even as profits fluctuated. These statistics indicated that firms prioritised consistent, guaranteed, financial returns to shareholders over everything else, including reinvestment. This reorientation from long-term success to short-term financial returns, in money, was referenced earlier as 'financialisation'. The neoliberal shareholder-focused corporate governance legislation determined this (Institute of Public Policy Research, 2018, p. 131).

Who were the shareholders? Although Thatcher proposed to create popular shareholding when she privatised the nationalised industries, the number of shares in UK domiciled companies held by individuals was down from more than 50 per cent in the 1960s to around 10 per cent in 2018. The number of shares held by pension funds and insurance companies was over half of all UK equities in 1990 and this number was less than 15 per cent in 2018. Individuals and pension funds have thus been replaced by various kinds of investment funds whose asset managers are generally rewarded on the basis of short-term gains rather than on the longer-term value of the companies in which they trade. The share market has developed in the way that Keynes (1936 [2017]) feared in his *The General Theory of Employment, Interest and Money*. It has become 'the casino'.

Even more worrying, however, is the rise of the ownerless company with few significant shareholding human people. This means that the majority of shareholders have neither the power nor the incentive to exercise control over management. In many cases, the day-to-day trading is done by artificial intelligence in the form of algorithms. The processes of our productive capacity were run mainly by machines and not by people.

Since the 1970s, neoliberal policies have created a two-tier economy, with high and rising inequality. The wealthiest 10 per cent of households owned more than 900 times the wealth of the poorest 10 per cent and five times more than the entire bottom half of all households combined. Wealth was even more unequally distributed than income. Unequal wealth and income distributions were increased by low levels of savings and high levels of debt, leaving many people with negative financial wealth. One in eight adults had no cash savings at all. One in ten households has over £10,000 of unsecured consumer debt, and 13 per cent of households spent over a quarter of their monthly income servicing debt or are in arrears (Institute of Public Policy Research, 2018, p. 189).

Home ownership rose with Thatcher and then fell again after the financial crash of 2008. So, while one in ten adults owned a second home in 2018, 40 per cent of adults owned no property at all. In 1990, half of those aged between 25 and 34 owned their own home. By 2017 this had fallen to one in four. In sum, the wealthiest 10 per cent now owned over 60 per cent of the UK's financial wealth, including stocks and shares. As Hayek (1944 [2001]) has pointed out, money determines power and freedom. When wealth was restricted and unevenly distributed, power and freedom were unequal and becoming more so. This was the result of neoliberalism in the UK.

Resistance and protest are not enough

It is clear that neoliberalism has not brought the prosperity or the stability that it has promised. Neoliberalism has, though, changed the meaning of politics and economics. Neoliberalism is the ideology of globalising financial interests and, as such, it has changed the nature of the state from one of mediating between the capitalist classes and the workers to one of only facilitating the exploitation and extraction of wealth from the workers by the financial capitalists within the global world economy.

Under neoliberalism, the state has become more authoritarian. Democracy has become a sham. For the first time in the history of capitalism, the workers, the people, are no longer the responsibility of the state. Communities, groups and society are discouraged in favour of family and individualism. Politics is becoming more and more limited by law and practice. Individuals and families are solely responsible for themselves in a world where competition for survival is fierce. Institutions are more important than people. We have lost our reverence for human life and for life in general, with dire consequences for the environment. Neoliberalism, the time of monsters, may very well destroy the world unless we can find a way out of it.

It is also clear that political opposition to neoliberalism must take on new forms. Resistance and protest by themselves are not enough to bring about the world yet to come. Resistance and protest are crucial. However, under neoliberalism, they only lead around and around in cycles. New forms of political opposition could be aimed at creating grass roots democratic, egalitarian and inclusive movements that are consciously fair and social, as well as alive and competitive. These movements are not only charitable.

Charity is important, but it also creates a power differential between receiver and giver. Grassroots movements must find ways of involving and evolving community self-organisation. Grassroots communities can remake the *polis*. They can do this through being able to have a group dimension which is coherent, as well as cohesive. This is a group dimension where difference is embraced and not simply tolerated. This means having groups that are strong and trusted enough for disagreement and conflict without violence and division. The politics of violent conflict, envy and revenge will only breed more violent conflict, envy and revenge. The politics of violence is not capable of bringing about a new world. The politics of denial, or turning a blind eye, is also not capable of bringing about a new world.

The politics of dialogue

The politics of dialogue, about to be lost along with the human condition, is capable of making a difference. If we continue the same, we will lose both humanity and the world. We need to be thinking, talking and arguing about what we do at all levels and at all moments. Neoliberalism has progressively colonised our cultures and our minds since the 1970s. We need to be thinking and talking with each other, including having disagreements, in order to decolonise. We need to use and value groups in order to learn about ourselves and each other. We need to think about how we create and destroy power in our relationships. Only then will we be able to reclaim the polis as politics which are capable of bringing about cooperative, collective and democratic change through dialogue and integration from the bottom up.

Arendt defined the modern age as having two characteristics. One was the capacity to destroy the world. The other was the capacity to destroy humanity. For Arendt, the capacity to destroy the world was linked to the dangers of nuclear war. We are now dealing with that and with even more drastic consequences of 'normal' productive processes, like climate change and major extinctions. The end of humanity, for Arendt though, was linked to the loss of our capacity to speak and to act together in the arena of the polis. She implored us to think together about what we are doing. It is now becoming clear that our capacity to destroy the world and our capacity to destroy humanity are related. These are two faces of the same process.

Arendt linked the demise of the polis to the powerful state that takes over responsibility for survival, elevates the labour of *animal laborans* and destroys the possibility of the work that is capable of creating stability in an everchanging world. She was thinking about a world which is run by machines leading to an irreparable loss of humanity. Along with the loss of humanity comes the loss of a sense of collective responsibility for our world, and, ultimately, the loss of the world itself.

In tracing the development of capitalism and capitalist economic thought through Smith, Marx, Keynes and Hayek, I have shown how figurations of interdependent individuals and groups can create a time of monsters that is not fit for humans. Arendt has given a better understanding of why neoliberal capitalism, though it frightens people and presents them with all kinds of monsters, is so difficult to change into a new and unknown world that could be made by humans in a different way. This world will include a polis that allows a multiplicity of ways of thinking, being, making words and taking actions.

The group as the basis for thought and action

However, although Arendt, unlike many other thinkers, leaves room for multiplicity and dialogue in her thoughts, I believe that she has not given enough consideration to the group as a thought, an action, and the basis of both thought and action. In reality, the group dimension has not really disappeared or even become only concerned with survival. In Parts III and IV of this work, I will show how the group, the plurality and dialogue between humans individually and together, is at the basis of humanity and human internal integrity. The group predates humans. The group is part of human physical being and is capable of surviving and changing even under neoliberal capitalism. In order to do this, it is essential to have group processes, including power relations, in our conscious and emotional lives. We must become more aware of groups, more aware of groups in ourselves and more aware of ourselves in groups. Arendt, Elias and Foulkes help with this understanding, each in their own way. Human evolution and neuroanatomy also help to see how humans are linked together, both evolutionarily and physically. Becoming conscious of these links is not always easy. The difficulty, though, is compensated by an increased sense of integrity, pleasure, freedom to make choices, and interest and excitement about the future.

Viewed in terms of groups, the history of the polis becomes one of a moving locus of group action. The feudal family house group has broken down into individual families. Women have largely taken on the work of animal laborans, even when they are also jobholders. Men are seen as *homo faber*, even when they are not jobholders. While the polis of the large houses has disappeared, dialogue continues in smaller, more personal circles, like the family and belonging groups in communities.

I believe that Keynesian economics continues to offer a way for dialogue and politics to develop in communities. Dialogues between men and women, and between minorities and majorities, at the grass roots level are crucial, though, for Keynesian economics to work in reality over the long term. Keynes offered a way for the interests of capital, the interests of work and the interests of egalitarian consumption to continue in dialogue with private ownership or maybe conservatorship. Keynes did not take the class struggle into account. He did not adequately understand how aggregation can lead to massification. He underestimated the power of class and vested interest. He virtually ignored the theoretical implications of the larger international financial community, though he also regulated it and created it. Keynes' theories are there to use, but he has not provided a blueprint to follow. There are too many missing pieces. Keynes must have known all this when he wrote his 'General Theory'. The General Theory is perhaps his version of a workable utopia left for us to implement in the future, or not. It is the capacity to make these decisions collectively that is most important and most at risk.

Norbert Elias viewed the changing nature of society and the psyche to be the result of the interactions of individuals and groups. 'Group' can be seen as the most realistic unit of human life, not individuals, culture or society. 'Groups' is a very big and vague term, though. It can apply to a myriad of different ways of humans being together. This is because groups and group behaviour come from very far back in the evolutionary past, as will be seen in Parts III and IV.

It is probably impossible to know everything about groups. What I hope to do in this volume is to make a start at turning human's most unconscious physical asset more conscious, enabling the creation and recreation of the 'polis' in everyday interactions and to create places where politics can be observed and practiced. I believe, as Arendt did, that this is the way out of neoliberalism and into a world that we can only know in dialogue together.

References

Friedman, M. (2002) *Capitalism and Freedom*. Chicago, IL: Chicago University Press.
Hayek, F. (1944 [2001]) *The Road to Serfdom*. London: Routledge.
Institute of Public Policy Research (2018) *Prosperity and Justice: A Plan for a New Economy*. Cambridge: Polity Press.
Jones, D. S. (2012) *Masters of the Universe: Hayek, Friedman, and the Birth of Neoliberal Politics*. Princeton, NJ: Princeton University Press.
Keynes, J. M. (1936 [2017]) *The General Theory of Employment, Interest and Money*. Stansted: Wordsworth Editions.
Wapshott, N. (2012) *Keynes Hayek: The Clash That Defined Modern Economics*. New York: W. W. Norton & Co.

Part III

The story of how humans evolved is the story of the group dimension

'I think we have gone through a period when too many children and people have been given to understand "I have a problem, it is the Government's job to cope with it!" or "I have a problem, I will go and get a grant to cope with it!" "I am homeless, the Government must house me!" and so they are casting their problems on society and who is society? There is no such thing! There are individual men and women and there are families and no government can do anything except through people and people look to themselves first'.

Margaret Thatcher (1987)

Figure 3 'On our way'

Chapter 5

Freedom before humans

Margaret Thatcher was wrong when she said that there were only individuals and families. She was not only wrong. She was creating a highly destructive ideology. A denial of the importance of groups and social life to humans outside the family is a crucial element of the neoliberal narrative. The consequence of this element is the splitting, fear and denial between people that allows authoritarian governments to be accepted and even to be desired.

An element to counter the neoliberal narrative can be found in the story of human evolution, with particular attention to the group dimension. The study of human evolution might seem a long way from the study of politics and from ideas about what actions are useful to and required of liberation movements. However, the kind of politics that will enhance and create democracies based on dialogue cannot happen without more general knowledge of what it means to be human in our evolution, in our bodies and in our emotions. Bringing to consciousness the group elements of ourselves in dialogue with each other counters the destructive splitting, fear and denial, outside and inside ourselves, that come from neoliberalism and from our participation in it.

Neoliberalism is a new narrative, created specifically to defeat the democratic ideas that came from the Enlightenment in 1770s' Europe and America and from the forms of capitalism that followed it. There is an idea of freedom underlying present-day neoliberalism. The freedom of neoliberalism is based on the freedom of choice given to those who have money. The group dimension brings a different understanding of freedom. This new freedom is also based on choice. Choice, in the group dimension, comes from knowledge and attention to the human body and mind. Freedom in the group dimension is an internal and external integration that creates organic coherent wholeness, as opposed to simple unity.

In *The Human Condition* (1958 [1998]), Hannah Arendt proposed a similar definition of freedom. The concept of individual freedom that we usually use is impossible for humans, she said. This is because the only way that an individual can be truly free is to be isolated. The Greeks and Romans called this the *vita contemplativa*. For the Ancients, the vita contemplativa was a desired and heroic state. However, the vita contemplativa was also a state from which a human did not, and could not, act in the world.

DOI: 10.4324/9781003350088-9

Humans who talk and act in the world can only do so as a plurality, Arendt said. This is what she called the *polis*. The polis is the plurality of humans who speak and act in the world. The polis is where politics happens. Arendt implicitly suggested that we accept a redefinition of freedom that may be competitive and individualistic, but is also contained and integrated in groups which are capable of coherent dialogue. These groups are made up of individuals who can be themselves with others, have their own voices and act in the world.

Arendt's descriptions of freedom and politics are very close to the way that Norbert Elias (1987) and S. H. Foulkes (1948) described group processes. Elias and Foulkes also focused on the group, not the individual, as the unit of humans. Elias and Foulkes, like Arendt, valued the action that comes out of plurality and dialogue. In fact, participation in groups where competition and individuality can safely be expressed and contained gives a particular kind of free and complete feeling. This is the feeling of the group dimension.

The group dimension cannot be seen directly. So, how real is it? It is not a usual, common-sense focus, since much of group behaviour is habitual, unconscious and taken for granted. In the group dimension, the proposal is that a focus on the human unit of the group is much more realistic than the focus that Adam Smith brought to the economic man. The change in focus from individual to group, though, requires a new kind of figure/ground turn of mind, where what is in the background can be brought to the fore. The change in focus also means looking into the unconscious and bringing it to consciousness.

The figure-ground Gestalt in the group dimension

The reward for this shift is a big one. A vision of the human condition allows thoughts about the polis as being possible in particular kinds of groups, both therapeutic and natural. It allows a new definition and feeling of freedom. Freedom becomes less competitive and isolating and more a sense of being oneself with others. The feeling of freedom becomes a feeling of being liberated with others. Collective solutions can be found, even when there are seemingly irresolvable conflicts.

Elias taught how individuals change cultures and how cultures change individuals. Foulkes taught about the specific dynamics of the life of groups, between groups and in groups. These understandings allow more thoughtful relating and better communication and cooperation, as well as safely and freely expressing conflict and competition. Peaceful situations can be worked out from warring ones. Energy and lives can be saved. Although this cannot be worked out all at once, we can start to think more clearly about how humans can learn to maintain their own environments and their own humanity instead of destroying it, and in the process, oppressing themselves and each other.

The 'group' is not just a vague concept needed to understand human relationships. The group is a present and historical reality. In order to show how the group dimension functions, it is necessary to understand that groups formed before the origins of humans in evolution. Presently, there are many kinds of groups. There are large groups and small groups. There are families who live close together in communities, as Margaret Thatcher identified. There are groups, categories or identities where individuals may never meet face to face. The very ubiquity of groups suggests that groups are at the heart of human integration and unity. The group is the most taken-for-granted human characteristic. The group is the most unconscious social process. We spend most of our time in groups, yet seldom think about them. In a real sense, groups are, at the same time, the greatest human accomplishment and the most basic part of human biology. How this biology works is the topic of Part IV. In Part III, I will look at human evolution with a particular emphasis on the group dimension.

In order to understand the present, we also need to understand the past. Understanding the long and varied past of human evolution will help to understand the human condition as it evolved from the animal social to the human social and political. The focus on the group dimension provides a coherent and substantive alternative theory and counter discourse to some of the accepted fallacies of the age of monsters.

I will tell the story of human evolution with particular attention to the evolution of humans in groups. In order to do this, I have used learning from mainstream palaeontology and animal studies. Palaeontology is the study of ancient remains of humans and animals all over the world. Many of these studies look at and trace the more obvious physical human characteristics, like walking on two legs. However, as well as looking for these more obvious characteristics to trace the human lineage, I will follow the palaeontologists who have also looked at the social arrangements of human remote ancestors. This is all relatively new knowledge that Arendt, Elias and Foulkes would not have had when they were writing. However, I have employed a method similar to theirs: that of looking for a beginning.

The beginning of humanity as found in *Dryopithecus*

I found the beginning of the specifically human group in a primate called *Dryopithecus*. Much of what follows comes from the work in Anne Russon and David Begun's *The Evolution of Thought: Evolutionary Origin of Great Ape Intelligence* (Russon and Begun, 2004). Russon and Begun are researchers in the field of palaeontology. Palaeontologists use scant and partial remains to hypothesise about physical and social origins of animals, including humans. Russon and Begun made a case for *Dryopithecus* as the last common ancestor of gorillas, bonobos, chimpanzees and humans.

As far as is known, life has only happened once. In evolutionary thinking, humans are one product of the process known as evolution, along with all creatures who live now and all those who ever lived in the past. Evolution is a continuous process. Evolution started with the first spark of life known as the Last Universal Common Ancestor (LUCA) about 4 billion years ago. It continues today.

Russon and Begun looked for the Last Common Ancestor of the great apes, the category of animals that includes humans. The search for the Last Common

Ancestor (LCA) involves a focus on certain characteristics followed by a search for physical remains, usually fossilised bones or teeth, which could have led to these characteristics. This process is like trying to identify parents when you only know what the children are like.

What did the parents contribute to the offspring? What did the offspring develop that was new and novel? Through this process of questioning and identifying relevant remains, Russon and Begun identified a group of species called *Dryopithecus* as the LCA of great apes. Then came the idea that all Eurasian hominids are hominins, in the line from Proconsul of 20 million years ago to present day humans (Begun, 2007).

To explain more: Russon and Begun proposed that the hypothesis of *Dryopithecus* as LCA of the great apes was better than other hypotheses. Their hypothesis is not so well known, but neither has it been seriously opposed and disproved. The investigation process followed by Russon and Begun included a focus on brain size and its corollaries, in preference to bipedality, in tracing lineages. In this respect, the *Dryopithecus* line of hominoids had an enormous brain for their time, 300 cubic centimetres, comparable to the existing gorilla, bonobo and chimpanzee brains. This brain size of 300cc was much larger than the brains of the other hominoids of its time, even of those with much larger bodies.

The Dryopithecus *suite of characteristics*

The story is as follows. About 17 million years ago, the Early Miocene Epoch, a warm period of time on the earth, came to an end. There was a great movement of land mass at this time, forming the Alpine and Himalayan mountains. Global turbulence followed with violent rising and falling seas, connecting and then disconnecting land masses. At some point, there was a land connection between Eurasia and Africa. This connection permitted animals and plants to cross from one to the other and back again.

One of the animals to cross over the land from Africa to Europe was a hominoid called *Griphopithecus*. As the earth started to cool, the lush early Miocene forests shrank and became patchy, first in Europe. *Griphopithecus* evolved into *Dryopithecus* in Europe in order to cope with patchy, as opposed to continuous, forest environments. *Dryopithecus*, like other primates, was a fruit eater. However, unlike some of the other hominoids, *Dryopithecus* survived most of the Miocene period in Europe by the conservative measure of residing in trees. This meant that *Dryopithecus* did not develop specialised land movement. Instead, *Dryopithecus* developed a speedier method of travelling through the trees by swinging under the branches, similar to orangutans that exist today. Rapid movement through the trees allowed *Dryopithecus* to remain a fruit eater all year round. As a consequence, *Dryopithecus* did not develop the larger intestines needed for lower quality foods that were the alternative. The consequent preservation of a small, hominid-like, intestine, Russon and Begun believed, allowed for the growth of a bigger brain because the smaller intestine used less energy, leaving potentially more energy for brain growth and maintenance.

Begun proposed a *Dryopithecus* 'suite of characteristics' which included the preservation of tree-living by a new tree movement and the identification of new foods, like nuts. New foods, like nuts, implied new learnings, and perhaps tools, for food preparation. Nuts, for example, had shells that needed to be cracked open. The suite of characteristics proposed by Begun included a small body with a bigger brain, similar in body and brain size to bonobos and chimpanzees. For Begun, the bigger brain implied primitive tool-making, tool use and inter-individual instruction like that witnessed in existing chimpanzees. Begun called this the beginning of culture, located in a qualitatively new and different part of the brain, the associational cortex.

None of these changes could have occurred without a further intensification of interbody relationships between individuals in groups of animals. *Dryopithecus* was certainly not a solitary creature. The species was also widespread. Close ties between individual animals were necessary for geographical migration and radiation.

The species-specific group

All mammals, in fact, have species-specific groups. So, it was not only the fact of multi-body and sexual relationships that were important and novel in *Dryopithecus*. It was the specific form of social organisation that was crucial to what came next. Part of this new and specific *Dryopithecus* group can be inferred from a change in another physical characteristic. Previous hominoid males were much larger than females, suggesting a gorilla type of social organisation, where many females form a group with one male. As *Dryopithecus* evolved, however, the evidence shows that females grew larger relative to males, along with the species-specific larger brain. In fact, *Dryopithecus* females and males are nearly the same size, like bonobos, chimpanzees and humans, yet unlike gorillas.

We can speculate that a larger, better nourished female was a necessary condition for giving birth to and caring for larger-brained babies with longer childhoods. Larger females, better nutrition, larger brains and longer childhoods all also point to the need for intense and stable inter-body, social organisation. *Dryopithecus* was the first ape to manifest this suite of characteristics. It follows that *Dryopithecus*, in a conservative solution to changes in their environment, originated the proto human group, also found in bonobos and chimpanzees.

These proto human groups involved intense relating. They were of mixed age and sex. They worked on what is called a fission and fusion basis. In present-day chimpanzees, larger groups sometimes reach numbers of 150. However, the individuals in the larger group spend much of their time in smaller groups hunting for fruit in the trees. This is the fission part of fission-fusion. When an individual or smaller group finds some fruit, they shout a signal and the others come to eat, have sex and rest. This is called 'carnival'.

The evidence shows that *Dryopithecus* probably had groups with these characteristics. This means that, in evolutionary terms, the need for a sociality that included close, intense, relationships created the beginnings of a big brain, along with the other conditions. This also means that the intense relationships and the big brain came before the other characteristics considered to be human: bipedalism, meat-eating and hunting of other animals. In this analysis, we had groups before we were humans.

Dryopithecus evolved, was successful, and spread widely throughout Europe. Eventually, though, some groups returned to the Rift Valley in Africa. The return happened around 10 million years ago. It was another turbulent time. Begun (2007) thinks that three ancestral line branched off quite quickly. Gorillas evolved from the line first. Bonobos evolved about 8 million years ago. Chimpanzees are thought to be a further evolution from bonobos. About 6 million years ago, the human line, *Ardipithecus ramidus*, branched away from the bonobos and chimpanzees, leading to *Australopithecus afarensis*, who is thought that be the most direct ancestor of humans found so far. Although there are many ancestors in between bonobos, chimpanzees and humans in evolution, all the others are extinct.

Dominance hierarchies

Although human brains are over three times as large as the great ape brain, the line of the *Dryopithecus* suite of characteristics is clear. In order to care for big-brained infants with longer childhoods, females needed better nutrition and collective childcare. This may have come from strong ties developed between females and also energy and food inputs from males. These groups developed further through the bonobo/chimpanzee line.

It is thought that the line of the gorilla returned to the strategy of descending from trees for lower quality food. Some of the other primate relatives of *Dryopithecus* also evolved in that direction. The brain size remained the same. However, gorilla male bodies grew both absolutely and in relative terms until they were over twice the size of female bodies. Gorilla groups are comprised of one male with several females and young offspring. Gorilla females do not bond with each other. Gorilla females bond with the group. Young males leave at puberty to roam solo or in pairs. They return to challenge the older 'silverbacks'. If successful, a younger male 'black-back' gorilla may kill the older one and also its offspring in order to take over the group. This is a tremendous cost of energy and life and occurs approximately once every ten years in each group.

In fission-fusion groups, like bonobos and chimpanzees, there are multiple males and females. This implies dominance hierarchies. I suspect that this group characteristic, or something similar, also first developed in *Dryopithecus*. Dominance hierarchies, especially between males, have obvious evolutionary advantage over gorilla groups. Dominance hierarchies are thus also significant for humans. In sum, modern humans inherited intense multi-body and mixed sex groups from about 10 million years ago. These groups imply dominance hierarchies and are part of human ancient biology. Male dominance hierarches saved both life and energy in evolutionary terms when compared with alternatives. They contributed to the possibility of male support for females with their big-brained offspring, though this possibility is not fully realised in bonobos and chimpanzees. These are the suites of characteristics that have defined the lineage of human deep history.

Grooming, bonobos and humans

Socially, both bonobos and chimpanzees have their strongest bonding between mothers and sons. Physically, bonobos and chimpanzees are both similar to *Dryopithecus* in body and brain size. There is hardly any difference in body size between males and females, even less difference than there is between modern human males and females. It can hypothesised that strong bonding between mothers and sons is part of the *Dryopithecus* suite of characteristics, inherited as humans, though, of course, there is no way to know this.

It is likely, though, that humans are more related to bonobos than to chimpanzees. Bonobo social arrangements are slightly different from the chimpanzees in important ways. Bonobos are known as the 'hippy chimp'. As well as the bonding between mothers and sons, bonobos show an intense bonding between females, who practice sexual rubbing as part of their grooming technique to reinforce social relationships. In fact, bonobos practice sexual grooming in all possible combinations. This sexual grooming is absent in chimpanzees, who groom by removing fleas and other insects. Bonobo sexual grooming indicates softer and closer social relations among the group as a whole. Chimpanzees are more male dominated than bonobos. Bonobos also spend more time grooming. This is not exploitative or abusive grooming. Although it may also be political, the grooming is, in essence, an external form of an internal connection that has become less visible in humans, or has it?

Bonobo females are more dominant, as a rule, than chimpanzee females. In sex, bonobo males and females often face each other and stare into each other's eyes. Males remain bonded with mothers in their birth groups. To observe exogamy, as most creatures do, females change groups at maturity. The close bonding that takes place between females is often with non-kin females. Brothers stay together.

Environment

Bonobos and chimpanzees have an only slightly larger brain size than *Dryopithecus*. However, as well as childhoods, bonobos and chimpanzees have a period of adolescence. There is no evidence of adolescence in *Dryopithecus*. In both childhood and adolescence, the brain continues to grow and develop outside the womb and in the company of others. It is, in fact, the company of others that grows and develops the brain. The baby chimp or bonobo attaches to the group. Fatherhood is thought to be unknown until much further along in human history. The most important male attachment is to brothers, who are all the males in the group. The social environment is as important, or more important than the physical environment. The group is a very real necessity for individual as well as for species survival.

Unlike *Dryopithecus*, who was a wide-ranging creature, gorillas, bonobos and chimps have adapted to specific environments. This adaptation limited the competition for food and habitat between them. Chimpanzees lived in the trees and ate mostly fruit. Bonobos lived on the edge of the forest and foraged in swamps. They found their environmental niches and remained there. They have not made any of the further changes. They may become extinct, though, in this most recent extinction event, especially if they are limited in the development of their adaptation to their changing environment.

What further defined humans in evolution was that they went into the savannah with their closely-knit and mixed-sex groups. It was in this environment where they stood and habitually walked upright. Consequently, these new hominoids could carry their homes with them. They also had home bases, which were temporary or cyclical. Their brains grew and developed. They lost their hair. They evolved even more intense inter-body bonds, including pair bonding within groups. Females developed a more muted, but constant, availability for sex and synchronised their periods of fertility which are signalled by menstruation. This means that the female body changed more than male body as group relationships become more intense and allowed the development of larger brains and extended childhoods.

These changes started to happen, initially, on the East side of the Rift Valley in Kenya, around 6 million years ago under environmental stress. To the West where the climate was less stressful, gorillas, bonobos and chimpanzees continued in their habitats. On the East side of the Rift Valley, the descendants of conservative *Dryopithecus*, called *Ardipithecus ramidus*, came down from the trees and entered the savannah. Begun estimated this at about 4.4 million years ago. Just one million years later, *Ardipithecus ramidus* became *A. afarensis*. *Ardipithecus ramidus* shared the *Dryopithecus* suite of characteristics plus a series of physical changes that allowed for the low quality back up diet. *A. afarensis* had a slightly more upright gait and a slightly bigger brain.

Australopithecus brain changes

As the human line developed, the elements of the human group of the present were laid down in layers, step by step, building on what came before to now. Modern humans make up much of their own environment. That process started with *Dryopithecus*, where childhood was extended by the turbulence of the physical environment, survival choices and consequences on brains, bodies and multi-body relationships. The process continued with *A. afarensis*, also known as 'Lucy' and 'The First Family'.

Capitalism is 800 years old. *Dryopithecus* dates from 9 to 10 million years ago. Gorillas departed from the line 8 million years ago and bonobos and chimpanzees about 6 million years ago. *Ardipithecus ramidus*, hypothesised as the ancestor who followed on from *Dryopithecus* on the human line, lived from 5.6 to 4.4 million years ago. None of these creatures post-*Dryopithecus* differed significantly from the initial suite of characteristics.

Australopithecines are generally accepted to be near the beginning of the human evolutionary line as defined by their bodies. *A. afarensis* was a physically small, bonobo-like creature. *A. afarensis* also had a comparatively small brain. However, this creature also had a mixture of climbing and walking capabilities far more human-like than the existing great apes. It is generally accepted that *A. afarensis* walked on two legs because footprints have been found in Tanzania preserved in fossil volcano dust. There are Laetoli footprints from 3.7 million years ago, the Lucy skeleton AL288-1 from 3.2 million years ago, and the first family AL333 from 3.2 million years ago. There are two larger sets of footprints, thought to be adults, and one smaller set, thought to be that of a child, all walking on two legs, like humans.

Besides physical proof of bipedalism, the fact that these three sets of footprints are found together certainly suggests a group, if not a family. These bi-pedal apes have acquired a name: Lucy. Another *A. afarensis* find consolidated the idea of groups. The First Family refers to a cache of fossil bones found together and dates from 3.2 million years ago, comprising nine adults, three adolescents and five children. Although there are many possible explanations for finding a number of individuals in one place, it is probable that these individuals lived together before they died. What kind of group might this 'First Family' have been?

The Australopithecines show a great diversity in size. Some are much larger than others. At first it was thought that this meant that there was a very high level of sexual dimorphism, indicating a gorilla-like social structure (Wolpoff, 1975). Size differences in fossil remains can be due to differences between species, differences between ages or sizes of individuals within species and/or differences between males and females, called 'sexual dimorphism'. Wolpoff (1975) interpreted the size differences as indicating high sexual dimorphism.

Later thinking, however, has concluded that the sexual dimorphism of *A. afarensis* was between chimpanzee/bonobo and human levels, in other words, very little size difference between males and females, exactly as is the case with *Dryopithecus* (Reno et al., 2010)

This more recent conclusion comes from analysis of the bones of the 'First Family'. The low sexual dimorphism and its clues as to social structure fits well with the arguments put forward in this work. Low sexual dimorphism, the equality in size between males and females, is an important indicator of group formation and relationship intensity, as has been seen in the differences and similarities between gorillas, bonobos and chimpanzees.

Further palaeontological evidence indicates that *A. afarensis* walked on two legs, but also sometimes used their hands, but not their knuckles, to walk. Chimpanzees and bonobos walk on their knuckles, not their hands. *A. afarensis* feet were even more human-like than their hands. It seems that human-like hands, in effect, were first liberated by human-like feet.

Controversial findings

A. afarensis showed one more, hidden, characteristic which was to change everything that came afterwards. This was a structural brain change. This brain change came before the dramatic changes in brain and body size that are often associated with humans. This brain change came before complete freedom of use of hands for making tools and before complete bipedality, hunting or any of the other physical changes and activities usually associated with the human line.

It is very difficult to see brain characteristics from fossils. Brains do not fossilise (Holloway, Broadfield and Yuan, 2004). The change was seen most clearly in the Baby Taung endocast, AL 162-28. Apparently, in this hominid, the placement of the posterior lunate sulcus, the anterior boundary of the primary visual cortex, close to Broca's Area 17 at the back of the head, changed its location. This information indicated that there was a structural brain change in *Australopithecus*. This brain change created a proportionately much larger posterior parietal cortex, taking brain space from the visual cortex. This change is also indicated in the size of eyes. A larger visual cortex means larger eyes and vice versa. *Australopithecus* had smaller eyes and a smaller visual cortex. Did something become more important for *Australopithecus* than vision to motivate and maintain this structural brain change?

The posterior parietal cortex is one of the 'associational areas' of the brain. Comparisons between modern humans, bonobos and chimpanzees show that other associational areas have grown relative to the great ape brains in the temporal and prefrontal cortex. The human cerebellum, associated with posture and movement, is also larger than in other great apes. Interestingly, primary sensory and motor areas in the cerebral cortex are similar in relative size between modern humans and modern apes. The primary sensory and motor brain areas are the connections between specific parts of the body and specific areas of the cerebral, associational, cortex.

The importance of the loss of visual cortex and the expansion of associational cortex at the back of the brain in afarensis is that it took place so early in human evolution, 3 to 4 million years ago. This was before fully developed feet for walking, before hands for making tools, and before the enormous size expansion of the other parts of the brain. This change happened, though, after 5 to 6 million years of the multi-body, fission–fusion foraging group (Holloway, Broadfield and Yuan, 2004).

Indeed, the fact of this brain change puts into question many of the accepted ideas about how human brain developed from technology and technical thought. It may not be technology, or even learning, that developed the brain. Brains may indeed evolve and develop with the intensity of social relationships and the requirement of thinking about them in groups. Interestingly, this brain change has been known for many years and has been widely resisted, but not disproved.

A second part of the importance of this change is that, not only is this structural brain change surprising to many palaeoanthropologists, it is also difficult to interpret. The area of the change in the brain, the posterior parietal cortex (PPC) is not well investigated or understood. What does it mean that the parietal cortex has grown at the expense of the visual cortex? What would give an evolutionary advantage to any creature that could replace the advantage of quality of sight?

Ralph Holloway (2008, p. 8) stated that 'I believed then and I remain convinced today that the earliest hominids, i.e., *Australopithecus africanus*, *A. afarensis*, and *A. garhi*, had brains that were definitely different from any ape's, despite their small size', and so 'natural selection had worked on more complex social behaviour as would be expected if the relative reduction in PVC (Primary Visual Cortex) signalled a relative increase in parietal association'.

This point may seem rather technical. It is of great interest and importance, however, especially in the light of how well *A. afarensis* fits into the human story being told here, which started with *Dryopithecus*. We cannot know for sure what was added or taken away with the internal structural brain change. However, it looks likely that it had to do with aspects of the afarensis social and group life. The visual cortex and the post parietal cortex are located next to each other at the back of the brain. Something was more important than vision for human survival. Something needed associational, rather than visual, cortex. What might this have been?

Experimentally and behaviourally, the posterior parietal cortex (PPC) has been linked to the planning and determination of the small calculations and judgments involved in physically throwing a ball to another person, for example. The PPC has also been linked to an internal visual perception, for another example, where parts of one's own body might be even when they cannot be seen. These provide some thoughts as to links with internal visual images as in dreams or imagination. There are clues in the importance of placement of self with others, as in throwing and catching balls. Could this brain change signal the entrance of the group physically into minds in a way that is particular to hominids on the human line?

The third position is self within group

It is not beyond probability that, in the deep history of *A. afarensis*, the sense of being an individual within the social network was born. The *A. afarensis* brain change allowed the representation of the human group in the brain. This was the sense of being able to see oneself in relation to others, sometimes known as the 'third position' or the 'third eye'. *A. afarensis* almost certainly had power and dominance hierarchies, following on from the *Dryopithecus* suite of characteristics. Dominance hierarchies resolved conflicts and saved lives in evolutionary terms. However, the more salient characteristic of human emotional and social life is one of belonging and being close, both physically and emotionally, to others.

Mammals are all group animals. In mammals, the primary care and emotional ties are between mothers and babies. Animal groupings take different forms with different mammals and the structure of the group is part of the physicality of any particular creature. With *Dryopithecus*, certain changes took place. Brains became bigger and the strategy of staying in the trees longer required that fission-fusion social structures evolved along with some new ways of finding and accessing more difficult fruit. With *A. afarensis*, human ancestors came to the ground and started to walk erect. *A. afarensis* was thus able to explore and exploit the new savannah environment that had developed while the more remote ancestors were in the trees.

When *A. afarensis* came down from the trees and into the savannah, the group became a multi-body finder of food. It is thought that *A. afarensis* was a scavenger. In the savannah, the group also became the main protection from predators. A creature alone on the savannah is easy prey for a lion or other predator. Three individual creatures together are safe from attack in most circumstances. Palaeontological evidence shows that *A. afarensis* was often the object of feline predators. This suggests that the natural selection process was active and acute. The group became a physical entity.

Thus, the *A. afarensis* structural brain change, which made the physical visual cortex and the eyes smaller and the associational posterior parietal cortex larger, is where the human group entered. This change pre-dates language. The advantage that the change brought with it was that *A. afarensis* was able to gain safety in numbers. Individuals remained physically close together. The close association of brothers and mothers to the group was necessary for survival. Mating was within the group and offspring were raised by the group, which contained both kith and kin. In order to practice exogamy, smaller groups needed to have other, larger kith-related groups around them too. I imagine this as larger groups containing smaller groups, which became arrangements of tribes containing clans later on. Without this kind of group, brains would not have been able to grow any larger than the 300cc of the *Dryopithecus* suite of characteristics. Solitary individuals in the savannah would have soon perished. *A. afarensis* would not have been able to survive as a solitary individual creature, or even as a creature with a fission–fusion kind of group.

With an internalised sense of self, each individual creature internalises a unique set of relationship connections. This happens most powerfully as infant and child. These internalised relationship connections, in turn, create an internal version or image of self with others. Early connections can be added to or changed later. However, from moment to moment, the internalised connections inform the individual about where they are and who they are with. This happens internally as well as externally. The group exists internally even when it is not present in the room.

The group exists as a set of relationship connections which are both inside and outside the individual at the same time. In other words, the connections are portable in each individual. The connections made in and with the group generalise to new environments, new groups and new individuals. These connections can be reinforced or contradicted, but they create a sense of the individual in the world and through time.

It is probable that this was the space that was opened in the *A. afarensis* brain change. This space was necessary to allow the exploration of the new savannah environment. It entailed a further transformation of the fission–fusion groups that went before. A closer, more intense, social environment was needed for safety. The groups needed to be intense, but also to avoid interbreeding. The kin relationships were diluted with non-kin, or kith. There was more integration between males and females, both as providers and carers of offspring. It was the growing complexity of these relationships and interrelationships that brought the exponential growth in hominid brain size, body size, and the use of tool which came immediately after *A. afarensis*.

Splits and controversies: Individual or group

Some of the findings that I have reported here are controversial in palaeontology and in other areas of study. Wolpoff (1975), for example, disputed the low sexual dimorphism of *A. afarensis*. The brain change was also a topic of hot disagreement between Holloway and colleagues. These smaller disagreements are part of a larger split in palaeontological anthropology. It is interesting that a focus on the group dimension emphasises so clearly only one side of the split. The other side of the split in palaeontology emphasises individuality and denies the importance of group behaviour and group life in evolution and in environments. This split includes disagreements on the political natures of chimpanzees and bonobos, the 'selfish gene', and others. My aim here is to bring to light the containing, inclusive and integrating power of the human group, as well as the forces that push humans apart. In any event, it is clear that there is no split between the individual and the group in evolution. The evolution of the human condition clearly shows that individuals grow from groups. Groups do not grow from individuals in evolutionary terms nor do groups grow from individuals in present everyday life.

Without a consciousness of the group, researchers in various fields emphasise what they call the Machiavellian and violent human potential. Ever more nuanced power dynamics are part of the *Australopithecus* brain change. However, at the more specifically human level, the social brain constantly senses and regulates relationships with others. The sensing and regulation of humans in groups always has to do with power and powerlessness. The sensing and regulation of humans in groups also always has to do with cooperation, belonging and rejection. Humans are, biologically and evolutionarily, nodes of multi-body groups or societies.

The splits in palaeontology have a hidden influence in determining how we think of ourselves and each other. Science is not free of politics and ideology, even though it also helps to inform us about the world. The works of Jane Goodall (1988) and Richard Dawkins (1976) have been highly influential in forming our individualistic and violently competitive images of ourselves and others. They are not the whole story and, in fact, their versions of human science have also been disputed (Power, 1991; Wilson, 2012). In the study of early humans, the group dimension is also missing. Following on from the findings about *Dryopithecus* and *Australopithecus*, however, the group dimension can still be traced through some really important physical changes to human bodies, particularly to female bodies.

References

Arendt, H. (1958 [1998]) *The Human Condition, 2nd edition*. Chicago, IL: University of Chicago Press.
Begun, D. (2007) 'Fossil Record of Miocene Hominoids', in W. Hanke and I. Tattersall (eds), *Handbook of Paleoanthropology, Volume 2*, pp. 921–977. Heidelberg: Springer.
Dawkins, R. (1976) *The Selfish Gene*. Oxford: Oxford University Press.
Elias, N. (1987) *Involvement and Detachment*. Oxford: Blackwell.
Foulkes, S. H. (1948) *Introduction to Group-analytic Psychotherapy: Studies in the Social Integration of Individuals and Groups*. London: Maresfield Reprints.
Goodall, J. (1988) *In The Shadow Of Man*. London: *Phoenix* Giants.
Holloway, R. L. (2008) 'The Human Brain Evolving: A Personal Retrospective', *Annual Review of Anthropology*, 37: 1–19.

Holloway, R. L., Broadfield, D. C. and Yuan, M. S. (2004) *The Human Fossil Record, Vol. 3*. Chichester, Wiley.

Power, M. (1991) *The Egalitarians – Human and Chimpanzee: An Anthropological View of Social Organization*. Cambridge: Cambridge University Press.

Reno, P. L., McCollum, M. A., Meindl, R. S. and Lovejoy, C. O. (2010) 'An Enlarged Post-cranial Sample confirms *Australopithecus afarensis* Dimorphism Similar to Modern Humans', *Philosophical Transactions of the Royal Society B: Biological Sciences 365 (1556)*: 3355–3363.

Russon, A. E. and Begun, D. R. (2004) (eds), *The Evolution of Thought: Evolutionary Origins of Great Ape Intelligence*. Cambridge: Cambridge University Press.

Wilson, E. O. (2012) *The Social Conquest of Earth*. New York: W. W. Norton & Co.

Wolpoff, M. H. (1975) 'Primate Models for Australopithecine Sexual Dimorphism', *American Journal of Physical Anthropology*, 45: 497–510.

Chapter 6

Early humans

The earliest remains considered to be human have been called *Homo habilis* and dated from three million years ago. Habilis remains have been found with stone flake tools, although these tools have also been found without bones and dated somewhat earlier. Stone flake tools are stones that show intentional workings and indicate that *H. habilis* made tools as well as used them. It is thought that *H. habilis*, like *A. afarensis*, added meat to the primarily fruit diet of primates. Meat was scavenged in the savannah initially, rather than hunted. Like *A. afarensis*, *H. habilis* remains often show signs of having been prey to large feline predators. This is evidence of the human expansion into the savannah as well as a suggestion that the consequent evolutionary pressures were immense.

H. habilis was small, like *A. afarensis*, on the pattern of the *Dryopithecus* suite of characteristics. However, what sets *H. habilis* apart from *A. afarensis* is the much bigger brain size of 640cc, as compared with the *A. afarensis* brain size of 300 to 400cc. The brain growth and structural brain change of *A. afarensis* may well have set off a series of conditions that grew both human brains and bodies exponentially. One of these conditions was an upright stance and free hands to make tools and use them. *H. habilis* was followed by *Homo ergaster* from 1.8 million years ago and *Homo erectus* from 1.9 million years ago, both with much larger bodies. It is thought that *H. erectus* made the early human migrations to Europe. *H. erectus* was the Last Common Ancestor of *Homo sapiens* in Africa and Neanderthals in Europe. The *Homo erectus* who stayed in Africa evolved into *H. sapiens*, also known as the Cro-Magnons of later migrations to Europe and Asia. These later migrations are dated about 65,000 years ago. The Cro-Magnons are understood to have had dark skins.

About the time of *H. habilis*, other human-like fossils have been found. Other species of hominins lived at the same time and in the same places. This suggests a radiation of different species into a new environment, much as happened with the Miocene great apes in the warm forests of Europe millions of years before.

The runaway brain

Hominin species were particularly 'evolvable.' This means that both variation and selection were acute, creating many different adaptations to a new environment and new environmental niches in relatively short spaces of time. There were some important developmental directions. In the time between *H. habilis* (three million years ago) and *H. ergaster* (1.8 to 1.3 million years ago), the hominins grew to modern human size, between 5'5" and 6'0". They became hairless. There were important brain changes. The 'runaway brain' grew exponentially in size to 900cc. There were also important structural changes. Cerebral asymmetries became more accentuated. The right and left brain, in other words, adopted specialised functions. One easily observable sign of asymmetry in the brain is right- and left -handedness, a division of labour between the hands and the sides of the brain. The left hand is associated with the right brain and with more emotional, cultural and artistic human aspects. The right hand is associated with the left brain and with language, rational and practical thought and action. There was some reorganisation of the frontal lobe, most often thought to be the centre of logical reasoning, although only when well-connected to other brain areas (Holloway, Broadfield and Yuan, 2004).

Homo sapiens

H. sapiens evolved from one million years ago. Anatomically modern *H. sapiens* remains have been identified from as long ago as 200,000 years. Brain and body changes are closely bound up with each other in evolution. The upright stance in the human lineage freed the hands and allowed tool use and tool-making, as we have seen. Free hands also enabled things to be carried from one locality to another. Home bases became possible within a culture of constant geographical movement. Hunters, foragers and gatherers could bring provisions back to the old, the young, the ill, the less able, and pregnant and lactating females. Childhood and adolescence could last longer. Home bases further defined the group identity. Upright stance and free hands enabled active hunting to replace or augment scavenging. Humans could wound or poison an animal and then track it until it died.

The upright stance enabled infants to be carried in adolescent or adult arms and on adolescent or adult backs without needing to clutch on to their mothers like the great ape babies. *H. sapiens* had lost the hairiness of the apes. Hairlessness enabled better cooling in warmer climates. Hairlessness controlled the lice that spread from close physical contact. Physical contact in humans was skin to skin. Babies and children could be more helpless because there were tribes and clans, groups, to provide care, as well as individual mothers and bonded pairs.

Female bodies

Female bodies evolved in ways that could only be an expression of the integrated, mixed male and female, intensely close community. Females became larger relative to males. Human female fertile periods and human female sexuality became nearly totally unlinked to each other. In chimpanzees, females are only receptive to sex when they are fertile. Fertility is clearly marked by swollen, red bottoms. Bonobos are somewhere in between chimpanzees and humans. In bonobos, receptivity to sex is not linked to fertility. Bonobos also have a long estrus that obscures their actual period of fertility, which is more like humans than chimpanzees.

In human females, fertility is well hidden. Human female receptivity to sex has a very weak relationship to fertility. Human female fertility is marked by the menstrual blood of periods. However, estrus positively marks fertility and receptivity to sex in female mammals. Human menstrual blood indicates the times when a human female is not fertile. The chimpanzee and bonobo marker is clearly saying 'yes' to sex and fertility and the human marker is saying something more like 'no', or 'no fertility now'. This leaves the actual period of fertility in human females unmarked, though possibly not unknown. In many hunter-gatherer cultures, the menstruating female is isolated from men during her period. Furthermore, when they are living together, modern human females adapt their periods to each other without willing it or even realising it. This synchrony of the fertility 'no' signal indicates that fertility belongs to the group, not primarily to the individual females. Camilla Power (2009) and Chris Knight (1991) were the writers who pointed out the importance of this evolutionary change.

Male and female reproductive strategies or the group dimension?

Power (2009) and Knight (1991) showed how evolutionary change in female bodies worked to attract and to keep males involved in maintaining the group. In mammals, group maintenance includes the care of offspring. Male mammals were driven to impregnate many females and take very little responsibility for infants, in general. Human females and babies, though, needed the support of adult males hunting together and the stability of their presence in order to give birth to, and to care for, the big-brained human infants. Human mothers were not capable of evolving big-brained babies without male group involvement.

Mainstream human evolutionary studies assume that human males and females have conflicting sexual strategies. Females want to secure life for their infants and males want to impregnate, assure their individual paternity and flee. However, in the group dimension, where the group itself is a crucial element in human evolution, it was the female bodies that were evidently evolving along with the human brain. This was a product of evolution that could not have occurred without male evolutionary involvement in the group, including collective hunting and collective responsibility for mothers, infants and children.

Knight (1991) posited a female sex strike, which has the effect of only involving the males in fertility who will stay involved with the group. The synchronisation of fertility, signalled by female menstruation, has the effect of stopping male sexual strategies from dominating the only reproductive strategy necessary to maintain the group, the new female bodies and the big-brained infants.

The male strategy assumed in mainstream human evolutionary development would never have allowed the human brain to grow large, as evidenced by bonobos and chimpanzees, whose brains have not grown past the *Dryopithecus* suite of characteristics. Human female menstruation, the red blood, is a sign that says 'no' to immediate fertility, but 'yes' to longer term fertility, which is invisible and uncertain. Human females may be saying 'no' to sex by a bleed when they are not capable of being impregnated, but 'yes' to sex with males who stay, create and maintain home bases that include big-brained human children. The human reproductive strategy needed both females and males working together in order to create more humans (Dunbar, Knight and Power, 1999).

Division of labour

The other potential sources of sexual conflict are all around competition, power and envy. Competing males and females needed find ways of living together in close proximity to each other. Competition, greed and envy sometimes explode, as with chimpanzees. In humans, however, the underlying division of labour is about preserving life, not just an individual life. The life being preserved in humans, in terms of evolution, is an intensely-related group life. This group life evolved to be expressed as a group self, symbolised in kinship, names, rituals, totems and cave paintings. Totems and cave paintings that identify groups have been understood to indicate the origins of religion. The unconscious awareness of the group dimension might feel something like spirituality.

Within human groups, males and females created a division of labour which left them in slightly different environments from each other and became the hunter-gatherer groups. Some of these hunter-gatherers still exist today. These living human hunter-gatherers provide insight into what being human entailed up to 10,000 years ago.

Ten thousand years ago, the world population of humans was about 10 million individuals, all of them foragers. This was a successful and long-lived form of social organisation, perhaps from as as two million years ago ago. Hunters and gatherers dominated the human landscape until agriculture. Agriculture revolutionised social relationships. The very beginnings of agriculture date from about 15,000 years ago in the Middle East, the Levant.

The San

One particular group of African tribes is thought to be the closest to these first people. These tribes are collectively called the San. The San have a long history in Southern Africa. They were pejoratively called Bushmen by the Boers, who hunted them like animals and nearly wiped them out. Many San now live in the Kalahari Desert in Central Africa between Botswana and Namibia. Their presence in Southern Africa has been traced to at least 10,000 years ago (Lee, 1979, p. 77).

From the point of view of an industrialised individual, it is difficult to imagine how intense the hominid and early human groups needed to be in order to create the human. Existing hunter-gatherers, like the San, sit close together, skin to skin, when they are resting, for example. This gives a visual sense of closeness and oneness.

Richard B. Lee (1979), an anthropologist who lived with the San, and learned their language, described how they are always talking. They talk to each other, and also to the group at large. Lee cited one woman who went out in the middle of the night and talked to the whole village while everyone else slept. They tell each other and the group when they are happy or unhappy. Constant talking provides constant group maintenance, much like the grooming and sex practised by chimpanzees and bonobos. In human groups, the talking and grooming are more generalised, and more enveloping of the individual group members (Dunbar, 1996, p. 396). One person talking can encompass the whole group, which is different from the individually-oriented grooming practised by the other great apes. Talking in itself is a very powerful, plural activity.

Further, much of the San talk functions to keep individual group members from becoming aloof, arrogant, and from having too much power. This is the group talking to individuals. Lee described how he was quite hurt at first when his gifts were never good enough. It took some time, but he finally understood that the banter that hurt his feelings was designed to promote egalitarianism in the group. They were saving him from his own aloofness, they explained. If he had too much praise and he became aloof, he would be in danger because he would no longer be a part of them (Lee, 1979, p. 24).

San tribes might be described as aggressively egalitarian. Egalitarianism and reciprocity are the basic organising principles of San groups. The San practise an immediate-return economy where all food, both hunted and gathered, is divided and consumed immediately, and according to strict rules of distribution. Nothing is saved or owned individually. Everything belongs to the group (Lee, 1979, p. 118). The San employ a strict sexual division of labour. Women gather food sometimes together and sometimes alone. Men hunt food sometimes together and sometimes alone. Men sometimes gather food together, but not with the women. Their diet is omnivorous.

However, the women's gathering provides 80 per cent of the food for the community and the men's hunting only provides 20 per cent. Some anthropologists argue that hunting is less for food and more for male bonding, providing males with rewarding activity. Interestingly, and in contrast to the sexual division of labour, men and women share the decision-making and conflict resolution. There is a hierarchy of influence in accordance with age, experience and wisdom.

The San have a relatively stable population in terms of numbers. The women average just three births in their lifetimes. Infant mortality is high at around 40 per cent. There is some emigration. Babies are carried and breast-fed for four to five years. This extended breast feeding controls female fertility somewhat. Children reach puberty at about twelve years old. Marriage is at fourteen or fifteen years old. The married couple live with the wife's family for a few years, at least, while her parents help to train the young man in hunting and receive a significant share of his meat in return.

All food is brought back to camp. It is then shared out in strict accordance with the rules and consumed immediately with up to 30 camp members. Sharing rules create and reinforce reciprocity and sociability. The hunted meat belongs to the man who made the arrow that first hit or killed the animal. This is not necessarily the bowman.

Individuals in groups

Paradoxically, perhaps, the San are also fiercely independent. All adults are autonomous and highly individuated. Each is accepted for their natural variety of talents and abilities. Each adult individual is responsible for themselves. As mentioned above, there is a constant social pressure against any one person taking power and leadership. The existence of privilege, status, difference and hierarchies are discouraged interpersonally and constantly. There are no institutions of State, Church or Army. The group is everything.

When asked, a San might say that they do not depend on the group at all. The South African traveller, Laurens van der Post (1958 [2004]), described how he met a small San group wandering in the desert, far from water and food, and obviously suffering. After they had accepted and consumed food and water from him, one member of the group jumped up, and came back a few hours later with two old people. The original group had left the old couple in the desert to die, presumably. No one seemed to expect more or less.

The implication is that the elderly couple would not have expected that the younger ones would endanger themselves to take care of them. Intense group relationships do not detract from this sense of the limits of the care of the group for each individual. The individual is responsible for the group, as well as the other way around.

The San groups are not necessarily defined by their genetics. They are not families as families are understood in terms of neoliberalism, in other words. The home bases of the San are centred around their physical environment. Home bases are centred around each area's scarce resources. The most important physical resources are the standing water holes and local, basic subsistence, foods. The water holes carry the name of a central group member, usually an elder and is built around core siblings and their spouses, siblings of spouses and their spouses. Permission must be asked to use the water hole or other resources. It is always granted, creating a reciprocal debit, like a long-term investment.

However, San groups are also open and non-territorial. They are made up of both kith and kin who find that they can live and work together. The group remains stable, although the individuals change. So, the water holes remain the same, but the individuals in the groups, either staying or visiting, change. Each local group is part of complex networks of interacting, interbreeding, and linguistic communities. There are several related San languages with unique sounds, based on various forms of clicks performed by the movement of the tongue.

Kinship is an important, but flexible concept. Lineages are recognised although birth alone does not determine the membership of the living groups. There are other ways of relating, such as by a given name. Richard Lee (1979) described how complex kin relationships connect different groups together, as opposed to defining the boundaries of the group. For example, Lee was given a name as soon as he arrived. This name immediately placed Lee in a lineage with a mother, father and brother, some of whom did not live in the groups that he studied.

Indirect competition

The San groups function with a principle of indirect competition. Indirect competition is an avoidance of direct competition. That is, if someone is not happy in a group, temporarily or permanently, they go and join another one. Scarcity and conflict are resolved in this way. The potential for human violence is somewhat controlled. Some of the controls are denial of approval and the threat of ostracism from the group. Lee observed some violence and heard about some murders, which he thought were mostly about sexual betrayal and jealousy.

Families and living groups are not coterminous, but cross-hatch with each other to create peace and to preserve life. A wide and loosely-defined kinship system means that wherever someone wants to go, there will be a 'relative' to visit. Lee estimated that 13 per cent of the San had made a residential shift from one group to another. Thirty-five per cent divide periods of residence equally among two or three different groups. There is much visiting.

The maintenance of the San hunter-gatherer group is the most important activity of the group, bar none. In fact, this group maintenance, even in modern cultures, is so basic that it is often overlooked as a prime motivator of all kinds of behaviour, including the hunting and gathering in the San. The group is the human environment most immediately sensed, and from which all life grows. On the savannah, the group protects the hunter-gatherer from predators, and is the unit of survival. All the above characteristics are aimed at keeping the group together and on preserving life.

The lessons of how the San live are very precious indicators of human ancient biology and sociality. We know a lot about them, but also very little. Their living existence is gravely threatened at the moment. The remaining San were denied access to their territories by the Namibian and the Botswanan governments some years ago. Apparently, diamonds were discovered there. We may lose the San and the other living hunter-gatherers at any moment; they may already be lost as living reminders of a common human past.

Becoming attuned to the group dimension

Tracing human history across millions of years might seem unnecessary to some. However, I believe that this knowledge is necessary for a full appreciation of how humans are biologically social. The group dimension is real and physical. An understanding of the reality of groups and the mental processes related to them is necessary before people can become consciously attuned to them. Everyone feels the group processes and the accompanying mental processes as they are working.

This will be the topic of the next chapter. Keeping groups and the ways that they work in focus leads to productive dialogue about the factors that divide humans, like race, gender, sexuality, ability, equality, power and politics. In this way, we can begin to develop forms of discourse and narrative that enable a deeper dialogue over difference and conflict, without minimising or turning away. The San solution, indirect competition, is no longer sufficiently effective in the modern world.

Humans were not engineered by external forces or invisible hands. Evolution is a tinkerer, not an engineer. The fit between individuals and groups is full of imperfections. First, the *Australopithecus* brain change that created the ability to have a self and a specifically human group also created the human ability to deny, turn away, and turn a blind eye from reality. This turning away is sometimes regarded as a defence that leads to what is considered to be mental illness in certain circumstances. Dialogue requires that this tendency to turn away be resisted in the interests of enabling difficult feelings to be expressed and heard.

Second, the fit between feelings and thoughts is often problematic. Feelings can overwhelm thinking. Thinking sometimes does not allow feelings to be known by self and others. This imperfect relationship between thoughts and feelings leaves a space in which humans can deceive themselves and others, and they often do. Dialogue requires that attempts are made to include thoughts and feelings that are more difficult to express and to be heard. Dialogue is required, however, for knowledge of thoughts and feelings. Very often, perhaps always, feelings and thoughts can only be known in relation to others.

Third, infants are also relatively powerless and powerful, at the same time, for most of their early years and beyond. The combination of power and powerlessness experienced by human babies at birth and for most of their first six months feeds into the importance of power, sometimes insatiable power, in the time of monsters. Feelings, thoughts and actions intended to counter the infantile relationship to power in modern daily life are ubiquitous. Power and powerlessness are present in every interaction. People are capable of becoming more conscious of power dynamics and thus, more able to use this consciousness in dialogue with a better understanding of the group dimension.

Brain changes in human evolution created many contradictions in human life. The changes in female bodies created a sense of a poor fit between males and females living together in groups. The San people exhibit some ways of maintaining equality between males and females in ways that also allow differences and conflicts for example, the division of labour between them. Any power differentials coming from the division of labour are minimised by a culture of diminution and critique. In evolution, women's bodies clearly changed more than men's bodies. Mating instincts and signals have become more ambiguous in humans. These changes emphasise the importance of the group, and particularly, the importance of male involvement in the group.

Containing competitive and dominance hierarchies was, and is, particularly important. The competitive reproduction strategies of males and females is one example. Changes in women's bodies and the importance of the human male collective were problems that needed to be solved before big-brained babies could be born and survive. Changes in women's bodies and the importance of the human male collective are problems that need constant renewal and continuous attention if we are to find a way out of the time of monsters and move into a different kind of world to come.

These problems are ancient. A sexual division of labour between men and women may no longer be necessary because of technological and social developments. There are very few activities that require only men or only women. However, the problems of power and of conflicting sexual strategies still exist and dominate everyday human lives and are becoming more acute in the time of monsters, exactly because of the progressive obscurity of the importance and dynamics of the human group.

It may well be asked why there is not more general awareness of group dynamics as part of the human condition. Part of the reason is in the separation of the areas of knowledge of human sciences. While knowledge is done in silos and echo chambers, information has become more important than thought.

The neoliberal attack on the group dimension

A part of the reason for lack of awareness of the group dimension is the overwhelming emphasis on individuality and the importance of family in the neoliberal narrative. This was clearly stated by Margaret Thatcher in the epigraph at the beginning of this section of the book. The ideas of Jane Goodall (1988), for example, are accepted because she emphasised the violence of the chimpanzee bands that she studied. The findings of Margaret Power (1991), who disputed Goodall's findings, have been dismissed. However, what Power noted was that Goodall altered the environment of the chimpanzees by feeding them to attract them and then retracting the feeding. The creation of this relative deprivation may well have caused the violence that Goodall later observed and interpreted as genetic. This crucial point shows the importance of changes in environment to changes in group dynamics.

Another example is the controversy between Richard Dawkins and Edmond O. Wilson. Dawkins' (1976) *The Selfish Gene* has become not only a bestseller, but a central ideological idea about how human sexual selection operates. Dawkins posited that the gene only wants to survive and does not care about the beings that it creates. For Dawkins, the gene was the unit of evolutionary selection. At the same time, Edmond O. Wilson (2012) wrote that the group was the unit of natural selection and not the gene. Wilson's position has been all but forgotten.

There have been other controversies mentioned in the review that I have written here. One of them was around the difference in size between *A. afarensis* males and females. The other was whether the brain change of visual cortex and associative cortex took place in *A. afarensis*, or later. These underlying conflicts touch upon the importance, or denial of the importance, of groups in human life. This review of the importance of an understanding of human evolution to be able to see the group dimension has been written to redress this denial. The lens of the group dimension has also been shown to be important for a better understanding of human evolution and its consequences in everyday life.

In the meantime, humans are actually in danger of losing their sense of groups. Internet technology makes it possible to be easily in touch with ideas and people around the globe. This same technology isolates us from those closest to us physically. Families and communities are breaking down and being torn apart by fears, differences and conflicts. More conscious knowledge of groups would help to contain these differences and conflicts.

Increased poverty in the time of monsters means that the nuclear family, cared for by one mother at home with children, while father worked outside the home, is no longer the norm, if it ever was. At present, both parents must work, often leaving children at home on their own, or in the charge of other children. The technology of gene selection applied to humans means that those in power will soon be able to consciously determine what the next generations of humans are like in many respects. If allowed, the elites will do this in their own interests. The availability of pornography and the disinhibition created by online life further alienate the sexual strategies of men and women from each other, with loss to both. The effect of this on younger and younger humans means that it has become more rooted into the heart of human emotions.

Decolonising from neoliberalism

Arendt begged us to think about what we are doing. Thinking about the group dimension as the space where the individual and society meet and integrate is an unusual perspective. In order to see it, decolonisation from neoliberal individualism is necessary. It is a bit like squinting to see the figure and the ground at the same time in a gestalt visual image. Arendt, Elias and Foulkes thought and wrote about the group dimension, but they were few among many.

The deep history of group and human evolution is an important perspective in the group dimension. Through tracing evolution forward, like a story, it became clear that humans have a specific biological sociality. This is the human group dimension. The details of how the San groups live demonstrate how groups in deep evolutionary history have grown into more and more complex webs of individuals, groups and institutions through more recent and familiar histories. However, the basic dynamics of human sociality as unconscious strategies for preserving energy and life remain in many of the ways that humans think and feel. These strategies for collectively preserving energy and life are at the foundation of humanity.

The details about the San also provide some ideas about how politics can be recreated and renewed in what Arendt has called the 'social' in the present. The San are another example of the proto-polis that Arendt saw in Greek and Roman civilisations. In fact, it is less that the San were political and more that San politics are the essence of the politics that are central to human life.

In Part IV, I will describe the emotional and thinking processes of human big brains. It is important to know about these processes in order to have the dialogue in groups that creates and expresses each unique internal self-integration and the integration of self in the real, social world. These are the same processes that are involved in decolonising from neoliberalism. Having shown that human bodies are biologically social, I will describe how the brain is also biologically social. This biological sociability means that everyone feels social processes in everyday life all the time. Individual conscious feeling for these social processes nourishes the inter-individual processes of having better and more contained dialogues, even in the most difficult of situations. Only this consciousness will bring back a sense of the polis in politics without the uncontained violence of splitting, factions, fighting and war.

Neoliberalism, the most recent form of capitalism, has not worked as a policy either for earth or for humans. Forms of collective production processes will always be needed. However, we no longer need the mean heart of capitalism, which is production by means of a relationship based on exploitation, extraction and alienation between people. In other words, capitalist economics is not capable of working in the interests of human beings now, if it ever was. Capitalism has created great wealth for some and abject poverty for others. Capitalism has also created this time of monsters which affects everyone. In order to escape from the time of monsters, humans need a polis, a way of modulating power that is based on equality. In order to have a polis based on equality, humans need ways of having dialogues over difference and conflict. This is the Group Dimension.

References

Dunbar, R. (1996) *Human Evolution*. Harmondsworth: Penguin.
Dunbar, R., Knight, C. and Power, C. (1999) *The Evolution of Culture: An Interdisciplinary View*. Edinburgh: Edinburgh University Press.
Goodall, J. (1988) *In the Shadow of Man*. London: Phoenix Giants.
Dawkins, R. (1976) *The Selfish Gene*. Oxford: Oxford University Press.
Holloway, R. L., Broadfield, D. C. and Yuan, M. S. (2004) *The Human Fossil Record, Vol. 3*. Chichester, Wiley.
Knight, C. (1991) *Blood Relations. Menstruation and the Origins of Culture*. New Haven and London: Yale University Press.
Lee, R. B. (1979) *The Kung! San: Men, Women and Work in a Foreign Society*. Cambridge: Cambridge University Press.
Power, C. (2009) 'Sexual Selection Models for the Emergence of Symbolic Communication: Why They Should Be Reversed', in R. Botha and C. Knight (eds), *The Cradle of Language*, pp. 257–280. Oxford: Oxford University Press.
Power, M. (1991) *The Egalitarians – Human and Chimpanzee: An Anthropological View of Social Organization*. Cambridge: Cambridge University Press.
Van der Post, L. (1958 [2004]) *The Lost World of the Kalahari*. London: Random House.
Wilson, E. O. (2012) *The Social Conquest of Earth*. New York: W. W. Norton & Co.

Part IV

The social brain

'The first revolution is when you change your mind about how you look at things and see that there might be another way to look at it that you have not been shown.'

Gil Scott-Heron (1970)

Figure 4 'Gobleki Tepe man'

Chapter 7

Jaak Panksepp and his unique contribution

The evolutionary perspective taken in the previous chapters fits well with the other ideas of the group dimension. Looking at processes in the past and how these processes produced the present gives a very different view to other, more structural and functional, ways of understanding how individuals, groups and societies interact. Evolutionary principles and the group dimension reinforce each other. The group made the human body. Human bodies and minds have been shaped by human social relationships through the tinkering of evolution and, more recently, history. Nowhere is there more evidence of this than in the human brain.

In evolution, bodies and brains developed together. Each new body part that appeared in evolution had to have nervous system features to support it. Thus, body and brain are inextricably linked to each other. This is not visually apparent. Bodies are visible, while brains are not seen in everyday life. Nevertheless, body and brain are differently structured and functioning parts of the same creature, always in some sort of interaction with other creatures, the environments that they inhabit and the environments that they create.

Groups arose with mammals. Brains pre-existed mammals. The first nervous systems were found in spiny fish, some 410 million years ago. This long evolution is only vaguely apparent in lower human bodies, below the neck. However, the whole of the evolution of the human brain from spiny fish is not only preserved in each individual's brain architecture, but also appears in the process of brain development of every human individual from conception. The body organ that most defines individuals, the brain, is also the organ that is most connected to the human collective evolutionary past. Humans have this evolutionary past in common with all living organisms.

If these concepts are not familiar, it is because the group dimension, along with evolution, has been all but expunged from neoliberal human consciousness. Evolution and the group dimension are two interrelated ways of thinking. Together, they are capable of resolving many of the dilemmas and conflicts that result from splitting and polarisation on all levels of individual, group and society.

To all appearances, human beings are individuals stuck inside their own bodies and heads. The history of the idea of the apparently individualised relationship between brains and skulls is an ancient one and promotes ignorance about human

DOI: 10.4324/9781003350088-12

conscious and unconscious groups and their relationship to internal and external integration between individuals. This ignorance is no longer tenable. We need to know about both evolution and groups in order to regain the *polis* through dialogue and to retain our sanity in the time of monsters.

Present ideological considerations from neoliberalism deny the existence of society in favour of the ideological concept of 'individual freedom'. Perhaps as a consequence of this ideological lack of integration between people, intellectual areas of study and research are stuck in specialised, individualised, 'silos'. That is, people studying one specialised area of knowledge tend not to know what is happening in other knowledge areas. This process of isolation of knowledge and information into separate silos, also called 'echo chambers', creates a generalised ignorance that promotes polarisations, conflicts and violence between people. Many of these conflicts are apparently not resolvable in the neoliberal ideology.

The study of the brain and how it works is a victim of the 'silo' process. So, although the study of the brain is one of the fastest growing areas of science, it misses the most important function of the human brain which is to connect, rather than to isolate, people. There is, in fact, only one neuroscientist, Jaak Panksepp, who has broken through the neuroscience silo in his research of the understudied aspects of the human and mammal brain.

An important aspect of Panksepp's unique contribution to the understanding of how the human brain is a social brain is his starting point from the evolutionary view on the human body and on human sociality. Panksepp wished to make the results of his experiments accessible outside the neuroscientific community. He was particularly interested in making connections with psychoanalysis and the other 'psy' professions: psychiatry, psychology and psychotherapy. He was only partially successful in both these endeavours. Panksepp's findings, like Keynes' General Theory, have been reinterpreted. However, in the group dimension, where the focus is on how humans experience and live with their intense involvement with each other and with their human environments, a light can be thrown on the most unique and important aspects of Panksepp's findings; they also illuminate and clarify important elements of human conscious and unconscious sociality.

Life only happened once. Evolution is a slow and unconscious process. Human consciousness is capable of understanding this process, but we need to look and think together, as Arendt called on us to do. Panksepp looked, thought, and produced information which is capable of producing understanding and change in the world.

The problem of consciousness

Jaak Panksepp's work provided a firm scientific and experimental basis for thinking about what all of humanity has in common in the group dimension. This was not his primary intention. In his first textbook, *Affective Neuroscience: The Foundations of Human and Animal Emotions* (1998), he intended to build the foundation of a new kind of neuroscience. The new neuroscience would lead to a 'new psychology' based on a neuroscientific foundation (Panksepp, 1998, p. viii). What follows is how Panksepp's writings fit into and elucidate the group dimension while the group dimension also elucidates Panksepp's findings.

Jaak Panksepp was born in Estonia in 1943. His father was a landowner and the family fled from Estonia to Germany during the Second World War when Estonia became part of the Soviet bloc. Jaak emigrated with his family to America in 1949. At some point during these journeys, the young Panksepp was badly burnt and nearly died. The pain must have been tremendous because he was only calmed by the doses of opiates that saved his life. These early physical and emotional traumas would certainly have been important in his later struggles to put forward his new paradigm of emotions and emotional learning.

Panksepp's family settled in America, in rural Delaware. Panksepp attended a one-room schoolhouse with 11 students until the age of 14. Later, he began his university studies in electrical engineering. However, while a student, he took a job working in the wards of a psychiatric hospital. In this hospital, he discovered, to his puzzlement, that no one actually knew what emotions were. Yet, here were all these people suffering from emotions. Panksepp changed his course to psychology and then changed again to neuroscience. He had not found an understanding of emotions in his psychological studies.

As a neuroscientist, Jaak Panksepp went in search of emotions and found them in the midbrain as a 'unified experience-generating organ with no Cartesian dualities that have traditionally hindered scientific understanding' (Panksepp, 2012).

Panksepp went into a field based on electrical impulses, chemicals and chemistry, largely without words, wanting to connect with what is, in effect, universal human experience. In neuroscience, Panksepp found, and proved, experimentally and persuasively, that there are seven foundational feelings. These foundational feelings are universally shared by humans, all mammals, some birds and some reptiles (Bacha, 2019).

Early in his career, in 1972, Panksepp found his ideal professional situation at Bowling Green State University in Ohio. He has said that he was attracted to Bowling Green by their new and extensive animal laboratory. It was in this laboratory that he developed his experiments. These experiments were designed to find the origins of the emotions. He proceeded from the bottom up to link animal brains with human ones. Over his lifetime, these experiments triangulated results from subjective human mental states put into words, brain functions of animals by experimentation, and emotional behaviours that all young mammals exhibit early in life in order to survive (Panksepp and Biven, 2012).

Panksepp did not choose an easy life. Far from Panksepp's ideas being welcomed into neuroscience, he met with much opposition from established scientists and institutions. However, he thrived on opposition, up to a point.

After Panksepp published *Affective Neuroscience* in 1998 he met Lucy Biven in the UK and they embarked on combining Panksepp's neuroscience with Biven's psychoanalysis. Although this partnership produced *The Archaeology of the Mind*, it was not a happy pairing. Panksepp did not feel that Biven did enough to help him understand the links with psychoanalysis. Biven found him difficult and dogmatic.

They had problems making a connection. However, Biven's participation and encouragement did produce a further clarification and a more readable text (Panksepp and Biven, 2012). Panksepp died in 2017, like Keynes, very soon after this major work was published. During much of the time that he was working he was ill with the lymphoma that eventually led to his death.

Although the combination of Pankseppian affective neuroscience and psychoanalysis has resulted in a new field of neuropsychoanalysis, a full recognition of the revolutionary aspects of Panksepp's work for all of the 'psy' professions and practices has yet to be accomplished.

One reason that Panksepp's bottom-up thinking about emotions and the brain has been so slow to develop is that many neuroscientists and psychoanalysts have become involved in philosophical debates about the roots of consciousness. The group dimension redefines this problem. In the group dimension, it is not consciousness that is problematic but the forms and depths of the unconscious that need exploring and thinking. Thinking processes bring the unconscious into consciousness. Panksepp showed that thinking processes start with feelings. In investigating the origins of feelings in the midbrain, Panksepp also implicitly posed a question. This question is: How do feelings, which are conscious sensations, become unconscious feelings, thoughts and fantasies? Identifying and understanding the processes by which conscious sensations become unconscious feelings, thoughts and fantasies and the processes by which unconscious feelings, thoughts and fantasies can become conscious are the most important area for the 'psy' professions and for the group dimension.

There are other reasons that the implications of Panksepp's work have been slow to be felt in the 'psy' professions. Panksepp's results are revolutionary in terms of common everyday thinking about self and others, feelings and thoughts, inside and outside. Because Panksepp's ideas are revolutionary and deep, they radiate out into many implications and new ideas. It is thus difficult to know where to start. Also, as indicated above, both Panksepp and psychoanalysis need a group dimension perspective in order to be able to combine with each other. Perhaps it is the group dimension that was missing in the collaboration between Panksepp and Biven.

Feeling process layers

The basic or foundational emotions that Panksepp discovered clarify the nature of specific feelings known as primary process feelings. The fact that mammals and humans share primary process feelings is controversial enough in terms of what this knowledge says about animals. Are animals sentient beings, example? But, perhaps more importantly, what does the fact that mammals and humans share primary process feelings say about humans? Panksepp and his colleagues firmly believed that animals have feelings just like humans. They experimented on animals believing that they were doing this experimentation in the light of animal feelings and with the special care needed in order to better the lives of both humans and animals. Their writings clarify how animal feelings predate and underscore human feelings.

The primary process layer is the foundational layer of the brain and mind. The primary process feelings, those shared with animals, are at the source of three layers that humans recognise as feelings. The primary process, or foundational feelings, are already formed at birth. Panksepp identified them as instinctual, perhaps much like Sigmund Freud identified his category of 'instincts' as drives. The universality of facial expressions, written about by Charles Darwin (1889 [1999]), is also linked to the midbrain primary processes shared between all humans and animals. One important property of the foundational, or primary process, feelings is that they are always conscious. These feelings are always conscious because they are the links that define the unity of the organism and its relationship to its environments.

The middle layer lies above the primary process layer in the midbrain. It is called the secondary process layer. In the secondary process layer are learning and memory functions. These secondary brain processes are identified as unconscious by Panksepp and others. This is because we are not conscious of the processes involved in learning and remembering, even though the results of learning and memory can and do become conscious at particular times, of course. For the 'psy' professions, and for general human self-understanding, the fact that memory and learning are unconscious processes, while the foundational feelings are conscious, is quite profound. From infancy, or maybe even before birth, human brains are taking in elements from the world with sensation, but without thought. In this way, the human unconscious contains most of our memories and learning from our environments in a very direct and physical way, but without full consciousness of them.

The tertiary layer processes are located at the top of the three brain layers in the midbrain. These tertiary processes allow reflection on what has been learned from experience. The tertiary neocortical layer is generally thought of as 'the brain' in popular culture. At birth, this neocortical thinking cap is largely blank, while the feeling, primary process, layer is already formed. The secondary and tertiary layers of the brain are largely associational. They create webs of connections that change over time and with events. The primary layer is directional, made up of identifiable chemical and electrical pathways. The sensitivities of these pathways can vary over time, but not as much as the associational webs of the other areas of the brain.

According to Panksepp, while most neuroscientists are studying secondary and tertiary layers of human brain functions, it is the primary layer that best equips living creatures for immediate survival and immediate learning about the potentialities and opportunities of their environments (Panksepp and Biven, 2012). The evolutionary basis of the primary process feelings is the very deep evolution of soft touch on the skin. The skin and the brain develop from the same layer of cells in embryos. Individual human and animal immediate reactions to contact with their environments lie in the primary process foundational feelings.

Foundational feelings are primary processes

The specific primary process or foundational feelings that Panksepp identified are located in chemical and electrical pathways and processes. These pathways and processes react to elements in the environment and signal the immediate need for response. In humans, where the baby's environment is largely made up of other humans, these feelings facilitate the baby's first opportunities to learn about social involvements with the other humans around it.

Evidence shows that the consciousness of the primary process feelings is independent of language. These are the feelings that originate before words and are experienced as sometimes beyond words. These feelings have only a language of bodily sensations in the first experiences of them.

In both evolutionary terms and in terms of individual development, it is clear that the processes of the midbrain create and develop the cerebral cortex, the thinking brain. Part III of this book showed how the primary process feelings involved in the formation of human specific groups promoted the growth and development of the human cerebral cortex in the runaway brain. The cerebral cortex needed to grow in order to modulate the increasingly intense primary conscious feeling processes involved in intense social and group living. It was the group that created the thinking brain. Panksepp has provided the knowledge of the physical means by which this evolutionary process occurred.

Panksepp invented two terms to describe the difference and the unity of the cerebral cortex with the midbrain. These terms are 'BrainMind' and 'MindBrain'. With these two terms, Panksepp highlighted the fact that his neuroscience was not dualistic. He reserved the term BrainMind for the bottom-up direction of processes, from the midbrain to the cerebral cortex, which is the motivating direction. He used the term MindBrain for the top-down direction of processes of the modulating direction from the cerebral cortex to the midbrain. For Panksepp, mind and brain are one organ, much like body and brain are one entity. However, at the same time, it is clear that emotions originate in the BrainMind while the functions of the cerebral cortex, the MindBrain, are essentially to modulate the foundational feelings and enable abundant learning and thought, guided by societal and cultural group influences.

From the perspective of the group dimension, Panksepp's discoveries begin to make sense of how humans' individual bodies and minds are able to relate to each other so intensely. Panksepp's discoveries also allow people to begin to interpret themselves and each other in a more feeling and empathic way. Further thinking about these discoveries encourages more precise individual relating to bodily sensations and to the thoughts that accompany these bodily sensations. These lines of thinking are important in therapy, self and other care. They also help to think about creating the kinds of social and political institutions that will encourage these processes of relating in the world yet to come, which is as yet unknown. The world yet to come can only be decided when democratic processes can be based on dialogue informed by better general understanding of what it means to be human.

These lines of thinking also speak to an improved consciousness of the nature of the time of monsters that humans have created for themselves. Maybe we can find the words for the feelings in order to speak to each other about our experiences in the time of monsters. We can also find a narrative that will counter the individualism and the politics of splitting and projection leading to conflict, violence and war that come with the neoliberal project. We can know more about how the time of monsters uses human biology against humanity.

Because he lacked the ideas about the group dimension that have come out of human evolutionary development, palaeontology and archaeology (described in Part III), Panksepp missed some of the power of his thinking on the topic of human evolution. Although Panksepp linked his thoughts to both Sigmund Freud and Charles Darwin, he did not develop them further.

However, it is the link between Panksepp's foundational feelings with Freud's (1915) ideas about 'instinct' and with Darwin's ideas about universal facial expressions that led to thoughts about how these foundational, or primary process, feelings are emotionally contagious. That they are emotionally contagious means that humans and animals can know quite a lot about each other even without words. Emotionally contagious means that people quite easily and mostly unconsciously transmit and receive feelings from others. For the most part, they also have no object. They just are.

Panksepp recognised that there was a social or group dimension to his work. He described environmental, interpersonal and medicinal approaches to the treatment of mental problems.

> Overall, our perspective is that an understanding of affect is of critical importance for an understanding of human nature. Not only are our personality structures rooted in affect, but a remarkable number of societally important human issues need to be approached from affective as well as from cognitive perspectives.
> (Panksepp and Biven, 2012, p. 45)

Nevertheless, the group dimension in Panksepp is usually secondary to his preconception of individuality and the search for the location of self in human brains. Panksepp's importance to the group dimension needs to be actively sought.

The seven foundational feelings

Panksepp identified seven foundational feelings, shared by humans and mammals, and situated as pathways in the midbrain. Some of these emotions are unfamiliar, although they may easily be recognised. The recognition of these emotions can change the way that we view our minds. An identification of these foundational feelings also helps to identify and to think about what feelings actually are. It is often difficult for people to differentiate their thoughts from their feelings in the first instance. When asked about feelings, people often give their thoughts. Foundational feelings are particularly recognisable. They are conscious, powerful and contagious. They express an urge to action. It is difficult to resist acting on them in the moment. Other feelings, tertiary and more complex feelings from the cerebral cortex, are often more difficult to locate.

The seven foundational feelings identified by Panksepp are: Seeking, Fear, Rage, Lust, Care, Panic/Grief and Play. The first three are individually-based and interpersonal. However, Care, Panic/Grief and Play involve having and losing others. They are social and transpersonal. In terms of approach and avoidance, three of the foundational feelings, Seeking, Care and Play are essentially positive feelings leading to approach. Fear, Rage and Panic/Grief are negative feelings leading to avoidance. That is, the mammals that Panksepp studied showed these attractions and repulsions clearly in their behaviour and in their vocalisations. In humans, these feelings are equally as powerful, conscious and contagious, but behaviours and vocalisations are muted by the equally powerful modulating cerebral cortex thinking that is motivated by the feelings.

Panksepp's work has wide implications for self-understanding, therapy, intimacy, dialogue and the polis. In fact, all the foundational feelings motivate activity and development in the cerebral cortex. In turn, conscious and unconscious associational thoughts in the cerebral cortex modulate emotions. These emotions can feel both profoundly disturbing and profoundly comforting. The foundational feelings are the simplest of human emotions. The foundational feelings provide the exquisite feeling of human and animal one-ness. Human brains, which are apparently closed to each other inside human skulls, are, in fact, open to each other in ways that we 'know' about, consciously and unconsciously, but have not been able to understand.

With some attention, individuals can feel these foundational feelings along with the cerebral cortex modulation response processes. This makes any theory based on them potentially an experience-near theory. When feelings are conscious, it is easier to make decisions about how best to choose and maintain internal and external social relationships. Internal and external social relationships make all the difference to feelings. Being able to make decisions, individuals can create and maintain dialogue, especially when dialogue is difficult and they want to turn away, attack or explode. The biology of human brains is based in the group in terms of evolution. In the present, groups create human integration with internal selves and others, or not, through these brain and body processes. These processes occur at the same time as humans engage in conversation and dialogue with each other and with themselves.

References

Bacha, C. S. (2019) 'The First Revolution: Taking Jaak Panksepp Seriously', *Group Analysis*, 52(4): 441–457.

Darwin, C. (1889 [1999]) *The Expression of the Emotions*. London: Fontana.

Freud, S. (1915) 'Instincts and their Vicissitudes', in J. Strachey (ed.), *The Standard Edition of the Complete Psychological Works of Sigmund Freud*, Vol. XIV. London: The Hogarth Press and the Institute of Psycho-Analysis.

Panksepp, J. (1998) *Affective Neuroscience: The Foundations of Human and Animal Emotions*. Oxford: Oxford University Press.

Panksepp, J. (2012) 'The Philosophical Implications of Affective Neuroscience', *Journal of Consciousness Studies*, 19(3–4): 6–48.

Panksepp, J., and Biven, L. (2012) *The Archaeology of Mind: Neuroevolutionary Origins of Human Emotions*. New York: W. W. Norton & Co.

Chapter 8

The basic feelings
Seeking, Fear, Rage

The seven foundational feelings have both a physiological and an evolutionary order. In evolution and in mammal embryo development, the nervous system pathways develop from the bottom up and from the middle to the margins. Visually, the development of the cerebral cortex, both in evolution and in fetes development, looks like a flower blooming from a stem. The midbrain, which is where Panksepp concentrated his experiments, is the stem of the brain starting at the top of the spinal cord in the neck just above the pons and continuing up into the centre of the head. Each emotional pathway has its own specific architecture that interacts in inhibitory and energising ways with the other emotional pathways.

The evolutionary and developmental relationships of the emotional pathways to each other suggests that each one builds something more nuanced, specific and complex into bodies and brains in relation to environments. The interactions between the emotional pathways and the rest of the human body are complex. The interactions between the emotional pathways and the environment are also complex. However, these seven named foundational feelings are discrete and clear. They originate from remote evolutionary times. They are felt consciously and physically. They do not need words. They are generated from the environment, through the body, to, and not from, the cerebral cortex higher up in the brain.

Seeking is the feeling of life

Panksepp called the oldest, and most basic, foundational feeling 'Seeking'. Panksepp identified the foundational feelings in his writing by using all capital letters. I have decided to retain only the first letter of each feeling when I use it to mean the foundational feeling. Anatomically, the Seeking pathway runs from its base in the ventral tegmental area (VTA), at the top of the spinal cord, to the shell of the nucleus accumbens, and from there to areas of the frontal cortex and the amygdala at the front of the head. These areas connect via pathways of dopamine sensitive neurons. The Seeking pathway may be as old as the brain itself. In a word, it is the foundational feeling of life.

Seeking is unfamiliar as a description of a feeling. This particular pathway was at first misrecognised by early animal behaviourists as the brain's reward system. The early behaviourists discovered that animals will work to exhaustion to self-stimulate the Seeking pathway. More important than food or rest, the feeling of Seeking is described as a sense of energised expectancy or joyous aliveness. The body feels light and energetic. This feeling is involved in making plans and having dreams for the future. It is linked to the political feeling and attraction of ideas that offer freedom and liberty. It often lifts the more negative feelings of fear, grief and depression.

Seeking was an evolutionary development from older chemical pathways that were based on norepinephrine or noradrenaline, a neuropeptide that facilitates attention during every kind of emotional arousal and leads to feelings of euphoria. The opposite effect in the older pathways comes from acetylcholine which is felt as a negative feeling. Negative feelings are felt in the body as heavy and lacking in energy as in depression or despair. This is the feeling of low or absent Seeking.

Seeking is based on the dopamine neuropeptide. Although Seeking is also sensitive to other neurotransmitters, the Seeking feeling is synonymous with what is also called the dopamine pathway in the brain. Seeking accompanies practically everything that organisms do and helps to facilitate most other emotional urges. When Seeking is active, it runs underneath all the other foundational feelings.

Homeostasis: Between joy and despair

What the behaviourists termed 'rewards' from Seeking have been found to be sensory and homeostatic. The rewards from Seeking are like body temperature gauges that have limits up and down, but remain in a dynamic balance around a specific point. Seeking is most active in animals when there is a homeostatic need, like temperature, hunger or thirst, and there are opportunities to find good things in the environment to satisfy these needs. The Seeking feeling in humans expresses the anticipation and excitement of finding these good things, which can be anything from food to company, to sex, to love. to revenge. Seeking is linked to the feeling of enthusiasm and the impetus to explore new environments. It is the feeling of interest in the world. Seeking stops when the good things are found and consumption begins, leading to a need being satisfied, or not. The consumption phase in animals is often followed by satisfaction and sleep. After a period of time, the Seeking feeling returns.

Nothing happens without Seeking. Seeking is not a feeling that we are used to having in our consciousness. However, once described, it is possible to notice the feeling of Seeking and its ebb and flow through time. Seeking ebbs and flows also in reaction to events in the environment and thoughts, most often involving the human environment that mostly involves other humans.

Seeking is an essentially good feeling. It is the feeling of belief in the expectations of a good future. It is active. It is excited, and can be anxious, but not usually. The ability to recognise and consciously feel the Seeking feeling is important information about how individual humans are relating to their environments. Seeking is a rewarding feeling in itself. It is sometimes described as synonymous with curiosity, interest and expectancy. Seeking is related to wanting to know. Seeking is also related to hopefulness as well as to euphoria and sometimes to mania.

The absence of Seeking is akin to depression. For humans, Seeking is about more than just surviving. Seeking is surviving with the expectation of something good in the environment in the future. Seeking engages learning, but can be discouraged by bad experiences that also entail learning.

Seeking plays a dynamic supporting role to the other foundational feelings. For example, when a mother feels the urge provide care to her offspring, a positive (Care) feeling, she will Seek food and shelter. When a mother is feeling Fearful, a negative feeling, she will Seek a safe place to be with her offspring. Seeking engenders positive feelings in itself and these positive feelings are capable of counteracting negative feelings. Negative feelings can also counteract and discourage Seeking.

Like all foundational feelings, Seeking has no specific object. Seeking is a further development of forward movement without particular direction. Animals and humans become active agents in their natural environments, but without necessarily having a set direction. Seeking was probably originally connected to bodily and environmental needs in evolutionary terms. Now Seeking is also connected to all the other emotional pathways and, crucially, to all learning.

These unexpected findings have turned Seeking on its head. For Panksepp and in the group dimension, Seeking is no longer thought of as an internal reward system, but as something much more basic. Seeking is the feeling of health and wellbeing. It is the feeling that the world has good things that can be found. This is not a reward, as such. At its best, Seeking is a feeling of being all right and secure in the world. In this sense, Seeking is also connected with the most recent foundational feeling, which is Play, located at the top of the midbrain.

In humans, though, Seeking can include the Seeking for money (greed), information (science), revenge and, of course, love, as well as sex. Seeking responds to greed as well as to need. Humans can be enticed by good things which may not be good for them, like an extra piece of cake or the sexual affair. Seeking can be healthy, but it can also become addictive, as in mania, greed and narcissism, where consumption does not end Seeking and periods of satisfaction are not possible. Drugs such as cocaine and amphetamines facilitate Seeking. It is the feeling of being awake and connected. Seeking does not need these drugs. However, the withdrawal of the Seeking feeling, like the kind of feeling that occurs when coming off cocaine and amphetamines, is a kind of empty depression. This empty feeling often motivates the Seeking return to the addictions which can artificially return the Seeking feeling for a while in a cycle of self-medication. It may be that, far from Seeking being a reward, it is the withdrawal of Seeking without satisfaction that is deeply disturbing and uncomfortable.

Freudian ideas about the 'libido' relate to Seeking. Another psychoanalytic term related to Seeking is 'desire'; also related are the feelings of 'Triumph' and power. In fact, growing knowledge about Seeking helps to clarify these other terms and feelings and helps to recognise and understand the raw feelings involved. The absence of Seeking is unusually uncomfortable and different from the satisfaction felt when the good thing is found. Seeking can feel that it is 'bursting out'. However, Seeking is also working constantly in the background, even when there are no needs to be satisfied or obvious temptations. Mammals are continuously scanning their environments in order to discover where satisfactions lie or in order to find temptations. Seeking keeps humans and animals in a general state of engagement with the world, even when asleep and the physical actions involved in Seeking are immobilised (Panksepp and Biven, 2012, p. 102).

Seeking, memories and learning

The Seeking pathway is also heavily involved in making memories and learning on the secondary process level. Learning entails finding clues to where the good things, the things that satisfy particular needs or temptations, might be found. Learning occurs when cognitive influences descending from the medial prefrontal cortex, behind the forehead, integrate with the emotional energies that ascend from the lower regions of the Seeking pathway in the midbrain. The nucleus accumbens at the top of the Seeking pathway is involved in everything that humans desire and enjoy, from poignant music to the funny joke.

The Seeking pathway is sensitive to the internal environment of the body and its needs. The Seeking pathway also responds to novel events that occur in the environment. The nucleus accumbens is activated when the human or animal becomes more and more excited. When the human or animal becomes habituated to the change, the Seeking pathway no longer responds. However, the Seeking pathway can be reactivated by an individualised memory of a novel event. These novel events are free of value. Thus, Seeking can be involved in compulsive gambling, revenge and sexual urges, as well as by more substantive life accomplishments, like academic or creative achievement (Panksepp and Biven, 2012, p. 107).

Seeking is also activated by the passage of time. In fact, although Seeking is always operating in the background, the dopamine neuropeptide that fuels the pathway comes in waves, abating for a time and returning in anticipation of some promised reward. Thus, Seeking is, all at the same time, a foundational feeling, a neuropeptide pathway and a behaviour. It is the unity of the feeling, the neurological pathway and the behaviour that shows Seeking clearly as a basic mammalian feeling that unites animals and humans and entails specific behaviours.

Panksepp observed that, when Seeking is frustrated in animals, they begin to move around in regular, but non-productive ways. Panksepp called this 'auto-shaping' and likened it to delusional, ritual and compulsive behaviour. In auto-shaping, animals seem to believe that actions other than direct search will bring the desired results, as if by magic. In animals, the Seeking behaviour involved in direct search is usually sniffing. In auto-shaping, the sniffing stops and other random behaviours take its place. Panksepp likened these other behaviours to delusions in humans.

Panksepp also observed that dopamine pathways are especially sensitive to stress. The dopamine pathway can become over aroused and the alternative behaviours can partially alleviate feelings of excessive appetitive arousal to the exclusion of reality testing. He likened this to the basis of obsessive-compulsive disorders, as well as to schizophrenia. The medical facilitation or inhibition of the dopamine, Seeking, circuit encourages or inhibits some kinds of 'schizophrenic behaviours'. (Panksepp, 1998, p. 161).

Emotional contagion and the 'runaway brain'

Seeking is clearly linked to both learning and delusions. When Seeking is frustrated, it becomes overactive and can lead to mania. Seeking can be linked to narcissism and greed, as well as to depression. Seeking can lead to revenge and predatory behaviours, like sexual stalking. It can lead to addictions, like drugs, gambling, pornography and the internet. But mostly, Seeking is where human sociality starts. It underlies all the other basic emotions. It connects humans directly and emotionally with each other and with most other living things. I have called this emotional connection 'emotional contagion'. By 'emotional contagion', I mean the very basic way that humans can feel what other humans are feeling. It is a kind of feeling resonance based on Seeking that leads to mirroring and, eventually, to empathy.

The emotional contagion of Seeking can also lead to mass group behaviours, such as those at political rallies or evoked by the mass and social media. The emotional idea of freedom is at the basis of the hyper individualism of neoliberalism. Could the neoliberal idea of freedom be seen as a disturbance based on Seeking? In other words, Seeking is a good feeling that dispels bad feelings. However, Seeking may also be leading us further into the time of monsters and preventing us from achieving the world yet to come.

Seeking may also be leading us away from dialogue, even though we cannot have dialogue without it. When times are hard and satisfactions frustrated, Seeking responds to chronic stress with denial, the creation of phantasies and magical thinking. Seeking may be connected to religion. It may also underlie mass attachment to strong authoritarian political figures. Seeking provides an element of understanding for how humans get into each other's heads. In effect, humans are always in each other's heads, even though we may sometimes feel that we are individualised, alone and stuck inside our own skulls.

For humans, perhaps the most important aspect of Seeking is that it motivates approach actions to other humans. When Seeking becomes chronically underactive, humans cut off from others, leading to a lack of desire for approach.

The group dimension is crucial for a wider understanding of Panksepp. The group dimension links the emotional development of the cerebral cortex with the 'runaway' brain growth that led from hominids to humans covered in Part III of this book. Human brains grew to three times as large as the hominines in the *Dryopithecus* suite of characteristics over a comparatively short period of three million years. In that time, and more, other primates had very little brain growth. Chimpanzees and bonobos, for example, have brains that have stayed much the same over that period of time. Chimpanzees and bonobos have also kept to the social and physical environments in which they evolved, which is not true of humans.

Panksepp's findings suggest that it was the midbrain processes of feelings and the need for their modulation that drove and motivated this cerebral cortex growth. In terms of human evolution and in terms of understanding humanity, this is a profound thought. What was it that drove the 'runaway' brain? Panksepp's results provide a process by which the intensity of human relationships requires more and more refined modulating capabilities for the raw emotions than ever required of previously evolved mammals. This refined modulating capacity was needed in order to maintain the intense social relationships required by the close living in groups needed to leave the forests and to enter the savannah. These close and intense relationships are at the very foundation of what it means to be human; they are mediated and modulated by many layers of complex bodily and cognitive processes evolved over millions of years. It is crucial that we learn to understand them and to be conscious of them in order to avoid being misled by these processes into the actions that are now threatening life and humanity.

In other words, it was the requirement of the human group in the group dimension that motivated brain growth. As Panksepp clearly asserted, the cognitive capacities of the cerebral cortex do not have the capability of providing this growth for itself. Learning does not occur without the emotions – nothing occurs without the emotions. The major difference between humans and other animals, then, is not the existence of emotions, but the intensity of the cerebral cortex modulations that come with an intense and complex human environment. In other words, the development of the cerebral cortex comes from the grooming, politics, care and individual development required of humans in human groups. It comes from interpersonal attention, care, love, hate, anger and fear. This profound change of focus regarding human evolution is one of the reasons that neuroscience and psychoanalysis have not been able to make better use of Panksepp's conclusions until now. Panksepp's findings certainly fit into the group dimension as an important link between the human long history and the present time of monsters.

For mammals, by and large, the foundational feelings result in action. For humans, the power and consciousness of the foundational feelings to action has a big pull. However, humans in groups instinctively modulate these powerful feelings with language, thoughts, decisions, communications and disturbances. The process of these learnings is unconscious and needs a conscious meeting of cognitive processes with emotional ones.

Seeking and happiness

Another aspect of Seeking is that it becomes clear that consumption by itself does not lead to happiness. That consumption leads to happiness underlies the whole of the economic and social system of the time of monsters. It is not accurate. Happiness in the group dimension comes from the capacity to be satisfied and to rest. Greed and narcissism, where there is no point of satisfaction, are thus clearly social illnesses that lead to compulsions, mania and psychotic defences, including those of denial.

The image of the behavioural psychologists' laboratory rats stimulating the Seeking pathway to exhaustion and ignoring the temptations of food and water, is a powerful one. It led the behavioural psychologists to misinterpret Seeking as a reward. In the group dimension, it has become clear that Seeking is not a reward as such. It is the withdrawal of Seeking that is the feeling to be avoided because, for animals, the withdrawal of Seeking is the end of life.

Taking Panksepp's analysis of the Seeking pathway seriously helps to understand how the time of monsters has become so ingrained and difficult to change. The instinctual emotional processes that underlie the human group dimension have been unleashed and manipulated by neoliberal capitalism in such a way that they will eventually destroy humanity much as Arendt predicted. Arendt predicted the destruction of humanity through technology and through the abuse of the physical environment (1958 [1998]). The abuse of the human environment underlies both of these threats. Seeking becomes overheated from the lack of resources available in the human environment. Fear, Panic/Grief and the other foundational feelings diminish Seeking. Both too much power and too little power are destructive to human happiness. The madness of paranoid denial on one end of the Seeking spectrum and the madness of empty depression on the other can be pushed into overdrive. In the circumstances of unevenly distributed power relations, the real problems that require the Seeking of dialogues around issues of artificial intelligence, other technologies and the environment, become impossible. Dialogues between different abilities, races, genders, gender identifications and classes become impossible. Difference is acted out in conflict and violence.

In the world yet to come, Seeking feelings and instincts will need special care. This involves feelings of enough safety to feel able to take risks. Panksepp's summarised this as follows: 'The Seeking system is a spontaneous behaviour generator that takes animals to places, actively and inquisitively, where associated learning mechanisms allow them to develop knowledge structures ... to create more structures – which facilitate survival' (1998, p. 136). In this way, Panksepp proposed that Seeking motivated the evolution of the other, higher but less intense, foundational feelings as well as having motivated the evolution of the learning and thought processes that grew the cerebral cortex.

Fear is learning about bad things in the world

Knowledge about each of the other foundational feeling pathways brings new ways of thinking about the interactions of human feelings and thoughts in the group dimension. Fear and Rage are both closely related to Seeking. Their pathways are distinct, but they both come from midbrain regions that are physically close to each other and to Seeking. Rage processes become active when Seeking is frustrated. Fear is the learning from Seeking that leads to the anticipation of bad things in the world. Fear is the opposite of Seeking, which involves the anticipation of good things. Levels of Fear can vary from abject terror to chronic anxiety in intensity. The Fear pathway runs from the periaqueductal grey area (PAG) at the bottom of the pathway to the amygdala at the top and back again. This pathway is hierarchical. The PAG is involved in the most basic terror. Fear in the amygdala depends on the more powerful and basic terror that is located in the PAG, but is less intense.

Different Fears are reactive to different stimuli. With evolution, generalised feelings have become ever more specific and nuanced. When the danger is far away, the amygdala and the medial frontal cortex, which are higher regions in the brain, are involved. The animal might hide and freeze. When the danger is immediate, the PAG is activated and the behaviour is flight. Pain is most often the stimulus that evokes the response in the PAG. Another property of the Fear pathway is that pain is immediate, but the Fear lasts through time. Positive animal behaviours like play, feeding, grooming and sexuality are absent or diminished for a while after the experience of Fear. If the Fear stress continues for too long, animals exhibit depressed behaviour, similar to the lack of Seeking. In other words, Seeking is suppressed by acute and chronic Fear.

Fear is felt in an aroused autonomic nervous system. This means that heart rate increases and salivation decreases. Breathing becomes quicker. Sensitivity to sounds and sudden movements increase. Vigilance also increases. Humans and animals startle easily and may urinate and empty bowels. In extreme Fear, a human or an animal might be able to remain quiet or might freeze and be unable able to move or speak. Sometimes, the human or animal might not even be able to breathe. The neuropeptide most important in Fear is acetylcholine, which is the activating neuropeptide.

Fear is felt without an object. Electrical stimulation of animal brains leads to the full spectrum of fear responses, even before these animals have had life experiences. This means that learning from experience is connected to the world through the foundational feeling of Fear. The Fear circuits are designed to anticipate bad things in the future and can easily become overresponsive to threats in the world for this reason. Fear is an extremely powerful feeling and is felt widely throughout the body.

Pain produces Fear in all species of animal. Loud noises cause Fear in most animals. Mammals rapidly learn to respond to many stimuli that predict Fear-invoking conditions, including locations where Fear has been felt. Pain stimuli enter the PAG directly and there are also pain-inhibitory mechanisms there. Pain and pain relief are thus closely related to Fear. It is thought that the direct stimulation of Fear in the PAG promotes quick and long-lasting learning. Fear is related to, and is brought under the control of, life events and the environment in a direct way. It is the Fear-inducing capacity of the midbrain that promotes the learning. It is not the learning that creates the fear.

Fear itself and the search for chemical control

There are several transmitters, both neuropeptides and other neurotransmitters that facilitate the Fear pathway. Corticotropin-releasing factor (CRF), for example, is a neuropeptide that increases agitated arousal and diminishes feeding, sexuality, grooming and play. In general, CRF conditions the brain and the body to respond to stress and danger. Glutamate is a neurotransmitter that can lead to the profound terror that is sometimes called 'Fear itself'.

Interestingly, the search for chemical means of quelling fears and anxieties in humans has been largely unsuccessful. The most successful calming chemicals have been the benzodiazepines (BZs) and serotonin. BZs enhance a neurotransmitter, GABA, that generally inhibits the activities of neurons by reducing their rate of firing. Other GABA inhibitors are alcohol and barbiturates. It is thought that the BZs also inhibit CRF and thus have a generalised effect on the Fear pathway all the way from the amygdala to the nucleus reticularus, at the very bottom of the midbrain. BZs do reduce fear and anxiety. However, BZs are highly addictive and can easily cause overdoses.

A less addictive way to quell Fear and anxiety has been found in serotonin by means of a class of drugs known as selective serotonin reuptake inhibitors (SSRIs). Serotonin in general leads to less anxiety and less emotion. and also acts generally as a calming factor throughout the brain, not only in the Fear pathway. Thus, the chemicals that mediate the Fear pathway are also generalised for other pathways, suppressing all feelings, including Seeking (see Panksepp and Biven 2012, p. 187). To date, no specific or better chemical solutions to Fear and anxiety have been found.

The search for chemicals to control certain feelings mistakenly suggests that these feelings are the result of imbalances in brain chemistry. Clinicians often explain feelings in these terms. Starting from an evolutionary and Pankseppian point of view, however, it is apparent that human feelings are much more complex than brain chemistry imbalances. For example, more serotonin inhibits all emotions and less serotonin arouses all emotions, including Fear, but not only Fear. Benzodiazepines (BZs) diminish Fear, but they are highly addictive and can be dangerous. Further, BZs do not work to quell Panic, which is involved in the Panic/Grief emotional pathway. This is because anxiety and Panic come from two different emotional chemistries and they are thus two different feelings, although they can be easily confused with each other. Anxiety is related to Fear and Panic is related to Grief.

The sympathetic nervous system, related to Fear feelings, prepares both human and animal bodies for an active response to threats in their environments. The behaviour associated with Fear is flight. In the Panic/Grief pathway, it is the parasympathetic part of the autonomic nervous system that is active producing a more passive state. Heart rate slows and there may be tears, salivation and sex. In the parasympathetic arousal, there are feelings of weakness, lassitude, tightness in the chest and a lump in the throat. The behaviours associated with Panic/Grief are seeking the company of others and thinking thoughts of those who have been lost.

Panic anxiety and Fear anxiety are thus two different feelings, produced by different reactions to different environmental events and by way of two different chemical and electrical pathways. They warn of different factors in environments and they have different social, as well as chemical, solutions. Fear leads to avoidance and Panic leads to approach between people. In this way, Panksepp's animal studies help to think more clearly and accurately about human emotions and feelings. Human relationships, behaviours and experiences cause chemical changes. These changes are not imbalances, but feelings. These feelings alert humans to what we need from each other. To treat feelings as chemical imbalances reflects a lack of understanding about how human and animal minds function. Human and animal bodies have evolved to work inter-individually in order to maintain wellbeing. This is one of the major ways that Panksepp's findings can make a real difference in the human emotional world; the reality of the group dimension is felt in everyday life.

Only safe social relationships can quell fear

The Fear pathway can inhibit Seeking in destructive ways, as in extreme or chronic withdrawal, avoidance, denial or depression. To date, only human social relationships that provide safety have any lasting power to quell Fear in humans. Panksepp made the point that humans are the most fearful of animals yet they are also the most social. Could it be that the human relating with other humans is such a basic emotional dynamic? In any case, Panksepp's conclusions lead to a more accurate and nuanced way of looking at emotional issues compared to those conclusions drawn from the proposition of a simple chemical imbalance. It is also where the group dimension enters into a more complex and elaborated view of humans and their feelings.

Panksepp envisioned that his findings would bring about new ways of understanding human emotions and emotional issues. Initially, he was looking for the emotions in the ward of the asylum where he worked. I think that this new way of understanding human emotions has not yet happened to any great extent because the group dimension is crucial for understanding human evolution, human emotions and human emotional development along with neuroscience and psychoanalysis.

One of the ways that Panksepp's ideas lead to the possibility of a better understanding of human emotions is in the area of promoting understanding of how the various 'psy' professions (psychiatry, psychoanalysis, psychotherapy, psychology and group analysis) reflect the various aspects of complex human emotional life. Each of these professions has its own theory and practice with much competition between them, as well as between their subgroups. The 'psy' professions operate in their respective silos. Panksepp's ideas allow us to understand and appreciate how different approaches relate to each other. Panksepp was not able to do this but it is clear that some of the diagnostic categories that he employs, like schizophrenia, come from the field of psychiatry. The general idea that solutions for breakdowns in emotional wellbeing lie with the chemistry of brains also comes from psychiatry. It is interesting, then, that although he looked at the chemistry of the foundational feelings, Panksepp also saw that these chemical solutions were largely inadequate, even in their own terms.

Panksepp hoped that his work on the chemistry of emotional pathways would lead to more accurate targeting of medical therapies in psychiatry. However,

Panksepp's foundational feelings also provide a better and more accurate basis for diagnosis in psychiatry as well as in the other psy professions. Different people are sensitised in different pathways, both by birth and by experience. Certainly, the understandings and diagnoses that people might receive based on their own feelings will be closer to their experiences of themselves and enable more intense selfcare and care of others than the present basis of diagnoses that involve self- and other-observed behaviours called 'symptoms'. Over- or under-arousal of different emotional pathways contributes to the symptoms that bring people to the clinic. These are always felt consciously in feelings, even when they are not understood and even when they are immediately repressed into the unconscious.

Psychology is a profession that is based on a behavioural and cognitive model of Fear training and conditioning. Panksepp showed that results from psychology studies about the emotions and behaviour have misled researchers' understandings of animals and humans. Psychology and psychiatry are mostly about knowledge used in order to control or 'manage' feelings and behaviours. Cognitive and behavioural psychology provide one understanding of how the brain works in the cerebral cortex to quell feelings in general and Fear in particular. However, both cognitive and behavioural psychology are largely useless for understanding any of the brain functions in the lower areas of the brain, particularly around feelings. Panksepp's findings have opened up these lower areas to research and knowledge useful in the clinic as well as in everyday life.

Integration between and within individuals

Some of Panksepp's discoveries, especially those around the Seeking and Fear pathways are related to Freud's psychoanalytic ideas. Seeking is related to libido, for example. Psychotherapy and psychoanalysis are more in tune with information about how the brain works to produce, modulate and modify feelings. Psychotherapy, psychoanalysis and group analysis are primarily concerned with how human relationships contribute to feelings in the past and in the present. Panksepp observed that psychoanalysis was the longer, but more certain, route to effecting real emotional change rather than psychology or psychiatry.

Group analysis is psychoanalysis in the group dimension. Psychotherapy aims for people to feel better. Psychoanalysis aims for the 'ordinary misery' of contact with emotional reality. Psychoanalysis also centres on early life, sometimes before language. Group analysis aims for self and other understanding to be produced by communication and dialogue between people in groups. The proposition of the group dimension is that groups are where integration happens between and within individuals. It is this integration that supports emotional wellbeing and productive dialogue. This is why the knowledge of the emotions put in a way that is experience-near to humans and communicated in groups is so important in preserving the *polis* and, thus, humanity.

Panksepp's observations that humans are the most fearful of animals and also the most intensely social of animals give an idea of the evolutionary and biological importance of human groups for integration and emotional wellbeing in all human environments. Certainly, Panksepp's findings about the Fear pathway suggest that there is a close connection between Fear and the learning that produced and conditioned the cerebral cortex, as well as the further development of other emotional pathways. The psychology behaviourists discovered that fear was a powerful factor in what they called 'conditioned' learning. This led them to think that fear was also learned. Panksepp was able to show that the higher structures in the Fear pathway, like the amygdala, were dependent on the lower structures, the PAG and the hypothalamus, and not the other way around, '… the thesis here is that deeper parts of the emotional brain teach the critical structures to perform a variety of cognitive strategies related to emotional regulation' (Pansepp, 1998, p. 197).

For Panksepp, and in the group dimension, the key question is how we can develop social structures that promote networks that are 'prosocial' in the higher regions of human brains. Fear motivates learning, but also damages Seeking. In the group dimension, Panksepp's prosocial structures have always existed for humans and mammals and they are collectively called groups. In certain kinds of groups, positive social forces can substantially counter the damaging influences of Fear both in the present and in the past. Animals who become deficient in Seeking stop caring for themselves and die. Fear can kill, in other words.

There are reasons why the psy professions and group relationships are so important for modulating fears and for, consequently, enabling social and experiential learning. Some of these reasons are based in an understanding of how the primary process of foundational feelings relate to the secondary processes of emotional learning. These secondary processes are located in the amygdala, the nucleus accumbens and the bed-nucleus of the stria terminalis. It is in these brain regions, between the midbrain and the cerebral cortex, where memories are converted from fleeting experiences into short-term memories and then, with repetition, into long-term memories. This process is called 'consolidation'. However, this process does not just consolidate memories. Consolidation also transforms memories through time and experience.

Some memories, like riding a bike, are consolidated immediately. Others, like childhood traumatic experiences, are consolidated at an early age. These memories can be recalled or evoked later, however, and either reconfirmed or not. When the memories are not reconfirmed, they are stored again, but in a different form. In this way, positive feelings in the present can counteract negative feelings in the past. This modulates some of the Fear responses. In fact, there is an emotional reconsolidation of memories every time something is remembered. Even just having a conscious witness can change a destructive Fearful memory into a sad or tragic one.

Panksepp thought that the growth of the dopamine pathway, as in Seeking, guided human mental and cultural evolution. This is especially true for the more recent lateral extensions of the cerebral cortex which were part of human, runaway brain growth as humans evolved. These lateral extensions, Panksepp said, were a further development of the modulating capacity needed by humans for their intense relating. These evolved later than the more medial emotionally centred higher brain regions. Memories are found in complex networks of neurons in the cerebral cortex. They become more sensitised with repetition and can be changed by lived experiences, especially in psychoanalytic psychotherapy and psychoanalysis. This is the way that psychoanalysis and group analysis work. Psychoanalysis and group analysis work particularly well for those early memories consolidated with Fear before language.

Rage comes when seeking is frustrated

While Seeking involves the anticipation of good things in the environment and Fear involves the anticipation of painful things in the environment, the feeling of Rage comes when anticipated good things from the environment are suddenly withdrawn, threatened with withdrawal, or are insufficient. Rage comes about when Seeking is blocked or frustrated. Rage can be destructive. At the same time, Rage is energising and is also needed for many 'higher' social emotional tasks, like balancing power relationships, establishing boundaries with others and defining a coherent and integrated self. Therefore, the absence of Rage is not pro-social. Its presence communicates important things about ourselves and our relationships with others, and especially, about power.

There are many kinds of feelings that are identified as 'aggressive' in everyday life. Feelings related to Rage, hatred and revenge, for example, involve tertiary level, cognitive processes linked to attempts to restore and maintain Seeking. Hatred and revenge involve thinking and devising schemes for retribution. Rage is more immediate and direct. Rage is a pure feeling. It is a raw anger. Rage feels horrible, although also energising. Rage is not designed to punish so much as to bring others immediately into line with one's desires.

Animals demonstrate Rage towards others when competing for resources. This happens more often with animals of the same species or group than with other species or prey. Predatory hunting involves the Seeking processes, not Rage. Rage is a sudden feeling, felt and then gone. In this sense, Rage is unlike Seeking, which is a basic feeling that comes and goes. Rage is also unlike Fear, which is a feeling that lasts beyond its environmental stimulus. When Rage has been stimulated by electrical pulses applied to certain areas of the brain, it is often followed by an almost immediate return to Seeking in laboratory animals. Panksepp observed that, while Rage interrupts Seeking, animals return to Seeking behaviours when the Rage stops. He thought that this was because there are so many modulating immediate physical processes for Rage. Panksepp also observed that when Rage continues over time, there is something in the environment that is continually producing it.

Deprivation leads to rage

Rage can be sensitised by the deprivation of food, love, attention, money and other 'good' things. Socially, Rage can be triggered by sibling rivalry, for example, or sexual jealousy. Researchers have produced Rage in animals with electrical currents in a pathway that runs from the periaqueductal grey area (PAG) to the medial hypothalamus and through the stria terminalis to the medial areas of the amygdala. The Rage pathway is adjacent to both the Fear and Seeking pathways. As in the Fear pathway, the Rage pathway is hierarchical with lower areas responsible for more intense Rage.

Seeking, Rage and Fear may arouse each other. Animal behaviour related to Rage is rapid attack. This attack is usually accompanied by biting anything that is readily available. These readily available objects may, or may not, be the accurate cause of the Rage. When these Rage brain areas were stimulated in humans, people tended to clench their jaws and report feelings of intense anger. They did not understand why they had become angry. In humans, Rage is almost always closely followed by cerebral cortex thoughts, many times about cause and blame. The cerebral cortex modulation of Rage can be directed outward, inward, or both.

The chemistry of the Rage pathway, like the Fear pathway, is complex and personalised through individuals' histories. Chemicals that can promote Rage are testosterone, Substance P, norepinephrine (NE), glutamate, acetylcholine and nitric oxide synthase. Chemicals that diminish Rage are serotonin and GABA, both of which tend to reduce all forms of emotional arousal. Some chemicals have differing effects when they arrive in different parts of the Rage pathway. Substance P, a neuropeptide, for example, activates Rage in certain higher parts of the brain. In lower parts of the brain, Substance P produces a feeling of nausea.

Besides serotonin and GABA, the only neuropeptides that quell Rage are endogenous opioids and oxytocin (Panksepp and Biven, 2012). Endogenous opioids are related to pain relief and oxytocin is related to childbirth in females. Both of these neuropeptides promote prosocial behaviour in animals. Males and females have different sensitivities in practically all the emotional pathways, even when the architecture of the pathway is the same. In animals, females are biologically less prone to anger than males. This is because of the dominance of different types of hormones related to sex organs.

Testosterone makes males more assertive and aggressive than females. Testosterone also promotes male dominance tendencies. It influences several distinct forms of aggression. Panksepp pointed out that this does not mean that females are less aggressive than males. Panksepp thought that female aggression was more about social exclusion than physical strength. However, male and female Rage pathways are the same. Only the hormones that activate them differ with gender. Testosterone and the neuropeptides have more influence in the Seeking kind of aggression than in the Rage kind of aggression. Like the different kinds of anxiety, there are also different kinds of aggression, not all of them directly related to Rage.

The septal area of the brain, for example, modulates and inhibits Rage. The septal area, like the amygdala, sits at the crossroads of many important emotional and cognitive pathways and networks. This indicates that the septal area is especially important for interactions between higher cognitive networks and lower emotional pathways. In particular, the septal area is implicated in sexual arousal and the Lust foundational feeling pathway. In other words, the septal area in the Rage pathway is similar to the nucleus accumbens in the Seeking pathway and the lateral regions of the amygdala in the Fear pathway. When the septum is damaged, cortical inhibition is curtailed and animals become more irritable and emotional. However, eventually, they become even more calm and social than they were before. It seems that Rage motivates modulation from the cerebral cortex in progressively more effective ways and that this phenomenon involves unconscious learning and is connected to the Lust foundational feeling (Panksepp and Biven, 2012). In other words, Rage is a pure foundational feeling and action, but aggression is a much more complicated behaviour.

Forms of aggression in dominance hierarchies

In human social life, understanding and reconciliation are powerful forces for quelling Rage. These processes are different from the more immediate Rage modulations of finding causes, blame, guilt, retaliation, scapegoating, projection and revenge, which involve damaging and then restoring Seeking. Most importantly, though, as for the Fear pathway, there are no medications that work to quell a continuous Rage. Aside from powerful tranquillising medications, there are only social solutions, like knowledge of the consequences of Rage which often involve Fear. The modulation of positive social relationships on Rage are the most effective and long-lasting. An important difference between Fear and Rage, though, is that, while reactions to the Fear pathway enhance the feeling of Fear over time, the processes of the Rage pathway work to stop the feeling and return to Seeking. This is using Rage defensively. Rage can also be used defensively because it sometimes provides relief from pain and distress.

A Rage reaction that is immediately restored to a Seeking feeling might explain some of the sadistic thoughts and behaviours that are generally thought of as aggression. These include social aggressions, like politically polarising movements, sexism, racism and wars. However, Rage only causes more Rage. It may be that nothing good comes from the punishment of Rage except for revenge as it preserves the Rage but also revives the Seeking feeling. When children are exposed to their own Rage resulting from abuse and neglect, for example, they lose their capacity to trust and without it, these children struggle to benefit from the modulating social relationship possibilities in their worlds.

Rage is one of the most difficult feelings for humans to put into words. However, Panksepp has helped to arrive at an understanding of how the Rage pathway, as a reaction to interruption and deprivation, leads to evolutionary and historical cultural phenomena. Dominance hierarchies are one example. Other examples are those evolutionary and cultural phenomena related to sexual jealousies, envy and power.

In primate evolution, as seen Part III, dominance hierarchies had the effect of saving life. Dominance hierarchies in chimpanzees and bonobos was a distinct evolutionary advantage over a gorilla type of group in that it preserved life and led to mixed sex groups which eventually became capable of raising big-brained babies.

Dominance hierarchies are part of human evolutionary heritage. Panksepp's findings about Rage, Fear and Seeking suggest that the aggression implied in forming and maintaining dominance hierarchies is motivated by Rage feelings turned into Seeking and Fear, giving increased feelings of power and control for some, and feelings of powerlessness and Fear for others.

Panksepp suggested that the urge for social dominance was related to sexual supremacy and linked it to the Lust pathway. Certainly, Lust emphasises male and female emotional and brain sensitivity differences for the first time. Certainly, Lust or sexual jealousy and competition were noted to be at the root of most social conflict, violence and rage in anthropological studies of hunter-gatherers (Lee, 1979). Panksepp linked power to sexuality and testosterone in this way.

However, in the group dimension, it is clear that the deeper evolution of social dominance hierarchies was much more about enabling male bonding and cooperative scavenging and hunting, while also protecting the group from Rage. This may have entailed a process by which Rage was transformed into Seeking through a feeling of power or pursuit of power. Female bonding and female dominance hierarchies would have occurred before the male equivalent. These female hierarchies would have been based on oestrogen, progesterone and oxytocin, also linked to pregnancy, birth and child rearing. Certainly, this way of starting to think about the roots of the aggressive pursuit of power as an emotional process, and not just for males, in the group dimension, gives much food for thought about how Rage and power might be balanced and modulated in the world yet to come.

Rage, action and agency

In sum, Rage is the basic foundational feeling derived from the frustration of Seeking. Experiments with animals have defined it as an unpleasant emotion. Animals will try and avoid it and anything associated with it, including locations. Rage is different from other so-called 'aggressive feelings', which derive from Seeking. The Rage pathway is sensitised when people, especially as children, are subjected to deprivation, abuse and neglect. Panksepp also pointed out that Rage can be healed, but it cannot be healed through punishment. The best way to heal Rage is through consistently friendly and positive interactions that establish, or re-establish, a person's capacity to form and sustain warm and trusting relationships. Nothing comes from violence except more violence.

Panksepp quoted research that showed that, when Rage is treated with consistent and positive interaction, the animals studied became more quiescent and social. This suggests that the handling or containing of Rage is an important step in socialisation. Mammal sociality, their relationships in groups, created the remaining four foundational feelings. Modern humans need to be in contact with their Rage feelings in order to maintain a sociality that also includes individual boundaries. In modern humans, in the time of monsters, the levels of both Rage and Fear are so high that constant modulating effects are at the basis of a large part of interpersonal, group and cultural life.

Like Seeking, a positive feeling and Fear, a negative feeling, Rage is a feeling that can be felt and monitored both internally and from the outside. These feelings are conscious and thus experience-near. When Rage is felt in a way that is overwhelming, it is a negative feeling. It is a feeling that threatens loss of control. Rage often overwhelms thinking. In extremes, Rage is overwhelming, denied or immediately transformed into a return to Seeking through hatred and revenge. Rage, however, is important to action and agency in life tasks, like competition, creativity, and boundary setting. Rage is also a communication that something is wrong and needs to be heard. Unfortunately, Rage also creates Fear, just as Fear creates Rage, and these two basic feelings can be difficult to untangle internally, interpersonally and socially.

These three foundational feelings: Seeking, Fear and Rage come to us in the present from millions of years ago and they are still powerful in creating and influencing human lives. Humans are capable of understanding themselves and each other with openness to feelings and thoughts. These are the paths that lead the way to recognise diversity in human identities, social differences and cultural creations in the dialogues of the group dimension and in the world yet to come. Seeking is the feeling of life that we most desperately want to protect and return to when it is interrupted by Fear and Rage.

References

Arendt, H. (1958 [1998]) *The Human Condition*, 2nd edition. Chicago, IL: University of Chicago Press.

Lee, R. B. (1979) *The Kung! San: Men, Women and Work in a Foreign Society*. Cambridge: Cambridge University Press.

Panksepp, J. (1998) *Affective Neuroscience: The Foundations of Human and Animal Emotions.* Oxford: Oxford University Press.

Panksepp, J., and Biven, L. (2012) *The Archaeology of Mind: Neuroevolutionary Origins of Human Emotions*. New York: W. W. Norton & Co.

Chapter 9

The relational feelings

Lust and Care

A pattern has begun to emerge, though the group dimension is needed to see it. Seeking is a generalised, good feeling which is awful in its absence. Fear, particularly, depresses Seeking. Without Seeking, there is no joy in life. Without Seeking, there is no life. Rage overwhelms Seeking momentarily but reverts quickly back to Seeking if the frustrating factor can be removed. Rage can also be stored in Seeking, in the forms of revenge and hatred. This combination of Rage and Seeking is particularly socially destructive. The combination of Rage and Seeking may well be associated with Freud's (1920) 'death instinct' in humans. Mammal and human wellbeing depend upon the maintenance of Seeking, though, even when this combination can be so individually and socially destructive. The tertiary feelings of greed, also in narcissism, come from a Seeking that is both delicate and overheated.

Also involved with Seeking, in the foundational feelings in the midbrain, is Lust. Lust and Seeking are closely related, almost co-terminus. Lust, like Seeking, extends from the homeostatic pathways, hunger and thirst, as well as from the sensory affective pathways, smell and taste. Mammal Lustful emotional action readiness is specified in Lustful behaviours. Lust, as a foundational feeling, indicates that there are pleasurable species-specific others in the environment that we want to be close to. Lust can be thought of, in the group dimension, as a precise identification of the pleasurable others needed for sexual reproduction. Lust identifies the right species, the right sex and the right time for reproduction, just as Seeking identifies the right food and the right time for eating. These are conscious feelings.

What is new and interesting in the Lust pathway are the differences in the organisation of the pathway as well as the differences in the effects of the neuropeptides and neurotransmitters both between genders and between species. Between genders, the pathway and the actions of the neurotransmitters are so complex and delicate that, on an individual level, the gendered body and the gendered brain can become dissociated from each other. This potential, and sometimes partial, dissociation creates an infinity of gender and sexual relationship combination possibilities. Males and females have the same physical brain architectures. However, the sensitivities of the pathways vary between individuals.

DOI: 10.4324/9781003350088-14

Gender and sexuality in the lust foundational feeling

In the very basic terms of reproduction, it makes no difference if males and females are anything like each other or even if they like each other. The first cells reproduced by replicating themselves. There was no sexual difference. However sexual reproduction and the familiar two-sex sexual differences were soon the dominant form of reproduction, even in very early animals and plants. Sexual reproduction is the reproduction of significantly different individuals into offspring that combine their characteristics in infinitely variable ways. This method of reproduction maximised variety, and thus survival advantage, in a changing world environment (Lane, 2015).

In sexual reproduction, different, individual living creatures need to find each other and also need to find a way of combining their DNA in mitosis at the right time. The most general means of doing this is to have two sexes. One of the sexes carries a large sexual cell. This cell has the nourishment essential for promoting the life of the new genetic combination for a short time. The other sex has small sexual cells. Small sexual cells maximise speed of movement; having two sizes of sexual cells promotes the searching for and the finding of available others for reproduction. Females are defined as the sex that carries the larger sexual cell, the egg, and males are defined as the sex that carries the smaller sexual cell, or sperm. For most of their lives, creatures of the same species do not need to have anything to do with each other until it is time to get ready to mate. This is where Lust comes into the biological imperative of reproduction as a foundational feeling and urge to action.

The Lust pathway runs from the basal ganglia at the base of the midbrain, where orgasm originates in both males and females. Orgasm is felt all over the brain and body. Orgasm is not strictly a feeling of Lust, though it is implicated. The feeling of Lust is difficult to define except perhaps as a feeling of wanting to have sex or, on a softer level, the feeling of wanting to be close and perhaps merged with another creature. The orgasm origin and result are the same for males and females. Orgasm might be thought of as a marker and a reward for the sexual act of reproduction. The other components of the Lust brain pathway look slightly different for males and females and also function in different ways and levels within each sex.

Gendered bodies and brains

Male and female bodies tend to be different from each other. Male and female brain Lust pathways also tend to have sex differences. However, this small tendency to be different in the ancient midbrain yields a myriad of individual sex and gender variabilities in the interpersonal world. This is because the process of determining sexual bodies differs from the process of determining sexual brains. Thus, although the Lust chemistries are different for male and female, these differences are a matter of emphasis and there is much crossover between them. Besides, an anatomically female body does not necessarily produce a female brain. An anatomically male body does not necessarily produce a male brain. This is as true for mammals as it is for humans (Panksepp and Biven, 2012). For humans, these small differences have profound social and political implications.

In male mammals, the epicentre for primary sexual urges is in the medial regions of the anterior hypothalamus. The precise location varies a little from one species to another. In rats, the epicentre is in the pre-optic area (POA) of the hypothalamus. In humans the epicentre for primary sexual urges is in the interstitial nuclei of the anterior hypothalamus (INAH). This is the first species difference that Panksepp (1998) mentioned in the architecture of the foundational feelings in the midbrain.

In human females, the epicentre for primary sexual urges is in the ventromedial hypothalamus (VMH). Both male and female mammals have the same sexual brain architecture. The gender differences are in the differential activation of these areas by body chemicals. The activation of these specific areas depends upon the amount of testosterone and on the number of testosterone receptors present in specific sites. The pathways are similar between male and female, in other words. It is the chemical activators and transmitters that differ. The sexually-determined hormones and receptors in the brain sensitise various sensory input channels that promote the different copulatory reflexes of males and females. These copulatory reflexes are lordosis for females, which is a presentation of sexual organs for mating. In males, the copulatory reflex is mounting and thrusting. The pathways are the same for male and female bodies. The behaviours are different because of the different chemical facilitators involved.

In foetal development, the basic body is female. It is the amount and timing of the secretion of testosterone, a steroid hormone, from the Y chromosome that distinguishes males from females. When enough testosterone is secreted, the resulting body will be a male. When not enough testosterone is secreted, the foetus will continue their development as a female. The testosterone spike happens in the second trimester of pregnancy in humans, from four to six months. The amount and timing of the testosterone secretion is dependent upon the wellbeing of the mother and varies according to her levels of stress.

The Y chromosome secretes a chemical that determines the growth of the testes. The male testes determine the masculinisation of the brain and the body, but in different ways. In the formation of the male body, on the one hand, testosterone is converted to dihydrotestosterone (DHT) by way of an enzyme called 5-alpha-reductase. In the male brain, on the other hand, testosterone becomes oestrogen, by way of an enzyme called aromatase. Ironically, it is this oestrogen (usually thought of as a female hormone) that masculinises the brain. If there is no oestrogen cascade at the right time, even when testosterone is present, the foetus brain continues to develop as a female brain. Testosterone release may come too early. So, for example, if a mother is stressed before 20 weeks, it is possible that no testosterone is present or no oestrogen is produced from the testosterone and a human is born with a male body and a female brain (Panksepp and Biven, 2012, pp. 270–272).

In usual female, XX, development, the female foetus secrets alpha-fetoprotein. This substance depresses the female oestrogen chemical influence on the developing brain. Most of the time, the brain of the female foetus continues to develop as female. If the mother secretes too much oestrogen, or not enough of the moderating chemical, a human will be born with a female body and a male brain under the influence of the oestrogen. To confuse matters further, females produce some testosterone and males produce some oestrogen. What might seem to be clear-cut differences between human genders, then, are not clear cut at all. These male and female differences are infinitely variable and responsive to moment-to-moment environmental changes. The importance of environmental factors for the balance between male and female births suggests that a basic element in the determination of gender is a species or group, not individual or gendered, reproduction strategy for survival.

No matter what happens in the brain pathways, male and female sexual bodies continue to develop in utero and after birth. In adolescent females, the maturation of ovarian oestrogen and progesterone (steroids) herald puberty and menstruation. In adolescent males, the testicles begin to produce abundant testosterone and this, in turn, produces an intense sexual awakening.

Male and female bodies can be seen but male and female brains cannot. The complexity of the combinations and the determining moments of interaction between individual mothers and their particular social environments leads to the question of what might constitute male and female brains. Is Lust felt differently between males and females? Are the differences that important? Some think that the similarities between human males and females are much more important than the differences for the purposes of modern human life (Fine, 2011). It may be that in modern human life, for the first time ever, individual differences and similarities are more important than relationship and gender differences between males and females. Dialogue between people of different genders, gender identities and sexualities, as well as other differences like nationality, race, ability and class, is more possible and necessary in the *polis* on the basis of equality than it has ever been before. This dialogue may also be more challenging.

Gender fluidity and complexity

Panksepp identified the foundational feeling of Lust in females as the behaviour called 'lordosis'. Lordosis is the posture with which the female mammal offers her sexual organs to the male. In males, the behaviours associated to the feeling of Lust is solicitation, mounting, intromission and ejaculation. In the language of animal experimenters, active and passive behaviours of males and females respectively are thought to indicate differences in their feelings of Lust. Male sexuality is expressed as 'urges', or 'abilities'. Female sexuality, according to Panksepp, is more complex and less understood and is expressed as female 'responsiveness'.

Modern patriarchal and heteronormative cultures discipline both male and female sexualities into these strict, active and passive gender roles. Panksepp proposed that the masculinity or femininity of the brain had to do with identity. He observed that mammals often show cross-gender behaviours. Panksepp was concerned with demonstrating the biological reality of transgender identities.

The reality of transgender can be seen in the complex processes that determine gender in the body and brain.

That humans can quite easily become biologically transgender in various degrees is an important finding. The description of the processes involved in gender-based brain development indicate that the differences in gender-based, Lust foundational feelings between males and females may be very small and infinitely variable, whatever the appearances of the body. Panksepp talked about universal bisexuality, like Freud, but perhaps gender fluidity or complexity is a more accurate conception. This may be true for bodies as well as for brains. Sexual relationship and gender identity are both more like interweaving currents, sometimes concurrent, sometimes going in different directions from each other, sometimes changing directions altogether. This vision is very different to the constant images of male and female polarised characteristics required by a social, cultural and political patriarchal heteronormativity. Patriarchal heteronormativity separates genders, gender identities and sexualities from each other and makes dialogue difficult. Although this variability extends from the ancient, Lust foundational feeling, it has particular relevance to humans in the present.

Lust is where species variability comes into the foundational feelings. Seeking, Fear and Rage foundational feelings and actions are considered to be the same for all mammals, although sometimes with different emphases in different species. Human sexual behaviours and feelings, however, are different from those of other mammals in specific ways. In all other mammals, the receptivity to sex expressed by female lordosis is determined by the female's reproductive estrus cycle. In most animals, females are only receptive to certain males at certain times of the year. Male mammals are generally available for sex at all times for the right sex and the right species. Chimpanzee females, for example, have a visual estrus and time-limited availability for sex. Bonobo females are more generally available for sex with a less obvious visual signal.

Human females are more like bonobos. Human males are generally receptive to sex, like most other mammals. Human females have reproductive cycles, but these cycles are 'hidden' and human females are also receptive to sex, and to the Lust feeling, at other times. However, the evident feelings of Lust and the enjoyment and importance of sex in everyday life that humans have is quite different, even from other mammals and, most interestingly, from those mammals most closely related to humans, except for bonobos. In the group dimension, it is hypothesised that it was the evolution of the intensity of the human group that modulated and disciplined the Lust feelings with the consequence, probably unintended, of the development of the enlarged cerebral cortex of the human brain.

Sexual behaviour is only part of lust in humans

Although the focus of Lust is in the anterior hypothalamus for male mammals, this brain centre becomes less important through time and experience. The cerebral cortex learns and sustains emotional feelings, like Lust. These feelings then become independent of their foundational mid-brain pathways. Presumably males also learn from females and vice versa.

Panksepp noted that the female contribution to sexuality, based in oxytocin, is only pleasurable to mammals when there are concurrent and pleasurable social interactions. In these circumstances, he thought that oxytocin may enhance the endogenous opioids released in animal and human social interactions. Endogenous opioids are major 'comfort and joy' chemicals (1998, p. 260). In females, oxytocin is released as a calming response to stress. Males release aggressive vasopressin in response to stress. Oxytocin can be thought of as the 'tend and befriend' hormone, while vasopressin is the 'pushy and competitive' hormone.

It is clear that, perhaps as a further development of female sexuality, oxytocin promotes positive social interactions and evokes peaceful tendencies. Oxytocin promotes the retrieval of positive social memories and feelings of trust. It quells anxiety and stress in social interactions. It soothes tension where there might be conflict. Oxytocin diminishes insecurity about separation and leads to more friendly social interactions. It may be that it leads to confidence and thus to trust. Oxytocin is perhaps the most important basic emotional element in childcare, in the Care foundational feeling circuit and also in the promotion of the basis of social feelings.

Thus, the Lust ingredient of the basic foundational feeling circuits goes all the way from the first sexual reproduction to the present variability of the human feeling of wanting to be close and merge, which is at the same time sexual and social.

Lust in the group dimension

Reproduction only demands that males and females be able to signal to each other that they are the right species, the right sex and that it is the right time to mate. These are the simple biological imperatives that motivate and school first the mid-brain and then the hypothalamus, which produce the feelings. These biological imperatives then motivate and educate the cerebral cortex. Each species has its own form of organising this reproduction. In humans, these simple biological imperatives have also meant that males and females necessarily cooperate together to produce and raise human children. It was this imperative for further closeness between the sexes and between individuals in groups that evolved into humans and the human-intense social networks that produced the human big brain and the group dimension.

It is fascinating to realise that the group and care processes in mammals are based on a strict male and female division of labour expressed by the female egg as the carrier of offspring and the male sperm as the active fertiliser. This division of labour is written into the mammal brain, not as pathway but as differences in chemicals and placement of receptors. Male and female strict division of labour began to break down when the runaway growth of the cerebral cortex in mammals required maternal care in mixed sex groups. This could only happen because the modulating capabilities of the cerebral cortex included dominance hierarchies as a modulation and discipline of Lust.

Mixed sex groups must also modulate and discipline Lust to maximise exogamy. Different species do this in different ways. In humans, the sexual division of labour and pair-bonding in mixed sex groups was key to the migration into the savannah. It also survived into agriculture and the Greek, Roman and European 'civilising' tendencies (Elias, 1994). It is this division of labour that Hannah Arendt (1958 [1998]) wrote about in her ideas about work and the polis. In Arendt's world, the polis, where politics was based on dialogue, could only survive when *homo faber* could be free of the work of *animal laborans*. The man who makes things must be free of the animal who takes care of the needs of survival. This is another way of saying that, in order to have dialogue, thinking must be free of feeling. The work of animal laborans is mostly thought of as women's work, though for the Romans, it also involved slaves and sometimes children. The work of making things and getting together in the polis is mostly thought of as men's work.

Neoliberal capitalism and the time of monsters has required that the sexual division of labour, no longer necessary in the modern world, persist to the present. In the time of monsters, though, the same modulation and discipline of sexuality into the patriarchal heteronormativity that is deemed necessary to reproduce humanity is actually destroying it.

Care is much more than motherhood

The utter centrality of human motherhood in the age of monsters is the key to both the sexual division of labour and to the continuing discipline of Lust into patriarchal heteronormativity. In counter to this, Panksepp started his chapter on the Care foundational feeling with the observation that human motherhood includes the role of extended families in nurture (Hrdy, 2009).

In the group dimension, it has become evident that humanity does not exist without the role of the group, including, but not only, the family. Humanity also exists in networks of groups within networks of communities. The neoliberal emphasis in the time of monsters is on pair-bonding and the family. This exclusive emphasis on family enforces patriarchal heteronormativity. The exclusive emphasis on motherhood and the family in the time of monsters punishes identity and relationship fluidity.

The neoliberal time of monsters denies the importance of groups and communities outside of the family. The active social destruction that this denial implies leaves a gap which is evident, for example, in the insufficient practical and emotional support for motherhood with the demise of community and of the extended family. Motherhood is concentrated into one person in the age of monsters. However, one mother is both too much and too little for children. Mothers can never do enough and children are deprived. The denial of the responsibility for children in the larger world around the family produces and reproduces a predominance of the negative foundational feelings of Fear and Rage. Fear and Rage overcome the ability to think and to Seek. In order to emerge from the time of monsters into the world yet to come, the implications of these constructive and destructive processes around the foundational feelings of Lust must be understood and taken seriously.

The foundational feelings of Care, Panic/Grief and Play emerge from, and modulate Lust, Fear, Rage and Seeking. The three social feeling pathways, Care, Panic/Grief and Play, are the foundational feelings that maintain social bonds. These are the feelings that motivate and modulate the complex and conflicting social instincts involved in exogamy and groups. I wonder if Arendt actually meant to leave these more feminine and social foundational feelings out of the polis, as her theories and use of language suggest. In the group dimension, the more feminine and social foundations must be consciously included in the political dialogue that is needed before humanity can emerge from the time of monsters.

Care feelings and actions are the social in the group dimension

In mammals, males show more sensitive and active Seeking, Rage and possibly Play pathways than females. In turn, females show more sensitive and active Care, Panic/Grief and possibly Fear. However, all mammals have all the feeling pathways and are capable of knowing how others feel. All mammals are capable of feeling the feelings of others and of allowing themselves be penetrated by these feelings. Specifically, the Care feelings have emerged from the pre-existing brain mechanisms and feeling circuits of female Lust but have become also generalised to include males and offspring.

The idea that all mammals experience feelings of Care, as well as Care behaviours, is a profound one. Panksepp used the mother-child bond as the model for the Care circuit. As these are brain pathways, though, it makes sense to think about each pathway as being general to all genders and ages. All mammals have mothers. Foundational feelings are contagious and almost always reciprocated positively or negatively between mammals, including humans. The infant Cares for the mother as the mother Cares for the infant. Males are just as capable of feeling Care for children as females, even if the behaviour impulses are different. Mothers, fathers and babies all experience Panic and Grief when they are separated.

The Care feeling is very close to Lust and often called love. In humans, Caring is a deep feeling of attachment that is emotional and physical. For Panksepp, it is clear that the foundational feelings of the Care pathway start with female Lust, but go on to create the social. This means that maternal and play behaviours are not socially constructed as the behaviourists think. On the contrary, Care and Play feelings and actions are the social, as they are understood in the group dimension.

The Care architecture of the mammal brain is similar across ages, sexes and species. Brain and body chemistries coordinate the timings and responsiveness of the architectural connections. Brain chemistries involved in the Care pathways are oxytocin, prolactin, dopamine and opioids.

Panksepp traced the Care pathway back to the process of giving birth in female reptiles. This process is also involved in the Lust foundational feeling pathway. Reptiles do not have Care pathways in their brains and do not care for their young. However, they have a hormone called vasotocin. In reptiles, vasotocin is produced by the posterior pituitary gland and increases when the female reptile lays her eggs. Panksepp gave the example of the female sea turtle who lays her eggs on land and then covers them over. When she is finished, the female sea turtle returns to the sea and offers no protection to her many young when they hatch weeks later. The reptile young need to fend for themselves and many become prey.

The same vasotocin is present in birds, as well as in reptiles. Birds, like mammals, Care for their young. It is thought that, in mammals, vasotocin evolved into both oxytocin and vasopressin, which, as we have seen, are hormones that differentiate female and male Lust, respectively. In reptiles, vasotocin is part of the Lust circuit. Its mammalian derivative, oxytocin, is active in female Lust and in the labour part of the birth process. Oxytocin participates in the birth process by producing uterine contractions. Oxytocin also triggers the letdown of milk in mothers when the baby suckles on mother's nipples.

The emotional health, and thus the survival fitness, of all mammals is critically tied to the quality of this early Care. Caring, combined with Panic/Grief, is more sustained than Lust. Caring feels more like tenderness and intensifies instead of being satiated or diminished over time.

The centres of the Care pathway are similar to both Seeking and Lust. Oxytocin is the major neuropeptide involved in eliciting the raw Caring feelings and actions in the Care pathway. Again, as in the Lust pathway, there are male and female differences in chemistry, with similar architecture and crossovers between them. For example, oxytocin is produced from oestrogen in the paraventricular nucleus of the anterior hypothalamus (PVN) and in the dorsal pre-optic area (POA), close to the focal sites of female and male Lust respectively. Oestrogen and progesterone, the neuropeptides of female sexual arousal, control the number of oxytocin receptors in many regions where oxytocin is released. These include the bed nucleus of the stria terminalis (BNST) and the ventromedial hypothalamus (VMH). The Care pathway extends into widespread brain areas, including the VTA (the ventral tegmental area), the PAG (periaqueductal grey), the habenula (HAB) and the septal area (S).

Males and females have essentially the same brain architecture for Caring. All young mammals, after all, receive maternal Care. The difference is one of quantity, both of Care hormones and the hormone receptor cells. The POA as a centre of Care and its proximity to the centre of male Lust is interesting. It has also been seen that the Care pathway, based on oxytocin, once established, is sustained by prolactin, opioids and social learning. It is not dependent on oxytocin alone after a period of time. Maternal Care is hugely important, but it is not the whole story in mammals or in humans.

Co-creating

Mothers and babies adjust themselves physically to each other after the baby's birth. The baby's sucking encourages the production of oxytocin to the PVN, which then lets down milk. In this way, mother and baby form each other in a Caring couple. This interconnection of co-creation between individuals who are forming each other is the basis of all social interaction. This co-creating connection between individuals is a major function of mammal brains and bodies, and specifically, of human brains and bodies (Panksepp, 1998).

The Care pathway reaches down into the VTA, which is the centre of Seeking. The VTA has oxytocin receptors that promote a good feeling of Seeking and also certain kinds of Seeking behaviour linked to Care. The Care neuropeptides vasopressin, oxytocin and the endogamous opioids, involved in maternal and sexual urges, also help to create memories that form specific positive and negative social experiences. For example, males produce oxytocin after having sex. This makes them less irritable and aggressive. In general, physical closeness, touching and the free flow of intimacy lead to a lower valence for violence, particularly in males.

Conversely, Panksepp said, the restriction of sexual outlets for adolescent boys required in modern human society leads to more valence for violence. Certain characteristics in modern human societies, such as the patriarchal heteronormativity required by neoliberalism, restrict sexuality, rather than facilitating it. This restriction creates more violence and aggression. The representation of these processes in the brains of young males is the restriction of oxytocin and endogamous opioids. In males after puberty, the increase of testosterone creates more vasopressin, which is not a nurturant chemical. In this way, males become less sensitised to Care in adolescence.

At the same time, females become more sensitised to Care by means of oestrogen which produces oxytocin. Oxytocin and oestrogen are the nurturant chemicals, together with the endogamous opioids. Oxytocin enhances the effects of opioids. Opioids, in themselves, promote sociality at low levels. However, at higher levels, opioids produce social feelings without the necessity of social behaviour. In this way, the opioids as medication or self-medication become addictive and isolating. This suggests that social feelings and behaviour are rewarding in a similar way and could be thought of as addictive. It also suggests that the absence of social feelings and behaviour, through fear, rage, aggressive feelings and violence, is disturbing, painful and damaging.

The internal production of oxytocin and opioids enhances social interactions and diminishes aggression. Sexual interactions enhance and consolidate social attachments. Exposing pre-pubescent males and post-pubescent females to infants, for example, promotes Caring behaviour through the medium of oxytocin and small amounts of opioids. These exposures leave indelible imprints on a creature's way of being in the world. In this way, the initial maternal Care feelings and actions are generalised to others through the medium of the mammal and human group. Group exposure to infants by young males and females created and maintained mammal groups as the origin of infant Care. Infant Care in evolution never belonged exclusively to mothers until the time of monsters.

Bonding windows

Further, while Seeking, Fear and Rage are universal and similar for all vertebrate animals and humans, Lust and Care are variable between species as well as between genders. Bonding windows is an example of this species-specific variation in Care behaviour. This is where the species-specific group becomes important. Care is not only a matter of mother and child, as above, but a matter of a complex group matrix formed around birth and infant care.

In the variable species characteristic of bonding windows, prey species, the herbivores, like horses, sheep and cows, are born highly mobile. Corresponding to this high initial mobility is a bonding window that closes quickly after birth. That is, the space of time in which an infant can accept, and be accepted, by a mothering animal, the birth mother or another, is a matter of hours. Mother and baby are both mobile and must be able to have a powerful attachment in order to find each other if they become separated. The attachment is necessary for survival. The bonding window defines the specific attachment between specific individual mothers and babies. Bonding affects both.

The short prey bonding window is contrasted to a much longer bonding window for predators. Predators, like lions and tigers, are born with their eyes closed. Predator infants cannot wander. Thus, the species-specific Care window is open for a longer time and mothers can substitute each other over a longer period.

Humans have a very lengthy extended infancy and childhood. Humans have an evolutionary history of being prey and are born with open eyes, but like predators, cannot move or wander. Mothers bond rapidly. This is generalised to others who are exposed to infants. However, human babies take much more time to bond. Panksepp thought that human children are able to form generalised special attachments with others until six months to one year of age. Six months to a year is when humans start to move around. The human group bonds with the child and the child bonds with the group in the first instance. This is yet more evidence of the intense generalised group Care and bonding in humans.

Still further, ungulates and rodents bond by smell, whereas humans, for example, bond by sight, sounds, touch and especially gentle touch, as well as by smell. These stimulate brain opioid and oxytocin release when they are associated with good experiences. Human babies start bonding before birth through sounds heard in the womb. These are sounds not just from mothers, but from others in the mother's social environment, including music, culture and religion. Human babies are not only bonding with mother but with a much wider social environment, before birth and long afterward. Mothers and others are bonding with babies similarly. This is the human species-specific bonding window that admits the group as well as the individuals in the group.

In the group dimension, it is the group bonding that grew out of, but also underlies, the mother and baby couple. It is the group bonding that creates and integrates the individual human. It is the group bonding that promotes pair bonding within the group. The intensity of human group relationships, combined with the instinctual necessity of exogamy, creates the web of human relationships necessary to reproduce humans. One lone mother is never enough. These first bonds of Care lay a basis for the whole of human lives and future human reproduction. Once these bonds are formed, security of attachment is all important, as is consistency. It is the security and integration of these first group attachments that become generalised from the primary group to the wider human network as an integrated human self. This generalised self and early environment is the basis of what a psychoanalyst might call repetition compulsion and transference in daily life. It contains the positive and negative maternal, group, cultural, social and individual experiences in early childhood as they are preserved in sensitised foundational feelings, brain associational networks, conscious and unconscious memories.

Social landscapes and internal worlds

Panksepp pointed out that baby rats who received more licking from mothers did better in all areas of life with an ability for life-long emotional learning from experience. This was initially facilitated, he thought, by oxytocin. This is because oxytocin makes lasting changes in the underlying Care pathways in individuals. These lasting changes are associated with sensitivities for receiving and giving good Care. Receiving and giving good Care bestows the ability to deal with the world in more confident, effective and integrated ways. This ability can be called resilience and robustness, but also involves an acceptance of self and others as vulnerable and in need of care.

Specifically, the baby rats that received the most licking from their mothers were less anxious, suffered less stress and could learn better. They produced less corticotrophin-releasing hormone (CRF) and less adrenocorticotropic hormone (ACTH). These neurological chemicals are related to Fear and stress. The same baby rats had more GABA receptor sites. GABA reduces anxiety and the intensity of all feelings. They also had more receptors for glutamate and norepinephrine, neurological chemicals that promote learning (Gerhardt, 2004).

Animals without this abundant maternal Care became more emotionally fragile and thus more overwhelmed by life events. Panksepp observed that prairie voles, for example, were more nurturant and confident when they grew up with both parents and pups in their groups. Mother and father Care, Panksepp thought, combining nurture with protection, produce altruism, compassion and empathy in offspring. Experiences of unconditional acceptance, empathic sensitivity and full concern for emotional lives can recruit the healing power of the positive foundational feelings in later human lives. These psychotherapeutic values work. Some part of the emotional bonding window stays open in humans. Further, human foundational feelings are communicated and shared, sometimes in ways that evoke the ideas of contagion, especially in the area of human empathy. In the time of monsters, we are losing the experiences of unconditional acceptance and full concern for emotional lives. The rehabilitation of these experiences will need to be part of the polis and of political dialogue in the world yet to come if humanity is to survive.

In humans, it takes a village to raise a child (Hrdy, 2009). In the group dimension, it is clear that human big-brained infants have shaped the village or group as the unit of human Care, life, self-integration and reproduction. We are in danger of losing the consciousness of this part of our evolutionary history. Consequently, we are also in danger of losing the essence of this sociality in our present cultural emphasis on neoliberal individuality. In the group dimension, our brains, which appear to be individually packed into individual heads, are primarily social and only secondarily carry our individual relationship histories in infinite individual variations. These variations are felt and seen in the contexts of social landscapes that are also internal worlds.

References

Arendt, H. (1958 [1998]) *The Human Condition*, 2nd edition. Chicago. University of Chicago Press.

Elias, N. (1994) *The Civilizing Process*. Oxford: Blackwell.

Fine, C. (2011) *Delusions of Gender: The Real Science Behind Sex Differences*. London: Icon.

Freud, S. (1920) 'Beyond the Pleasure Principle', in J. Strachey (ed.) *The Standard Edition of the Complete Psychological Works of Sigmund Freud*, Vol. XVIII. London: The Hogarth Press and the Institute of Psycho-Analysis.

Gerhardt, S. (2004) *Why Love Matters: How Affection Shapes a Baby's Brain*. London: Routledge.

Hrdy, S. (2009) *Mothers and Others: The Evolutionary Origins of Mutual Understanding*. Cambridge, MA: Harvard University Press.

Lane, N. (2015) *The Vital Question: Why Is Life the Way It Is?* London: Profile Books.

Panksepp, J. (1998) *Affective Neuroscience: The Foundations of Human and Animal Emotions*. Oxford: Oxford University Press.

Panksepp, J., and Biven, L. (2012) *The Archaeology of Mind: Neuroevolutionary Origins of Human Emotions*. New York: W. W. Norton & Company.

Chapter 10

Panic/Grief, Play, integration and social homeostasis

It may be as a result of traumatic early experiences, that Panksepp's chapter on Panic/Grief in *Affective Neuroscience: The Foundations of Human and Animal Emotions* is one of the most important, but also one of the most puzzling of his writings (Panksepp, 1998). The chapter is full of information and intriguing thoughts, but without the evolutionary underpinning so important in the other chapters. Unlike the other chapters in the book, Care and Panic/Grief do not have clear diagrammatic pathways.

Care and Panic/Grief are obviously foundational feelings, however. Care and Panic/Grief mammal behaviours are clear. In humans, there are definite Panic/Grief feelings that promote urges to act. Most of the knowledge about how Panic/Grief is expressed in human brains as foundational feelings comes from studies where chemical medications and self-medications have been used. Panksepp would have benefitted from a knowledge of the group dimension but the group dimension can still benefit from Panksepp's thoughts about how Care and Panic/Grief together form the feelings and behaviour urges that create and maintain social homeostasis.

The addition of Seeking as the basic state of this homeostasis in the foundational feelings adds to the clarity of how human social brains evolve, function and feel. Homeostasis is a delicate balance around an ideal point, like a temperature gauge. Homeostasis is never, in fact, static, but tends to move and balance around this point. Homeostasis is based on processes that are in dynamic equilibrium rather than being in more rigid and stable structures.

For Panksepp, the neuroscientist, the Panic/Grief pathway is at the heart of the Care pathway. Panic/Grief is thus at the heart of social relations in the group dimension. Panic/Grief and Care form and enhance each other, while also remaining separate foundational feelings, each involving its own complex interactions of pathways and neurochemicals.

The Panic/Grief pathway has its roots in pain

Panic/Grief in mammals is indicated by 'distress vocalisations' (DVs). When mothers and infants are separated, the infants call for their mothers for a long time, and then fall silent if she does not appear; the infants do not move during this time, which has been likened to depression, the absence of Seeking. Eventually, if the mother does not find the infant, the infant dies. Mothers call for their infants too. This is also Panic/Grief. The Panic/Grief pathway, the distress feelings associated with separation, are the other side of the attachment feelings that are expressed as the bonding process in the Care pathway. Care and Panic/Grief are the two sides of this attachment. Humans have a constant and lifelong oscillation between them. The shock and pain of even momentarily losing a child is a prime example of the Panic/Grief feeling. The amazing, joyous and loving feeling of finding the child again is the feeling of the renewal of the closeness of the bonding. The pain of not finding the child again is unbearable, not only for the mother. In neuroscience terms, nothing involves the whole of the human brain like the pain and sadness associated with Grief.

The Care pathway stems originally from gentle touch; the Panic/Grief pathway has its roots in pain. The pain of the pathway comes from an ancient part of the midbrain, the pain centre, the ventral tegmental area (VTA). Panksepp proposed that all warm-blooded vertebrates have Grief-based social needs: '… even though early investigators did not believe in the existence of intrinsic social processes within the brain, it now seems likely that a great deal of higher brain organisation evolved in the service of promoting social behaviours and sustaining feelings of social homeostasis' Panksepp (1998, p. 276). Once again, this is the group dimension in the brain. Humans' needs for each other are addictive by their presence on the one hand, and distressingly painful by their absence on the other. Panksepp described the pain of Grief in relation to a Grief opioid, dynorphin, as 'disorienting and dissociated, like losing one's mind'.

The Panic is aroused in the midbrain area of the periaqueductal grey (PAG). The PAG is also involved in Fear and Rage. Other areas of brain architecture involved in Panic are the dorsal medial thalamus, the ventral septal area, the dorsal pre-optic area (dPOA) and many sites in the bed nucleus of the stria terminalis (BNST). The dPOA and the ventral septal area are also the sites of Lust and Care feelings and behaviours.

In brief, separation activates corticotrophin-releasing hormone (CRF) that produces the Panic. Reunion activates endogenous opiates and oxytocin that quell the panic and reinforce Care. Like the other foundational feeling pathways in the midbrain, the Panic/Grief pathway evolved from the Seeking pathway. Panic/Grief inhibits the production and reception of the Seeking neuropeptide, dopamine, as well as the endogenous opiates that might relieve the pain. Chronic Panic/Grief leads to depression. Depression is the absence of Seeking. Seeking is the feeling basis of all life.

One of the major Panksepp findings is that Panic/Grief and Fear come from different emotional brain pathways. Grief is painful, sometimes unbearably so. Loss can produce Panic as well as Grief. In Panic, humans report feelings of weakness, difficulty breathing and a lump in the throat. CRF is involved in both Panic and Fear. Fear is more of a feeling of apprehension of hurt or harm in the future. Loss might be Feared, but the actual loss itself causes Panic. Chronic arousal of the Panic pathway leads to despair and depression. More CRF and adrenal activities (stress chemicals) suppress the production and reception of the brain chemicals associated with good feelings, namely, norepinephrine (NOR), serotonin and dopamine.

Two different neural pathways are involved in Panic and Fear respectively. It is clear that the feeling of being isolated and lost, Panic, is different from the anticipation of injury or death, Fear. Both Panic and Fear, however, can lead to depression. These are two different depressions chemically but both respond to the healing aspect of Care in the group dimension.

Panksepp identified the distress of the Panic and the pain of the Grief. However, he gave little attention to the processes involved in Grieving and separation. Panksepp thought that separation enhances Care in mammals. This is because the major social chemicals, the endogenous opioids, lose their effect after a period of time. The distress of separation renews the Care bonds through the distress of panic and sadness. In other words, Grief renews relationships and develops new ones. This is how loss and Grieving are experienced and modulated in social humans. This is why loss and grieving are so important in the clinic and in the psy professions.

Depression lifts when Seeking is restored. Sadness is a modulation of depression. When Panic is quelled, loss can be acknowledged with Grieving, which involves Care, and Seeking returns. Like the other shifts in the foundational feelings, this shift is clear and consciously felt. Grief and recovery through Care is a ubiquitous, human, homeostatic life process. Grieving and Caring are paired social processes that are happening continuously in human life.

The relationship between Care and Panic/Grief pathways again emphasises the homeostatic nature of human feelings and involvements. Panksepp used the terms of systems in his writing. However, he was not describing systems. He was describing moment to moment processes that respond to often very tiny changes in the human world. Panksepp also wrote about chemicals and medical chemical treatments for feelings. However, he clearly described how these medical chemical treatments, such as benzodiazepines for anxiety and antidepressants for panic, do not work as well as renewed human social relationships based on Care. Panksepp's discussion of the Care and Panic/Grief pathways brings into focus the importance of the Seeking pathway as the homeostatic feeling basis of life itself and depression as the feeling of chronic Seeking interruption or loss.

The importance of play in the group dimension

Panksepp became best known as the man who tickled rats and made them laugh. Panksepp's seventh foundational feeling was 'Play'. He observed that there are certain Play behaviours and sounds. These are the so-called 'rough and tumble' Play noises that are innate, rather than learned, in rats and all other mammals. Play is a foundational feeling that is exclusive to mammals and some birds. Mammals who are young, healthy and feeling good will almost always Play. Panksepp described the feeling of Play as the urge to Play. This urge to Play is most visible in the establishment of social relationships with peers in humans and other mammals. The feeling might also be called 'Playful'.

Rough and tumble rat play is something like professional wrestling. The Play noises that rats make are analogous to human laughter. These Play behaviours, like the other urges to action related to the foundational feelings, come through the neural pathways that prepare, form, challenge and motivate the cerebral cortex. Play promotes certain kinds of neuronal growth and may also encourage the integration of the various levels of feelings, thoughts and actions in mammals. Play is essentially social. It is about the interplay between dominance, submission, difference and equality between individuals. At the same time, Play is about internal integration. Play is where the link between interpersonal integration and intrapersonal integration is most evident in Panksepp's writings. The observation of the identity processes – interpersonal, between people, and intrapersonal, within individuals – is crucial to understanding and valuing the group dimension.

Play is closely associated with Seeking. The major Seeking neurotransmitter, dopamine, is one of the neuropeptides associated with Play. The play foundational feeling is not the same as Seeking, though. Play is more like a hunger that can be satiated. Play is more like food, that which is Sought. Seeking is part of Play, but not all of it. Play and Seeking are actually more like alternative neural pathways. An increase in Seeking activity leads to a decrease in Play activity, in fact, even though dopamine fuels both.

Play is closely associated with touch. Rats and mice have some spots of skin that are especially sensitive to tickling. Tickling these sensitive spots produces rat laughter. Touch and tickling are important indicators of the Play urge. And, as Panksepp pointed out, no one can tickle themselves. There is something of the unexpected in Play that produces pleasure. In other words, Play needs an 'other'. Play is intrinsically social, even in solitary Play.

Play can be defined as the foundational feeling of joy associated with free and present, moment-to-moment, pleasurable contact with others, primarily peers. It is the feeling of being able to freely compete. It does not matter so much who wins or who loses. However, Play is also about dominance, submission and equality. Panksepp observed that, even with mis-matched playmates, dominant rats will only win, at most, 70 per cent of the time. In other words, dominant rats will control how much they win if they want to keep playing. This is because the subordinate rats lose interest in Playing unless they win at least 30 per cent of the time. Playing produces friendships between equals and resolves dominance hierarchies. Play teaches both winners and losers to accept defeat. Mammals practice cooperation by Playing. According to Panksepp (1998, p. 280), 'Play helps to stitch individuals into the social fabric that is the staging grounds for their lives'. Other feelings associated with Play are carefree, dynamic rambunctiousness and joy in social exchange with a strong competitive edge.

Play contributes to social homeostasis

In humans, Play only happens in a secure base, a familiar environment, and usually starts with parental involvement. Fear and hunger eliminate Play. In mammals, the females are more Playful than the males, who are often too aggressive. In humans, males and females appear to Play in very different ways. Males are thought to play more aggressively with children. However, too much aggressiveness stops Play, as does too much Seeking. When other emotional states come into Play (Fear, Anger, Lust, Panic/Grief and Care), Play stops. In Play, feelings are practised without actually having them. When the feelings become too powerful, Play stops.

Neurochemically, Play is the most complex of the foundational feelings. Acetylcholine, glutamate, and the opioids arouse Play. Serotonin, norepinephrine and GABA reduce Play. Physically, Play may have evolved from the pleasure of soft touch, like tickling.

Most sensory systems, including touch, divide at the level of the thalamus on their way to the higher regions of the brain, with some of the information directed towards the neocortex, while the rest of the information influences the lower reticular regions of the brain. These lower regions convey the affective impact of sensory inputs. The touch components that promote Play do not generally go directly to the neocortex, but rather to the more ancient midline thalamic regions.

Panksepp pointed out that there is a growing body of evidence that the primary urge to Play, is an important influence in helping 'programme' higher brain regions to produce happy adults with abundant creativity and zest for life. This wellbeing is '… profoundly dependent on a cortex that listens intently to the ancestral messages from below' (Panksepp and Biven, 2012, p. 365). These are the messages coming from all the seven foundational feelings. So that, far from well-being or emotional health coming from a cortex that repels or ignores these feelings, emotional health and happiness come from a cortex that listens to feelings and can think about them, integrate them and temper them without eliminating them. This is what Play facilitates.

Besides dopamine, vestibular, cerebellar and basal ganglia are also necessary for Play. These last nerve centres are involved in general control of movements. There is a widespread release of opioids during Play in the medial pre-optic area, also important in sexual and maternal behaviours, Lust and Care. Oxytocin and CRF (cortisol-releasing factor) reduce Play. Social deprivation, isolation, increases the necessity for Play.

What emerges from these empirical findings about Play is that it originates from the somatic sense of touch, much as Grief arises from the somatic sense of pain. Like pain and Grief, Play connects the higher regions of the brain, the cerebral cortex and the thalamus, with the lower regions of the brain, specifically, the lower reticular regions in the pons. Play is the link between these lower regions to the non-specific midline regions of the Thalamus. These observations suggest that Play has a very ancient origin, in touch, with a more recent evolution, in mammals, specifically.

Play, seeking and dreaming

When creatures are deprived of touch, the Play urge arises as if it were a hunger. This indicates that Play is related to the consumption part of Seeking. Seeking stops when consumption begins. Play stops when the Play hunger is satisfied. This aspect of Play is similar to Lust, as well as to hunger. The Play urge comes when dopamine is depleted. Play produces dopamine and when the levels of dopamine increase beyond a certain point, Play becomes Seeking. This also suggests that Play relieves depressive feelings by restoring dopamine-induced Seeking from low levels. Play, Seeking and the exercise of power without coercion are related. Play fighting is enjoyable for all, until someone gets hurt. Play laughter is aroused by Playfulness. Dark laughter, when someone is hurt, humiliated or embarrassed is a different kind of laughter that may well be related to the revenge processes in Seeking. A revenge process in Seeking might be Seeking in order to wound.

The same neuropeptides, acetylcholine, dopamine, norepinephrine and serotonin involved in Play are also involved in dreaming. Panksepp thought that dreaming and Play perform similar functions of integration of complex affective information. He thought that Play performs this function in waking life and proposed that: '... in ancient evolutionary history, raw primary-process consciousness might have initially existed as a kind of dreaming-type wakefulness – one that is full of emotional arousals, which is then superseded by more cognitive frames of mind' (Panksepp and Biven, 2012, p. 377).

Play produces epigenetic changes

Play may also be involved in the epigenetic creation of mental lives. Epigenetics is a new discovery. Epigenetics describes the way that environments influence living things to make genetic changes that can be inherited by future generations. This means that evolution in general does not rely only on chance mutations. These genetic changes involve the stimulation of some already-existing genes to switch them on and off. Like genetic changes that come from mutations, epigenetic changes are transmitted across generations. Inheritable environmental influences can happen much more quickly than previously thought.

Social Play activates the neural growth factors, the Brain-Derived Neural Growth Factors (BDNF) in the frontal cortex and in the amygdala. Dynamic brain changes evoked by Play facilitate brain growth and maturation, epigenetically creating prosocial circuits of the brain. This means that Play is not only social in the moment. Play also creates social pathways in the neocortex. This implies that the long-term gene expression patterns that go through the generations are a consequence of experiences created by Play, or not. According to Panksepp, Play is involved in the construction of sophisticated social brains that can understand the emotional states and motives of others. This opens the doors to social cooperation, camaraderie, compassion, empathy and solidarity. These are a further development of the emotional contagion of each of the foundational feelings. They are part of the modulating processes involved in the interchange between midbrain and cerebral cortex interactions.

Panksepp proposed that rough, physical, Play, with adult supervision, is a developmental necessity for human social life. He observed that children who are deprived of Play are depressed and envious and that Play is needed to mitigate self-serving greed. Panksepp focused his thoughts on the importance of all children experiencing high levels of social rough and tumble Play with adult supervision. Adult supervision is necessary to keep Play within boundaries and to sort out relationships when Play crosses over into the other feeling areas. Panksepp was concerned that human children were not getting enough Play. He proposed that adults needed to train children to contain and quell the powerful foundational feelings with Playing, thinking, speaking and listening.

Modules, layers, interaction, integration

The behaviourists of the 'psy' professions based their theories on the idea that the human brain is a 'black box', meaning that no one could see inside it. Since no one could see it, no one needed to think about it. According to the behaviourists, and contrary to human experience-near sensations of self, it was only learned, 'conditioned', and unlearned, 'unconditioned', behavioural responses to stimuli that were open to knowledge and thought. Behaviourist thinking was that humans act and react in accordance with emotional rewards and punishments. Thus, humans can best be described en masse, observed from the outside and in numbers. This behaviourist thinking has become part of the neoliberal ideology, where numbers count more than quality and where norm counts more than the specific. In neoliberalism, humans are counted in and counted out. Neoliberalism deals in statistics, averages and probabilities.

Panksepp's experiments have opened the 'black box'. For the first time, it is possible to see and know the workings of the mammal mind. It is also possible to extrapolate from the mammal mind to the human mind. There are many directions to go with Panksepp's findings. Much of neoliberal psychology has been directed towards mass manipulation economically through the marketplace and politically through the media. This has produced the psychology of the time of monsters which is more focused on control than the alleviation of suffering.

Panksepp ended his life searching for chemical solutions to alleviate the suffering caused by neoliberal political and psychological manipulations that encourage extreme individualism and enhance the manipulations of the mass. One possible direction is to think about how Panksepp's findings help to understand how this same neoliberal mass behaviourist psychology is driving people into depression on the one hand and into manic denial on the other, causing the very suffering that Panksepp hoped to be able to alleviate.

Another possible direction is to look for ways of informing the various 'psy' professions with the knowledge created by opening the 'black box'. Panksepp's thoughts and experiments work well with other 'psy' theories, confirming some theories and disconfirming others. His findings also make 'psy' theories more available for experience, thought and action in the clinical professions. Both of these ways of understanding and digesting Panksepp are valid. Both ways of understanding Panksepp, as alleviator of suffering and as provider of basic concepts imply power relationships where some people know and others do not.

Singularities and coherence

To have a new world in the group dimension presupposes more than good and effective therapy. To have a new world in the group dimension presupposes that each human person has access to the maximum amount of knowledge about self and other. Without widespread and accurate knowledge, experience and practice of self and other, there is no freedom of choice. Any democracy based on ignorance of self and other is a fallacy. So, while the time of monsters works on choices made in terms of numbers, averages and statistics, in the world yet to come decisions will most often be made in terms of singularities and integrational coherence, based on dialogue. It is hoped that, with becoming more conscious of these singularities and their integration through dialogue in groups, the seeds of a new world will evolve. This is the first time in human history that these particular seeds can be planted. This particular historical moment is a singularity.

The first singularity, though, is life. Life only happened once on earth. Further, as far as is known, life has not happened anywhere else. Humans collectively may be responsible for all life in the universe.

With life itself, each individual human has access to the feeling called Seeking. Seeking underpins all the varieties of life that have evolved since the first autonomous and reproducing cell. Humans experience Seeking as a pleasurable, forward-moving action feeling of the expectation of good things in the world.

The second singularity is that, apart from humans, when Seeking stops as a response to a particular environment, life ends. For humans, the loss of Seeking is a horrible feeling. Humans have many ways of preserving and returning to Seeking. Not all of these ways of maintaining Seeking are individually healthy and socially constructive. However, what makes humans different, singular, from other animals is that the intensity of human relationships with each other is such that each human can be helped to recoup Seeking by others. When other animals can no longer care for themselves, they die. The feeling of the absence of Seeking in humans is depression. Only the gift of human relationships with each other can dispel depression and encourage a return to Seeking. The experience of losing and recouping Seeking in life is a uniquely human one.

Life and the preservation of life

Between these two singularities, life, the feeling of life, and the feeling of the absence of life felt by humans, there is the complexity of millions of years of evolution, all of which are preserved in the architecture, feeling pathways and chemistries of brains as Panksepp described. At first, these principles seem relatively simple. Seeking has produced, by evolutionary tinkering, ever more precise and sensitive, but less powerful, feeling reactions and actions to preserve the life/Seeking/desire force.

Seeking first produced the Fear of pain. Fear diminishes Seeking and informs it. Extreme fear or terror stops life altogether. Fear also preserves Seeking through experience and learning. Rage comes when Seeking is interrupted or frustrated. Rage stops Seeking, but also enables actions that soon allow its restoration. Lust facilitates finding mating possibilities, thus ensuring reproduction.

These foundational feelings come from the midbrain, translating and facilitating the reality of the environment to meaning and basis of action for individual living creatures. Midbrain processes are slow and long-lasting. However, with the evolution of mammals, a second sensory and learning structure in the brain, with faster and more flexible associational learning, developed. This second, and qualitatively different structure, improved translation and facilitation of environments to meanings for individual creatures. Cerebral cortex learning from the feelings in the midbrain entailed modulation of these feelings for more effective, life-preserving, action. Effective, life-preserving action entailed not only reacting to elements in the creature's environment, but also sometimes not reacting, hiding and thinking. The more rapid processes of the cerebral cortex were capable of modulating the foundational feelings and their consequent actions. These processes also supported a speedier return to Seeking from Fear and Rage.

Complexity

Everything changed with the first mammals and with the new cerebral cortex brain architecture. Babies were carried inside mothers to term and were no longer limited in their development by the nourishment that was stored in eggs. Babies could be nourished by mothers before and after birth. The variation in the ways that these processes developed through evolution created the variety of ways that mammals produce each other, reproduce and evolve. Individuals were no longer simply representatives of their species, but also representatives of their groups and group processes. These developments came from the evolution of the female Lust pathway into the Care pathway. Foundational feelings had to be further modulated by the requirements of living together in groups. These are the processes that grew the cerebral cortex.

With singularity comes complexity. Seeking and life preservation also depend on the lasting Care processes. Lasting Care processes involve Panic/Grief. The Panic/Grief foundational feeling preserves Care and Care preserves Seeking when there are losses, including changes, in the environment. On the one hand, Care protects Seeking by quelling Rage and Fear, on the other, the group demands of Care cause hurt/Fear and frustration/Rage. Fear, Rage, Panic and Grief reduce levels of Seeking. These are all complex and dynamic homeostatic processes. In the tensions between these processes, each individual mammal born into a group becomes a singularity that, in turn, creates the group.

The group dimension in humans, so powerful that it can sustain life beyond Seeking, is full of complex levels, qualities and strengths of feelings. Panksepp's foundational feeling of Play and dreaming are two ways that these complexities come together as integrated whole selves and groups. When these integrations do not work well enough, various feeling and relationship difficulties emerge. It is then that conscious thinking and dialogue are needed.

Thinking and dialogue

Thinking and dialogue are closely related. Thinking and dialogue are only possible when the singularities and complexities of being an individual human in the group dimension are sufficiently integrated. They are not always integrated. To add to the complexity, the seven foundational feelings, identified by Panksepp, are conscious but without obvious value or objective. It is the process of learning from the foundational feelings that is unconscious.

In the group dimension, consciousness is not the problem. The human problem in terms of dialogue and integrated thinking is the problem of the unconscious. Some part of learning is unconscious. Memories are made and then also remade to eliminate some feeling or knowledge that is more difficult to integrate into a particular, working-model self. Some feelings are felt and then banished from consciousness. For some people, who are abused, deprived or neglected as children, experiences and learnings from the foundational feelings are so frightening and painful that an integrated self cannot exist. Some memories exist only as feeling without words when they come from experiences that were had as babies and before language for thought and communication. In less extreme childhoods, the conscious and unconscious are formed individually and collectively into each person as complex and singular entities, since growing up as an intensely-connected human is already complex and singular.

The world of feelings and the unconscious is not of the same logic as in the associational networks of the human cerebral cortex. Peoples' feelings and unconscious minds have their own logic. The truth of the processes, though, as Panksepp revealed them, is that no thinking or dialogue can exist without feelings and words to communicate the feelings internally and to and from others. There is no self without feelings, however unintegrated, chaotic and inconsistent these feelings might be (Matte Blanco, 1988).

These are thoughts and understanding drawn from Panksepp's experiments and writings. They are congruent with experiences known to therapists in the analytic areas of the 'psy' professions who have the most experience listening to, and thinking with, people about their feelings and their relationships. Freud, the originator of psychoanalysis was first a neurologist and knew about the differing structures in human brains. He also had a theoretical and physical model of the human mind, as well as a psychic one. However, with the understanding of the contents of the 'black box' from Panksepp, together with the evolutionary understanding from human evolution in particular, it becomes apparent, and even obvious, that some of Freud's amazing insights into the human psyche are, in essence, group processes derived from feelings.

An important element of group processes derived from feelings, is that the foundational feelings, although conscious, have no intrinsic object, value or direction. In the complexity, there are no meaningful aspects of good or bad, or even any evidence of the behaviourists' rewards and punishments. The foundational feelings are powerful reactions to elements and events in the human environment consisting of other humans. These powerful feelings evoke whole networks of possible meanings, associations and memories in the cerebral cortex before they become thoughts, decisions, actions or inactions. The foundational feelings are given meaning in both conscious and unconscious processes which come from past conscious and unconscious learning and possible predictions of the future which are specific to each individual.

In the group dimension, the only value or direction of thoughts, decisions, actions and inactions that come from the foundational feelings is if they are constructive or destructive to good social relations between individuals and others. Even on this plane, the identification of goodness and badness is complex. When the foundational feelings are powerful enough, they overwhelm some of the thinking and modulating processes. When this happens, feelings become mis-attributed as to their meaning (Stacey, 2003).

Power, dominance hierarchies and psychology

The mammal world of groups, motivated by the foundational feelings of Care, Panic/Grief and Play in the group dimension, created the dynamics of power. Care, particularly, is an unequal relationship of power and powerlessness. The mother and other carers have power while the baby, physically at least, is helpless and dependent. Human babies are helpless in varying degrees for the first two years of their lives, until they learn to say 'no'. The evolution of the Care foundational feeling and subsequent mixed sex groups created dominance hierarchies as a way of preserving and enhancing life. Humans would not have evolved without these characteristics in their last common ancestors. With mixed and cooperative males in human groups, power is an important social dynamic, only modulated somewhat by the equality and peer aspects of Play. In the group dimension, foundational feelings are always modulated and directed by power relationships. In the family of neoliberal capitalism, these power relationships start with the parents.

Where the power differences are perceived as extreme, feelings can be misdirected or, when they feel dangerous, physically or psychically, they can be perceived as coming from somewhere other than their accurate origin. This dynamic is linked with the possibility of internal or external blame. In psychoanalysis this psychological process, discovered in therapeutic experiences between analysts and patients, is called 'projection' (Klein, 1986). In everyday life, some reflection on where the feelings are located and what they mean in relationships is always helpful.

In circumstances of even more extreme power differences, humans can act in such a way as to elicit these unwanted feelings from someone else, thus freeing themselves of these unwanted feelings. This is a power relationship in itself. This process is often seen as manipulative. It has great political use as the mass media have powers of manipulating emotional environments and do so daily. In interpersonal relationships, an individual who regularly gives their feelings to others soon loses all sense as to who they are themselves. This is often in the service of maintaining Seeking in the face of chronic Fear and Rage. These individuals were often on the extremes of situations where they were powerless as babies or young children. The psychoanalytic terms for these intra- and inter-personal processes are 'projection' and 'projective identification'. The psychic processes of projection and projective identification often become addictive and feed on themselves, if not scrutinised and reflected upon. They are almost always self-defeating.

In 'projective identification', the manipulation is so powerful that the person receiving the projections identifies with them. In other words, the projections become a part of their identity. These projective processes were discovered in therapeutic relationships. They are, though, also in wide use in the time of monsters, most often used unconsciously as a way of defending against thoughts and feelings that are disturbing and destructive to the maintenance of Seeking.

The psychoanalytic concepts of 'transference' and 'countertransference' were also discovered in therapeutic relationships between therapists and patients. One of the first psychoanalytic patients, Anna O, taught Freud and his colleague, Breuer, that some authority figures in the consulting room evoke psychic connections with others outside the consulting room and in the past. This is 'transference'. 'Countertransference' is the corresponding feeling in the therapist. Therapists are trained to be attentive to the feelings that their patients are giving them to hold or as communications. These phenomena were discovered in the consulting room, but are not confined to it. In the group dimension, they illustrate how permeable humans are to being interpenetrated by others around them. It is in the consulting room that these phenomena were discovered and also have become objects of reflective, emotional and conscious modulation. They are part of the intense group relationships that created the human. They are also part of the human capacity for feeling others' feelings as contagious feelings and as empathy.

Neoliberal individualism destroys the group

In terms of evolution, humans were not made for the pressures of the time of monsters that humans have collectively produced over the last 800 years of capitalism. It is part of the specificity and complexity of this historical moment that the group dimension has become both intensified and obscured by neoliberal individualism. In neoliberal individualism, communities and groups have been broken down by economic and political demands into nuclear and single-parent families. Fewer and fewer resources of time and thought are spent on raising human children, who are often left alone to raise themselves and their siblings and peers. Life experiences have become more and more individualised, ironically, as they have become more and more massified. Increasingly, Seeking for most individuals has become inconsistent and disappointing, leading to the Seeking-damaging foundational feelings of chronic Fear, Rage and Panic (Wodak, 2015).

More projective and denial defences are needed in order to maintain a sense of Seeking, as the loss of Seeking is akin to living death. Human group relationships, felt as being increasingly dangerous, complex and difficult, are being replaced by technology, artificial intelligence and the internet, as Arendt predicted. Soon, even Lust will no longer be necessary to make babies. However, human babies still need human relationships in groups in order to maintain, integrate and reproduce a good enough human environment. Increasingly, this also includes emergency measures to renew and maintain the human physical environment of the planet.

Human and physical environments are inextricably linked. The capitalist relationship of worker and employer-owner of the means of production, particularly in its most recent neoliberal, unmanaged, form is not good enough to reproduce humanity. It cannot be good enough because of its emotional as well as economic and health consequences. Power feeds on itself.

It is increasingly important to find some other ways of modulating power and dominance hierarchies into more equal and democratic forms of groups. Whatever the world yet to come is called, humans need to find a way of creating, maintaining, integrating and reproducing themselves and the world together under conditions of multiple and varied internal and external identities. This entails a new kind of democracy, coming from the grassroots, inclusive of everyone and valuing of difference. It depends upon people being able to think, live and work together with an interpenetration made more conscious by active dialogue and decision-making with thought and reflection. These dialogues have their roots in the group dimension. Group processes give birth to individual processes, both evolutionarily and developmentally. These need to become more conscious and available for dialogue to lead to an understanding of how we interpenetrate and make ourselves through others. This will not be easy. This is what Elias and Foulkes saw in groups and figurations.

References

Klein, M. (1986) *The Selected Melanie Klein* (edited by J. Mitchell). Harmondsworth: Peregrine.
Matte Blanco, I. (1988) *Thinking, Feeling, and Being*. London: Routledge.
Panksepp, J. (1998) *Affective Neuroscience: The Foundations of Human and Animal Emotions*. Oxford: Oxford University Press.
Panksepp, J., and Biven, L. (2012) *The Archaeology of Mind: Neuroevolutionary Origins of Human Emotions*. New York: W. W. Norton & Co.
Stacey, R. (2003) *Complexity and Group Process: A Radically Social Understanding of Individuals*. Hove: Brunner Routledge.
Wodak, R. (2015) *The Politics of Fear: What Right-Wing Populist Discourses Mean*. London: Sage.

Part V

Figurations and groups

'Although we will not avoid theoretical questions, it is practice that is the key and what we can learn from psychoanalytic clinical practice connects with the practice of liberation.'
Ian Parker and David Pavón-Cuéllar (2021)

Figure 5 'Woman, Life, Freedom'

Chapter 11

Seeking is the foundational feeling of life

The group dimension, as a dimension, pre-existed humans. It operates inside each of us. Groups are ubiquitous in everyday life. It is the purpose of this work to bring all aspects of groups to consciousness as continuous processes. This consciousness is a crucial part of decolonising from the extreme individualism of neoliberalism. It is also a crucial aspect of liberation, in both the individual and the political senses. We will not break free of neoliberalism without better internal and external communication and a more refined dialogue leading to a democracy that is able to hear and to attend to all human voices as a priority and in a coherent way.

Group processes existed before humans. In fact, humans arose from group processes. The study of primates and early human evolution suggests that this is the only way that human evolution could have happened, through the group to the social brain that modulates emotions in order to maintain the group. In fact, maintaining groups is a large part of being human.

It remains, though, that groups are the implied collective. From a more detached perspective, groups can be implied through actions of individuals. Jane Goodall (1988, p. 239) first described this in her book *In the Shadow of Man*: 'A greeting between two chimpanzees ... re-establishes the dominance status of the one relative to the other.'

The group, in other words, is carried by the individuals in their relationships with each other. In the group dimension, groups can be discrete, with boundaries and closed, like the family and therapeutic groups. They can also be overlapping and intermingling like they are in organisations, with interdependent sub-groups. They can be implied, like identities. All of these groups have a reality because they are carried inside animal and human social brains. They are defined and regulated by the feelings that lead to actions, as Jaak Panksepp's findings show. Groups exist in the present moment reality because each person's feelings alert them and describe to them what is going on in their global group context. This is a return to the idea of figure/ground, where both individuals and groups exist at once. People know that groups are there because they are felt consciously and physically, as feelings and urges.

DOI: 10.4324/9781003350088-17

Groups and their contexts: Jane Goodall and Margaret Power

What happens in groups is defined by their contexts and changes in their contexts. This is what Norbert Elias (1987) termed 'figurations'. Figurations refer to the constantly changing relationships between interdependent individuals and groups. Jane Goodall, who observed that individual chimpanzees carry the group inside, also made the discoveries that identified chimpanzees as aggressive, murderous and warlike. These findings from Jane Goodall have become one of the bases of neoliberal views of chimpanzees, and thus of humans, as aggressively individualised. The neoliberal view, however, is a partial view.

Jane Goodall (1988) chronicled her time with the chimpanzees at the Gombe Stream Research Centre in Tanzania. She was one of three young people sent to observe primates by Louis Leakey, the paleoanthropologist who demonstrated that humans evolved in Africa. Leakey wanted to send non-scientist observers to describe and document the social lives of primates in the wild. He wanted non-scientists because he felt that they would be more open to their observations and experiences than trained academics.

Goodall took on Leakey's challenge and devoted her life to the Gombe chimpanzees as sentient beings, starting in 1960. Goodall was the first observer to name the animals and interpret their behaviours as individual personalities and as individuals in relationships, mostly power relationships, with each other. She showed how it is possible for a human being to come close to, and be accepted by, non-human creatures in their natural habitats. However, in the process of getting to know the troop of chimpanzees and becoming part of their lives, Goodall changed the nature of their social context by establishing feeding stations. Goodall later described how aggressive the chimpanzees became with each other, finally ending in a split, murder and a war. Aggression increased inside the group as well. That chimpanzees are capable of aggression, murder, splitting and war became the 'scientific' finding of the time, confirming the neoliberal trope, 'It has always been like this.'

Margaret Power (1991), in *The Egalitarians – Human and Chimpanzee: An Anthropological View of Social Organization*, wrote a critique of the Goodall findings. As well as the aggressive group behaviour that Goodall observed, Power also traced very different behaviours through 'naturalistic' primate studies, without feeding stations, and early anthropological studies of hunter-gatherers, including the San mentioned earlier in this work. In humans, these have been described as being based upon kindness, generosity, affection, hospitality, cooperation and egalitarianism. These, Power said, are essential for what she called the 'dependence' group.

Jane Goodall also reported peaceful chimpanzees from 1961 to 1965. It took her fourteen months of following before the chimps became accustomed to her. It was a further eight months before one of the chimps, David Greybeard, visited her camp. Later he came with two others, lured into the human camp by bananas. From 1962 to 1965 Goodall fed the chimps who came into camp by placing bananas around the camp. Even with this feeding, there was no direct competition or possessiveness between the animals. Consequently, however, by the end of 1964, there were 45 chimpanzees regularly visiting the camp along with 60 baboons, who were also reluctantly fed by the researchers (Power, 1991, pp. 27–28).

It was decided at that point to ration the bananas. They were hidden underground in feeding boxes, access to which was controlled by humans. The consequence of the various limited feeding regimes that were tried, was more and more aggressive competition, mainly between the chimpanzee males for food or even for control of the empty boxes. When other researchers from outside the Goodall team appeared in 1967, the Gombe chimpanzees and baboons were very different in their relationships with each other than they had been in 1965 (Power, p. 29).

Immediate return vs delayed return: aggression as displaced frustration

Power compared the importance of the context of the Gombe chimpanzee group to their relationships with the changes in context of pre-agricultural human hunter-gatherers who organised their economies as immediate-return. Immediate-return is contrasted with the delayed-return economies of the more complex human social processes linked to agriculture. In immediate-return groups, all members are considered of equal worth and entitled to equal access of the goods, rights and principles of their society. These equalities are not just taken for granted, but are constantly reasserted. Individual members are skilled in some things and less skilled in others. Another word for the quality of these group relationships could be 'coherence' of differences, as well as 'cohesion' of similarities. In general, in these groups, there is a great amount of concern for the reduction of the human, violent potential for aggression.

Power then went on to describe more fully the deterioration of the relationships between the Gombe animals. They continued to come into camp, but with increasing frustration of their expectations. Power described the changes in their relationships. In one particular incident, the feeding boxes were closed when 60 baboons also came to feed. The human researchers had closed the boxes in the hope that the baboons would leave. This was common procedure at the time. The animals could all smell the bananas. The chimpanzees and the baboons started to become aggressive with each other. The boxes opened, closed and then opened again. The researchers believed that they were minimising competition. However, at one point, Mike, one of the chimpanzees, snatched an infant baboon, killed it and fled. Power interpreted this behaviour as 'displaced frustration' brought on by the feeding regime.

Power observed that territoriality was also affected. Between 1960 and 1962, Jane Goodall had not been convinced that there were two groups in separate communities. In 1968, it was noticed that the group ranging further south no longer came regularly to the feeding station. In 1970–71, there was still some interaction between the groups, but by 1971, they were mainly separate. This evolved into border patrols by 1972. There were killings and war zones. Sexual relations changed too. From a situation where females were able to choose their sexual partners and sex looked to be mutually consensual between males and females, male aggressive sexual behaviour became more usual with less female choice. Sex became more violent and injurious to the females. Even the nature of childcare changed from gentle to aggressive. Infants were recorded being used as 'display objects', like tree branches, and were injured in the process, whereas earlier records showed males to be generally gentle and protective with infants and females. Power linked this later behaviour to the change in the context of the chimpanzee groups brought about by the frustration of processes of deprivation at the feeding stations and in the feeding regimes.

Feelings as conveyors of evolutionary links

The work of Goodall, Power and others is important because it shows how some of the principles analysed by Panksepp, Elias and Foulkes came down through the ages and stages of evolution. The conveyors and indicators of these communications through the ages are feelings. When the context of the relationships of groups with each other changes, the carriers of the groups, the emotional inner and outer relationships of the individuals that are touched by these changes, also transform. What Elias referred to as 'figurations', are also related to his ideas about the 'civilizing process' (1994). Feelings are the medium by which these processes occur. Feelings link individual and group processes in complex ways that can be understood. Becoming conscious of these feelings and their meanings in relationships is the liberation and the revolution in the practice of the psy professions. In this section of the book, I hope to begin the work of translation from the learnings found in the practice of the psy professions about feelings into useful knowledge for everyday life, dialogue, the *polis* and the world yet to come.

Elias's figurations and Foulkes' (1948) ideas of 'matrix' capture the ever-changing interdependence of groups and individuals. In many ways, Elias provided the theory and Foulkes provided the practice. What I hope to show in this work is how these abstract and distant concepts of theory and practice can be expressed in such a way as to describe and make conscious how feelings, thoughts and actions between people can increase understanding of, and coherent integration with, self and others. The process of this increasing consciousness is liberation. This increasing consciousness is also essential for maximising the possibility of dialogue in moments of stress and conflict. In its turn, maximising the dialogue is essential for metabolising aggression into something more contained, peaceful, integrating and useful for informing what happens next. The big social processes are always influencing individual thoughts and feelings. Elias, Foulkes, Arendt and others help us to learn about how individual moments of feelings and liberated decision-making can affect these same powerful social currents in their turn. This is where the revolution needs to begin and develop. Resistance is important, but it is not enough to bring people out of their individualised neoliberal isolation into coherent and cooperative assemblies with dialogue externally and into a coherent, integrated and liberating internal sense of well-being or rightness. Resistance by itself is not enough to emerge from the time of monsters and into the world yet to come.

Involvement and detachment

Elias, again, has provided some crucial understandings. In *Involvement and Detachment* (Elias, 1987), he began with the question of why we humans are so reluctant to examine ourselves in the same way that we examine nature. He contrasted the ways in which humans approach analysis of non-human processes in science with the ways in which humans mostly ignore, deny, and disavow the harms that we do to each other in everyday life. Like Margaret Power, Elias was concerned about how war and the dangers of war become self-feeding processes that appear to be out of human control but are produced in reality by human interactions. Here, Elias was particularly concerned about the Cold War between the US and Russia.

In effect, *Involvement and Detachment* is a plea for people to distance themselves from 'traditional' attitudes and identities in order to be able to ask with curiosity: 'what does this interaction mean?' rather than 'what does this interaction mean for me?'. This is what Elias means by 'detachment'. Part of the detachment that Elias thought was so important was what he called 'time perspective'. He accused systemic sociologists of ignoring that 'present social conditions represent an instant of a continuous process which, coming from the past, moves on through present times towards a future as yet unknown' (Elias, 1987).

For Elias, times of growing danger are also times of growing involvement and these exert a pressure towards a shortening of the time perspective (1987, p. xvi). Emphasis of structure over process is an example of the denial of how these processes move and change through time, sometimes quickly and sometimes very slowly. Elias then went on to show how detachment, even with natural phenomena, has been a position that has been hard-won through time, and part of the 'civilizing' process. Elias's argument is for detachment through restraint, observing that this restraint is easier when there is a 'strong and permanent external authority' (1987, p. lxviii). Further, Elias observed that weaker and unstable central authorities may be matched by strong and stable self-regulation by their members. In the case of the Cold War, there was no effective authority that could regulate a process of integration between the US and Russia. More self-restraint and detachment at all levels are needed 'to maintain humanity permanently in a pluralistic condition' (Elias, 1987, p. lxix).

Double-bind figurations

Further citing the Cold War, Elias went on to describe what he called 'double-bind figurations'. In double-bind figurations, two powerful parties are locked together by their indissoluble interdependence which, in the last resort, dictates the actions and decisions of both. The plans and actions of both sides are determined by the dynamics of this figuration. The two powers are bound together in such a way that each constitutes a deadly danger for the other. Alongside the Cold War, Elias cited the example of the situation in Palestine/Israel. When these figurations are obscured, all parties become helpless to control the dynamics of negative feedback between them. When these figurations can be identified, they can be lessened and broken up. In other words, double-bind figurations can be lessened and broken up by the identification and understanding of the figurations as processes happening through time. They are co-created. 'Problems of the double-bind can be lessened if attention is focused on connection and integration as well as on separation, isolation and on processes, rather than on fixed and frozen states' (Elias, 1987, p. 114). This means changing some group beliefs into something more 'reality-oriented'. Connection and integration are key. How do we maximise connection and integration in order to dissolve double-bind figurations and facilitate dialogue?

Elias's insistence on detachment might seem to be in sharp contrast with what I have referred to as feelings. The processes of the psy professions and of therapy are about involvement as well as about detachment. Foulkes, in the group analytic world, might seem to be on the opposite extreme from Elias when he makes communication the focus of emotional and relationship well-being. In truth, if Elias's double-bind figurations, which are familiar at all levels of social, political, relational and emotional life, can only be dissolved by integrating, coherent, communication through dialogue, then both involvement and detachment are needed. Apparently, Elias later conceded this point. This way of approaching the problem of conflicts and double-binds is much more effective than simple self and other restraint. Experience and history have shown time and time again that restraints only leave the conflicts bubbling under the surface, to pop up unexpectedly when the restraints are lifted or in seemingly unrelated other ways.

The problem then becomes how to attain an involved understanding of feelings and also maintain enough detachment to find the words and to communicate them in such a way as they can be heard. An associated problem is how to find the involvement and the detachment to hear, in depth of feeling, what is being communicated. This process also entails taking learning from the practice of the therapy rooms of the psy professions, particularly psychoanalysis and group analysis, and translating the learning in a way that is experience-near enough for people to be able to use it in everyday life for themselves and with each other.

Experience-near concepts

Experience-near is a concept that was popularised by the psychoanalyst Heinz Kohut (1971) in his writings on narcissism. In effect, most of the knowledge about human emotions and social processes comes from a detached perspective. Very little of the psy professional discourse is described in terms of feelings. However, psy professional practice is based on them. Most of the psy profession concepts are abstract and derived from observation. Even when it is admitted that observation between people cannot be totally 'objective', the therapist and/or group are thought to be interacting from a third perspective. The idea of experience-near concepts is to help people to have access to their own conscious and unconscious mental and social processes. Experience-near concepts also help people to know how to make use of the knowledge that others have about them. This is useful knowledge in the psych consulting rooms, for therapists and patients. It is also useful knowledge for people in relationships and figurations in everyday life.

How do we get access to our own mental and social processes? One place to start is with the reality-based, and detached, idea that the foundational feelings are conscious and that they only become unconscious when they are faced with social internal or external sanctions. That the foundational feelings, Seeking, Fear, Rage, Lust, Care, Panic/Grief and Play, are both conscious and contagious has come out of Panksepp's writings, as well as from psychoanalytic and group analytic practice. That these feelings are conscious means that, at least for an instant in the present, they are felt. That they are contagious means that they are available for others to feel them also in that instant. Often, others can feel the feeling more powerfully as a feeling than the person from whom it originates. This is what is called projection and the projective processes in the psy professions. The projective phenomena can be observed all the time in the psy professions and are happening all the time between people. They are usually experienced as unconscious communications.

The foundational feelings are felt and communicated in an instant of the present moment. In certain circumstances, both self and others can perceive feelings that have not been voiced, as well as those that have been voiced. This is the communication that makes a connection. This is the communication that makes a difference and a change.

Sometimes these feelings are fleeting and very quickly modulated by thoughts and actions. In these instances, the actual feelings can still be perceived through their modulations. However, the process of perceiving feelings through their modulations entails analysis of the modulations in their present moment context. In other words, conscious and unconscious involvement are needed to notice these processes. Sometimes the modulations provide reassurance or comfort, for oneself or for someone else, for example, when the underlying feeling is Fear. The Fear is expressed as a comforting 'don't worry, it will be fine'. Sometimes the action modulation is an angry expletive or snide comment. The modulation might also be an urge to Care or a caring act. One common modulation of a Panic/Grief feeling is to enact Care for someone else.

Repression and the unconscious

Another of these actions is the mental action of repression into the unconscious. In the unconscious, feelings and thoughts are away from direct awareness. The unconscious also has some logics of its own. Perhaps 'psycho-logical' is a good word for unconscious processes. Ignacio Matte Blanco (1988) wrote about the unconscious in terms of mathematics, and for him, in the unconscious, time does not exist. Feelings from the past can be felt, evoked, in the present moment as if they belong to that moment. Matte Blanco also described unconscious logic as 'symmetrical', which means that cause and effect are interchangeable. Man bites dog is the same as dog bites man. Caring for you is the same as caring for me. Conscious processes are usually termed as logical and are asymmetrical. Dreams, slips of the tongue and re-enactments in relationships are all communications from the unconscious into conscious awareness. However, they are disguised. They require analysis. An overemphasis on detachment leads to processes that involve repressing feelings from the present and from the past into the unconscious.

This is where detachment is not enough to make dialogue work. Involvement through self and other knowledge is also required along with the detachment that expresses curiosity about meaning and process. We need to be in touch with how the here-and-now feels (involvement) as well as to be curious about what it means (detachment). All this happens in the moment, which is a complexity, but is also capable of being understood, once the moment has been expanded into a process. In psychoanalysis and group analysis, the experience of 'transference' from figures and relationships experienced in the past is brought into the consulting room as a projective process. The practice of tracking 'countertransference', the therapist's feelings in relation to the patient or client, is also an example of these processes. These projective processes are going on all the time between people in everyday life as well as being distilled and observed in psy professional consulting rooms.

Panksepp's (1998) foundational feelings and their interactions are one place to start to understand both the involvement and the detachment required for dialogue. Of the seven foundational feelings proposed by Panksepp, the most foundational was the first feeling that has taken the place of the reward and punishment system proposed by the behaviourists. The reward and punishment system and the black box brain were ideas asserted by the psy professional behaviourists. They are now an important part of neoliberal ideology. Alternatively, for Panksepp, the first foundational feeling is Seeking, the feeling of life. Seeking is also linked to Freud's (1920) ideas about libido and, perhaps also, to the 'death instinct' in an understanding of how its absence is as important to humans as its presence.

While Seeking is not a feeling that is traditionally named as a feeling, it is instantly recognisable. The Seeking foundational feeling is homeostatic and based on the neuropeptide dopamine. It can vary from euphoria on the positive side of too much Seeking, to the total lack of Seeking, which is felt as depression, sadness and grief. Seeking subsides with consumption of what has been sought. Consumption ideally leads to satisfaction, as when eating a good meal that quells a hunger. Like hunger, though, Seeking returns with time. In its normal homeostatic state, Seeking is always active in the background, even when combined with sleep. All learning is based on Seeking.

Maintaining awareness of losing and restoring seeking

Tracking the Seeking feeling is one way into the unconscious through feelings. Tracking Seeking is an analytic and dialectic process. What follows is how thinking and maintaining awareness of the conscious Seeking feeling can help preserve contact with the realities of an individual's relationship to their environments. An individual's relationship to their environments is mostly awareness of their social/group environment of other people, their reality. Seeking is an indication of the involvement part of the process. 'What does this mean for me?' An individual can feel the loss and return of the Seeking feeling in relation to what is happening to them in their environment in the here-and-now. All the other foundational feelings have their specific effects on Seeking. The loss and gain of the Seeking feeling and its relationship to the other foundational feelings defines each person's unique emotional reality in that moment.

Seeking can be lost at the extremes in two ways, both of which are felt as disturbances. On the euphoria end of the feeling, when the Seeking urge does not provide the expected results, Panksepp observed something that he called 'auto-shaping'. In auto-shaping, animals looked like they were trying to produce the desired outcome as if by magic. In humans, this might be thought of as fixed ideas, obsession-compulsion or the loss of a process of testing reality, often just by asking questions and hearing answers. Loss of reality testing involves losing a sense of a process by which the close connection between what is going on inside and what is going on outside is broken. This can happen in the psychiatric professional diagnoses of schizophrenia, mania, denial, obsessions, compulsions and other fixed ideas. Euphoria also has its attractions and is a way of defending against or denying some of the more painful feelings that influence Seeking. It is defence from pain by overstimulation. Sometimes it is difficult to give up the mania because that means facing unbearable pain.

The foundational feelings of Fear and Rage diminish or stop Seeking. These are both feelings that are disturbing, unpleasant and sometimes dangerous. However, they are also essential communications from the human environment, which is most often other humans, and interpreted through learning from past experience. Fear and pain promote learning about bad things in the human environment. These can lead to fight, flight and freeze urges. Social Care and reassurance, from inside or outside, modulate and mitigate Fear and Rage. If these are not available, then addictions can also restore Seeking.

In all cases, it is the frustration, deprivation or destruction of Seeking by other means that is the disturbing factor and the restoration of Seeking that is the desired factor. Addictions, narcissism and greed are conditions or social feelings where there is no point of satisfaction. In these conditions, Seeking is never allowed to stop or rest. Social disturbances like addictions, narcissism and greed might be thought of as modulations or defences against losing Seeking through Fear and Rage. Addictions can include drugs, especially opiates, gambling, sex, and sexual obsession. Rage and the urge to excessive power over self and others, including revenge, are also disturbances of Seeking and defences against the disturbances. When Seeking is working to enable people to be open to the outside without having to defend, close off or be overwhelmed, Seeking feels like the capacity for happiness, for satisfaction, for satisfactory activities and for rest. These are the feelings of liberation. All of these feelings are emotionally contagious. Sometimes others can better see and feel the feelings on the euphoria end of Seeking. The restoration of Seeking feels like relief, no matter how Seeking is recouped after loss. On the depression end of Seeking, modulating and mitigating are also difficult. Humans are the only creatures who can lose Seeking and go on living. This is because humans are preserved by the care of other humans when the feeling of life is absent. It is more basic for humans to preserve life than to take it. The reason that Seeking is an experience-near concept is that its ebb and flow, especially in relation to Panic/Grief and loss, is consciously and continuously felt.

Seeking is value free. This creates some confusion in the psy professions and this aspect of Seeking is exploited by neoliberalism. If it feels OK, then it is OK in neoliberalism. However, some restorations of Seeking for self and others contribute to positive consequences for self and others and some strategies for the restoration of Seeking contribute to negative consequences for self and others. Addictions are one example of actions that lead to negative consequences, but restore the feelings. Hatred and revenge restore Seeking from the feeling of Rage, but also lead to negative consequences for self and others. Narcissism maintains Seeking but steals energy and life from others for the maintenance of self. Greed is a similar process of maintenance and extraction. Seeking is value free. However, some values are needed to promote life and growth, rather than extraction and death in the group dimension. These are the values that are absent in Neoliberalism. They are a fundamental part of the group dimension that defines humanity.

Individuals as group nodes, where all voices need to be beard: Group analysis

Every individual is unique in their own reality, as in the view taken above. Every individual is also a node in matrices, networks and figurations of groups in the modern world. As a node that carries these networks, each individual, in their unique reality, also carries pieces of the groups in their lives. The groups are not complete without all the pieces or fragments, the individuals in them, being voiced and known at any specific moment. Conversely, each voice in groups is only one piece of the depth of conscious and unconscious connections that are being made in that moment of that group. Each person speaking in a group is speaking for themselves and also for others. In the modern world, where an individual might belong to several groups simultaneously, the task of remaining integrated is a major emotional achievement. Belonging to groups that are integrated, coherent and capable of dialogue makes this task easier. The group members together accomplish this. It is not always easy, but liberation is dependent upon it. Working together cooperatively and the continuation of difficult dialogue in the polis are also dependent upon coherence and integration.

Much of what follows about groups has originated in group analytic, as well as in psychoanalytic, consulting rooms. Group analysts spend their time observing people in groups, as well as facilitating their communications, conscious and unconscious, with each other. Group analytic groups are discrete entities with well-defined boundaries of meeting and confidentiality. They thus capture, in part, the sense of the whole world happening in the group, as in the example of the San people in Chapter 6 of this book. People who come to group analytic groups are those who have lost their sense of liberation and are intent on finding it again in positive and social ways. The concepts that have formed and come out of these encounters between therapists and group members are, at the same time, unique to analytic groups and general in everyday group life, which is formative and formed by the emotional, social and political life of individuals.

These group analytic concepts will be unfamiliar to most people. This is because group analysis is comparatively new. Psychoanalysis, barely more than fifty years older, rejected groups and became the study of individuals existing in isolation and inside their heads. Elias termed this '*Homo clausus*'. Psychoanalysis became the treatment of people in dyads, the therapeutic couple. Freud followed a sociologist called Gustave Le Bon (1896) who saw groups as produced by the 'dangerous classes' involved in the French Revolution and the Paris Commune. The French Revolution called for maximum freedom for the abstract individual. Le Bon influenced Freud's group texts, *Totem and Taboo* (1913) and *Group Psychology and the Analysis of the Ego* (1921). Le Bon, writing before and during the First World War, developed ideas about the 'psychological crowd'. The phenomenon of the psychological crowd was that it created a collective unconscious or group mind that robbed every individual member of their opinions, values and beliefs.

This 'group mind' was based on anonymity and contagion. Anonymity facilitated a loss of personal responsibility where each individual person yielded to the instincts of their unconscious mind and followed their emotions. Contagion, for Le Bon, occurred when individuals sacrificed their personal interests for the collective interest. Both these processes increased the suggestibility of the crowd and susceptibility to the strong voices produced by it. Like Freud, Hitler and Mussolini also read Le Bon's writings. Le Bon's ideas were part of the legacy of the First World War. Groups became identified with the mindless mob. Riots were the language of the unheard.

It was only during the Second World War that the smaller group processes became an object of thought and study. The unconscious and taken-for-granted groups, which were always there, started to become more visible. Of course, they were always there, in the Church, the armed forces, the family, friendship and work groups, the pub, identity groups, national and tribal groups. As this work has shown, groups are the important element of human emotional life. Up until the Second World War, however, they were virtually ignored and considered dangerous as an object of therapy, study and thought. Groups were taken for granted and, thus, have been operating in the unconscious, powerfully affecting social and political processes, as well as lives, without being open to reflection.

The Northfield Experiments: The group analytic moment

This changed during the Second World War. There were some lessons from the First World War and the period between the wars that laid the ground for what might be called the 'group analytic moment'. This term has been used by Dieter Nitzgen (2008) who has contributed substantially to an understanding of how this moment came about. The group analytic moment centres on what has become known as the Northfield Experiments.

The ideas behind Northfield started with W. H. R. Rivers. Rivers was a psychiatrist who treated 'shell shock neurosis' in the First World War. It was understood that once soldiers had left the battlefield, it was unlikely that they would return. Northfield was a rehabilitation unit in Birmingham UK and was a place of return and treatment of soldiers with severe non-psychotic mental disorders. Northfield had a medical wing and a military wing. John Rickman, a psychoanalyst, arrived in 1942, sent by the military. Rickman had studied with Rivers and had been psychoanalysed by Freud and by Melanie Klein. He was a Quaker, a conscientious objector and had driven an ambulance in the First World War (Coombe, 2020).

Rivers and Rickman represented one element of the group analytic moment. They represented the psychoanalytic element. Rickman soon brought in what Tom Harrison (1999) has called the 'Invisible College'. These were medical psychoanalysts from the Tavistock Clinic, both before and after the war. Wilfred Bion (1961) was part of the 'Invisible College'. Rickman had been Bion's training analyst. Bion's parents were diplomats and he spent his early childhood, from the age of 8, in boarding school. At 21, he was a tank commander in the First World War and afterwards taught at boarding school before training as a psychoanalyst. In 1942, before he went to Northfield, Bion had been involved in an experiment using small group situations for selecting officer candidates for the War Office. At Northfield, Bion recognised that the army was made up of groups and he wanted to remind the men that they were soldiers. Before Bion, most of the treatments were by sedative medication. Bion devised a group treatment whereby the soldiers were all in a battle against their neuroses. It was thus important to keep up a good group spirit. These ideas were combined with a passive, Quaker-style leadership, or no leadership, and an emphasis on the here and now. Democracy and ideas around community involvement as therapy were in the mix.

Also in the mix were the ideas of the American Kurt Lewin, where the group-as-a-whole was the unit of observation and analysis. Every individual in the group acted out of a field of forces. In his practice, Bion spoke in the group only very rarely. He analysed only his relationship with the group-as-a-whole, as if the group were an individual into which each of the individual group members fitted in various positions of leadership and followership (Hinshelwood, 2018).

Bion's basic assumption: The assumption of dependency

When Bion wrote about groups later, published in 1961 as *Experiences in Groups and Other Papers*, he described his 1948 post-war experience of being asked to take therapeutic groups by the Professional Committee of the Tavistock Clinic. What Bion first met when he 'took' the groups, was the assumption of dependence on the leader of the group and a feeling of entitlement to leadership on the part of the group participants. Frustrated dependence might be likened to frustrated Seeking. Bion went on to describe three patterns in the group that he called 'basic assumptions'. These basic assumptions are something like Panksepp's auto-shaping in that they do not have any specific sense of an effect on reality. Bion's basic assumptions were: dependence, fight and flight, and pairing. They all get in the way of the group doing the work that the group is meant to do together cooperatively. Bion described the basic assumptions as always being just under the surface of the group at work.

Bion's basic assumptions were defined as being instinctual or emotional dynamics that get in the way of doing good cooperative work in groups. The consequences of his techniques of group leadership, however, brought more disturbance than therapy. They illustrated the presence of disturbance under the surface of groups, but they did not contribute to better understanding of how these disturbances might be ameliorated or made useful. The combination of passive leadership, long silences from a position of denial of leadership, combined with the encyclopaedic interpretations about the group-as-a-whole only in relation to the leader, brought with it a high level of anxiety. The high level of anxiety caused angry outbursts, sometimes directed at the group leader. The leader was often removed from the group room physically by the group. Bion groups were not pleasant places to be. What Bion groups did show is that groups can be dangerous and anxious places. Bion only emphasised what was already the received wisdom about groups.

Bion and Rickman pursued their experiment for six weeks. The combination of passive leadership and the pressure to self-discipline meant that the soldiers' behaviours spiralled out of control. The idea was that order would be spontaneously restored by the soldiers assuming responsibilities for themselves and for their groups. The men themselves would restore control, theoretically, by a process of detachment from their need for dependence. Before this happened, the military lost patience and asked Bion and Rickman to leave.

S. H. Foulkes and the second Northfield Experiment

The experiments were not finished, however. In 1944, the second Northfield Experiment began with S. H. Foulkes, Harold Bridger and Tom Main. S. H. Foulkes considered himself a civilian, even though he had a military rank. He had served in communications with the German Army in the First World War. Foulkes was born in Karlsruhe in 1898, the youngest of five children. His father was a timber merchant who loved Wagner and who named all his children after Wagnerian characters (Nitzgen, 2014). Foulkes was named after Sigmund, an especially complex Wagnerian character. Foulkes was told that he was an unwanted child by his mother who had a difficult confinement with him and was unable to nurse him, so he had a wet nurse. He was the one in the family who did not belong.

As 'Dr Heinz Fuchs', S. H. Foulkes completed his psychoanalytic training in Vienna. He worked in the same building as the Institute for Social Research, what became known as the Frankfurt School. There, he knew Norbert Elias and Karl

Mannheim and their sociological ideas. It is unclear how much Foulkes was influenced by the Frankfurt School. It is clear, though, that the Frankfurt School was a crucible of progressive ideas made possible by the socialist revolution in Russia in 1917 and the failure of the socialist revolution in Germany in 1919. A combination of Marxist economics, politics and psychoanalysis were deeply embedded in the ideas that developed from the Frankfurt School. 'The actual dynamics of society, the rate of social change, cannot be derived from the economy alone, but depends on the specificity of cultural institutions and even special effects of these on personality structure' (Piccone, 1982 [1988], p. vii). These were the ideas that obviously influenced Elias, who worked with Mannheim at the Frankfurt School when Foulkes was there and, later, directly with Foulkes in the UK in the early days of group analysis after the war.

One element of the ideas that Foulkes brought with him to the UK was that the group is more fundamental than the individual, an idea echoed in the group dimension work here. Another was the idea of an expanded unconscious and the important distinction between the not knowing due to repression and the not knowing which is simply out of consciousness.

In 1933, Adolf Hitler became Chancellor of Germany. Foulkes, with his family, left Germany in order to avoid surrendering his passport, a requirement made of Jews in Germany at that time. Foulkes had stayed in Germany long enough to witness first-hand the 'successful' group dynamics of the Nazi takeover. Nitzgen maintains that Foulkes never desired a return to Germany.

Foulkes began his private practice in Exeter in 1937 and completed training in the UK in 1938; he also changed his name again to the final version. Nitzgen (2014) speculates that this last name change was a sort of declaration of his commitment to groups, as Foulkes is pronounced 'Folks' in German. In 1940, he was facilitating his first psychoanalytic group in his private consulting rooms in Exeter. Foulkes is credited with being the first group therapist in the UK (Hinshelwood, 2018). By 1944 he was leading the second Northfield Experiment. He published his first paper on groups, also in 1944 and stayed at Northfield until 1946.

Among the second group of experimenters at Northfield, Foulkes was the most experienced therapist of groups. He let the patients organise themselves. He did very little therapy but went between the groups to lend a hand. There were other activities in the hospital and Tom Main instituted a total culture of enquiry involving everyone in the unit in the work of analysis and rehabilitation. This moment is credited with being the first therapeutic community.

Communication is the therapy: Free-floating discussion

Working together on these activities at Northfield revealed many conflicts. Foulkes approached the group-as-a-whole in a completely different way from Bion. Foulkes had wanted to be a neural psychologist at one point in his life and understood how the human cerebral cortex works with networks, neurons and nodal points. This understanding was one of the bases of his theories. Foulkes emphasised the patterns of communication between individuals in the group as well as between the group and himself. The leader of the group is also a node in the group. This was a completely different approach from Bion's. For Foulkes, patterns of communication included unconscious communication and they were generalised to all the members of the groups, including the conductors. As a psychoanalyst, it was these patterns of communication that he wanted to facilitate. So, while Bion had a more military idea of the task at Northfield, Foulkes followed with a more psychoanalytic and social idea of the task. Foulkes took elements of psychoanalysis into thinking about what was going on in groups with a view to using groups for therapy. This, too, was a different sort of project from Bion's. Foulkes understood that the group was in the individuals, as much as the individuals were in the group. For Foulkes, the key to understanding and treatment was in a form of free association that he called 'free-floating discussion'. The neurotic was out of key with the group but could be brought back into communication as an individual who could express their individuality in the group context. This was the therapy with healing power because it was social healing.

From 1945, Foulkes led weekly seminars on group therapy at Northfield. There were 15–16 members, which included the majority of the psychiatrists who had groups on their wards. One of the things that the psychiatrists learned from each other was that the groups penetrated the psychiatrists, as much as they penetrated the patients. The facilitators were also group members, but members with special responsibilities.

Psy practitioners from the first Northfield Experiment, influenced by Bion, were still in the services. Thus, there were two different approaches to groups in the seminars, those from the first experiment and those from the second. Tensions and conflicts built up from the two different approaches and they led to the gradual decline of the seminar. Instead of being able to dialogue, the psychiatrists and psychoanalysts of the two currents of the Northfield Experiments simply turned away from each other, leaving two separate and polarised bodies of group theory. This is another example of Elias's double-bind figurations: this specific double-bind kept the two group theories separate and apparently in competition with each other. It might be speculated that they needed the group dimension to bring them into dialogue.

In the interests of maximising connection and integration between these theories, it is relevant that there was a third figure at Northfield, Patrick De Maré (De Maré, Piper and Thompson, 1991). De Maré was part of both the first and second Northfield Experiments. He qualified as a doctor in 1941 and was trained by Rickman and Bion in the first Northfield Experiment. However, he then spent most of the war working in exhaustion centres on the front lines. The aim of the exhaustion centres was to keep the soldiers at the front and engaged in war. The main idea was that the experiences of war were not totally unspeakable but were largely inaudible. The exhaustion centres used groups to create new social links through speech and hearing, emerging from the absolute isolation of the battlefield. In these centres the only possible response to mass violence was collective dialogue.

De Maré brought these experiences to Northfield, joining Foulkes near the end of the war. He was surprised and critical of Foulkes because there were no large groups at Northfield. For de Maré, Foulkes carried the large group around in his person. For Foulkes, the large group did not represent any dynamics that were different from the small group. At the end of the war, Bion and the others from the 'Invisible College' returned to the Tavistock Clinic. Foulkes, Main, Bridger and de Maré, along with others, like Norbert Elias and Ilse Seglow, both from the days of the Frankfurt School, founded the Group Analytic Society in 1952. This is how currents of group thinking and theorising have become separate and have stayed institutionally separated.

De Maré championed the large group and its dynamics in the new Group Analytic Society. He defined the role of large group convenor as different from the small group conductor. The convenor of a large group encourages freedom of dialogue. The convenor also makes interpretations about the nature of the social and cultural pressures in the group as on a different level from those of a more personal and historical emphasis. For de Maré, the large group was identical to the field of the investigation of conscious interactions, differentiating it from the small groups where the dynamics were those of the family. This is what he had learned from the exhaustion centres. The traumatic effects of panic, grief and mental pain combined with hatred, anger and fear, to liberate the energy needed to be able to dialogue as a brotherhood, which he called 'Koinonia', after the Greek word. De Maré's use of koinonia is closely related to Arendt's use of polis. Like Bion, however, and different from Foulkes, de Maré emphasised the negative emotions and the feelings of utter isolation that can happen in groups, along with the necessity of their recognition and resolution to attain dialogue.

Synthesis in the group dimension: Group size as silo

Patrick de Maré's ideas about working with large, standalone and continuous large groups never worked out. Large groups have been held most effectively when they are embedded in courses and workshops. Where there are small groups before and after the large groups, the disturbing dynamics of the large size of the groups can be contained and reflected upon outside the groups themselves. De Maré ended up working with what he called 'median groups'. Foulkes, however, maintained his scepticism about the effect of the size of the group on its dynamics. In fact, Foulkes has been quoted as saying that it is the conductor that makes the group dramatic or traumatic, not the size. Most recent writings in the area of applied group analysis agree with Foulkes' position. The dynamics of the groups are the same, whatever the size of the group. The emotional impact of the size of the group on the dynamics of the feelings of the group members are relative to each other. In other words, a small group can be as terrifying to someone unused to, or traumatised by groups, as large groups are to people who are more at ease and have had good experiences in groups (Thornton, 2019).

It may be that the size of the group has become a kind of silo in which to store some aspects of group analytic dynamics which could help to maximise connection and integration between the ideas of Bion, Foulkes, de Maré and also, later, the anti-group of Morris Nitsun (1996).

It has become clear from this review of the events around the Group Analytic Moment at Northfield, and those that followed, that Foulkes brought his ideas into the crucible of Northfield nearly fully formed. Foulkes had formed his ideas about groups before he arrived at Northfield and he was not going to be swayed from them by others. The other ideas that he met at Northfield were about continuing the war and conflict mentality as group metaphors. They were the accepted ideas about groups. Foulkes' contribution came from somewhere else: the crucible of the Group Analytic Moment, the Frankfurt School, embodied in Norbert Elias and Ilse Seglow, together with Foulkes' own experiments and experiences.

In effect, what Foulkes was looking to find and convey was that groups were not only a place of war and conflict. Foulkes wanted to investigate how they could be convened, facilitated, and conducted, in such a way as to accomplish the maximisation of connection and integration, as contrasted with simple cohesion, aggregation and massification (Hopper, 2002). The maximisation of connection and integration are the ingredients that are needed to resolve conflicts, heal wounds and to produce collective working and decision-making. The maximisation of connection and integration are needed to encourage the democratic re-invention of the polis. The maximisation of connection and integration is crucial for keeping people together in rooms with the possibility of dialogue.

Foulkes found the group space for personal and social integration: The heart of the group dimension

For Foulkes, this is the therapy. Foulkes was looking to find the positive integration in human groups that also facilitated internal integration for each human group member. This was Foulkes' greatest contribution. He found the techniques that created the group space in which the personal and the social integrate in and between individuals. He found this space and he protected it from other, more conflictual, ideas. He found the space in which groups are therapeutic and capable of attaining the liberation of the reconnection of individuals to each other in the group dimension. Group analysts and group analytic group members experience the power of the therapeutic group space. They also participate and witness how people work to heal themselves and each other through connection and communication. This is what Foulkes knew and brought to the Northfield Experiments and then to the Group Analytic Society (GAS), later, to the Institute of Group Analysis (IGA).

It is important to keep this 'good' group space in mind, of course. The good group space is at the heart of the group dimension. However, it is also important to bring back and highlight the 'bad' or negative conflicts that occur in groups all the time. The blurring of the focus on these more difficult or negative aspects of groups in group analysis has limited group analysis to a purely therapeutic silo. Conflicts are not absent in group analysis. However, there are levels in which conflicts are very carefully avoided. The avoidance of conflict, one of the consequences of the more Foulkesian ideas, including 'trust the group', keep group analysis from entering the world of ideas about everyday life, politics and experiences.

Bion's ideas about the basic assumptions in groups, which are dependency, rage (fight), fear (flight) and pairing, and de Maré's ideas about hatred, panic and grief in large groups must be included and considered, along with Nitsun's ideas about the anti-group. This integration is more evident and necessary now that we have the background of the group dimension. In the group dimension, groups are the focus of everyday life and responsible for the formation of the integrated human individual. What Foulkes has made possible is the conscious understanding of groups and their dynamics in people's lives, in the processes of liberation, continuous reform and continuous revolution. This understanding has not been possible before now. It needed the group dimension to distinguish the different levels of human evolution in groups and their enduring importance in the much more complex societies that we have built for ourselves.

For Nitzgen (2008), Foulkes made the decisive step away from psychoanalysis in 1948 when he brought the community into the consulting room. Foulkes showed that both social conflict and personal repression form the contents of the unconscious. This means that the community, as well as the family, are accessed through Foulkes' version of free association. Foulkes called his version of free association 'free-floating conversation'. This modification made it the task of small therapy groups to access all conscious and unconscious connections. In therapy groups, the minds of strangers respond to each other with instinctive understanding, contagion and empathy. In groups and group fractions in everyday life these responses are also always happening. The appearance that individuals exist in isolation, in other words, is a fallacy.

References

Bion, W. (1961) *Experiences in Groups, and Other Papers*. Hove: Brunner-Routledge.
Coombe, P. (2020) 'The Northfield Experiments: A Reappraisal 70 Years On', *Group Analysis*, 53(2): 162–176.
De Maré, P., Piper, R. and Thompson, S. (1991) *Koinonia: From Hate through Dialogue, to Culture and the Large Group*. London: Karnac Books.
Elias, N. (1987) *Involvement and Detachment*. Oxford: Blackwell.
Elias, N. (1994) *The Civilizing Process*. Oxford: Blackwell.
Freud, S. (1913 [1912–1913]) 'Totem and Taboo', in J. Strachey (ed.), *The Standard Edition of the Complete Psychological Works of Sigmund Freud*, Vol. XIII. London: Hogarth Press and Institute of Psycho-Analysis.
Freud, S. (1920) 'Beyond the Pleasure Principle', in J. Strachey (ed.), *The Standard Edition of the Complete Psychological Works of Sigmund Freud*, Vol. XVIII. London: Hogarth Press and the Institute of Psycho-Analysis.
Freud, S. (1921) 'Group Psychology and the Analysis of the Ego', in J. Strachey (ed.), *The Standard Edition of the Complete Psychological Works of Sigmund Freud*, Vol. XVIII. London: The Hogarth Press and the Institute of Psycho-Analysis
Foulkes, S. H. (1948) *Introduction to Group-analytic Psychotherapy: Studies in the Social Integration of Individuals and Groups*. London: Maresfield Reprints.

Goodall, J. (1988) *In The Shadow Of Man*. London: *Phoenix* Giants.
Harrison, T. (1999) *Bion, Rickman, Foulkes and the Northfield Experiments: Advancing on a Different Front*. London: Jessica Kingsley.
Hinshelwood, R. D. (2018) 'Northfield for Ever', *Group Analysis*, 51(4): 434–441.
Hopper, E. (2002) *The Social Unconscious: Selected Papers*. London: Jessica Kingsley.
Kohut, H. (1971) *The Analysis of the Self: A Systematic Approach to the Psychoanalytic Treatment of Narcissistic Personality Disorders*. New York: International Universities Press.
Le Bon, G. (1896) *The Crowd: A Study of the Popular Mind*. London: Ernest Benn Ltd.
Matte Blanco, I. (1988) *Thinking, Feeling, and Being*. London: Routledge.
Nitsun, M. (1996) *The Anti-Group: Destructive Forces in the Group and their Creative Potential*. London: Routledge.
Nitzgen, D. (2008) 'The Group Analytic Moment Sixty Years on: Revisiting 'Introduction to Group Analytic Psychotherapy' by S. H. Foulkes', *Group Analysis*, 41(4): 319–340.
Nitzgen, D. (2014) 'Lost in Translation? Reading Foulkes Today', *Group Analysis*, 47(3): 213–226.
Panksepp, J. (1998) *Affective Neuroscience: The Foundations of Human and Animal Emotions*. Oxford: Oxford University Press.
Piccone. P. (1982 [1998]) 'Introduction' in A. Arato and E. Gebhardt (eds), *The Essential Frankfurt School Reader*, pp. viii–ix. New York: Continuum.
Power, M. (1991) *The Egalitarians – Human and Chimpanzee: An Anthropological View of Social Organization*. Cambridge: Cambridge University Press.
Thornton, C. (2019) (ed.) *The Art and Science of Working Together: Practising Group Analysis in Teams and Organizations*. London: Routledge.

Chapter 12

The role of groups in everyday life
Synthesis with Panksepp

The role of groups in everyday life and the increased consciousness of groups and their dynamics is a great discovery in the group dimension. S. H. Foulkes contributed a set of concepts about group dynamics and Panksepp's findings add other layers of understanding through which to view the concepts that Foulkes proposed for understanding groups. The keys that bring these ideas together into useful formulations are the foundational feelings. In terms of therapy and communications, the naming of feelings and their contagious nature together create conscious and unconscious connections between people, fractions of groups and groups. They also create connections through time.

Thinking reflectively and analytically about these conscious and unconscious connections is needed to produce the understanding necessary to identify, dissolve and resolve Elias's double-bind configurations and other kinds of conflicts. In practice, as we know in the psy professions, the curative here-and-now moment of emotional healing happens when a feeling is named, spoken and heard. This is what therapists witness in their consulting rooms. Different kinds of therapists might have different names, images or languages for the impact of this connection. Klein (1986) and her followers refer to the naming of projections and introjections as 'part-objects' with body descriptions as metaphors. Freudian psychoanalysts refer to 'mutative interpretations' (Strachey, 1934). Other analytic psychotherapists discuss these moments as 'emotionally corrective experience'. Group analysts might refer to emotional processes that are being shared in a group. Again, these processes are not limited to consulting rooms. We know about these processes because our patients teach us about them and bring them to the consulting room from their everyday lives to be heard, understood and thus transformed. These projective processes happen all the time in everyday life, often named as 'love' and sometimes as 'hate'. The nature of the connection, though, is communication. For Foulkes (1948), it is the communication that is the therapy.

Communication starts with the foundational feelings. These feelings are conscious and contagious. The feelings happen in the present here-and-now moment and sometimes only last a fraction of a second, particularly if they are to become repressed or projected for individual, social, cultural or power reasons. All feelings are a connection with the environment, which, for humans, is essentially, the

DOI: 10.4324/9781003350088-18

human environment. However, it is not always clear what it is in the environment that produced the feeling. The feelings themselves have no clear cause or object. This is true especially in the rich and complex environment that is the human group inside and outside the human being. The foundational feelings are, in fact, a non-specific warning. When a feeling happens, it often must be captured and named before it disappears, becomes projected, denied, disavowed or repressed for whatever reason.

Naming the feeling

When the feeling is captured and named, it can be communicated and reflected upon in solitary thought and in thoughts and conversations with others. The naming is important. In capitalism, humans are trained to disavow, reject, project, ignore, and repress feelings, in favour of all forms of cognitive thinking. The psy professions, even those that recognise the importance of feelings in practice have not challenged this. This is the importance of Panksepp and his understanding of how the foundational feelings alert humans to what is happening in their environments.

The foundational feeling motivates thinking and combines with thinking to both modulate and express the feeling. Thinking alone cannot produce the necessary physical/emotional charge that we need to understand what it is that is happening to us in the world. The accurate name of the feeling is its container (Bion, 1961). Without the name, the feeling is wild and chaotic. Bion called these feeling 'beta elements'. When the feeling can be named and contained, it becomes suitable for internal and external communication. These more contained feelings become 'alpha elements'.

These are the 'alpha elements' of Foulkes's concepts of the communication that is the therapy. Foulkes speaks about this as the symptom murmuring to itself in isolation. The therapy includes the naming and the communication of the symptom in the free-floating discussion, where it is shared with others and the group member is no longer left alone with it. The feeling named and shared also becomes part of the conscious and unconscious dynamics that are happening between people in the external and internal group of the group's members. It becomes an emotional element and a voice among others.

Communicating feelings in groups adds another level that Foulkes called 'resonance'. In resonance, the contagion of the communicated feeling reverberates around the group, touching and evoking feelings that have associated evocations and meanings in every group member. This property of resonance feeds and expands the free-floating discussion into a symphony or cascade of interrelated communications that are rich in both empathy and association. To use a musical metaphor, a note can become a melody or even a symphony. The resonance of the feeling opens a condensed space of unconscious and conscious connections that can inform the reality of the present moment in the group. These moments can be both intimate and conflictual. These are two of the Foulkesian concepts of 'resonance' and 'condensation' related to finding the 'location of the disturbance.'

The location of the disturbance

Naming the feeling is not always easy. Most people have become deskilled in distinguishing thoughts from feelings, for a start. Often, people offer thoughts when asked for feelings. When feelings can be recognised and named, they often appear to be about, or to originate in, other individuals. An example of this is 'You (they) made me feel …'. Another example is the use of the concept of 'triggering'. In 'triggering', the feeling is assumed to come from the event that evoked it. When the evoking event is avoided, the more analytic questions about the dynamics of the 'triggering' are difficult or impossible to ask. The idea of 'triggering', which implies the foundational feelings of Fear, Rage and Panic/Grief, ends in an avoidance which becomes part of a set of restrictive solutions to emotional problems, as compared to facilitative solutions, which imply the possibility of curiosity combined with communication (Stock Whittaker, 2000). Making these feelings bearable to become part of communication can be aided or hampered by others in internal and external groups. When avoiding the 'triggering' urge, Care takes the form of protection and the cascade of communication and connection is interrupted. Sometimes this is necessary, as with young children, but it does not facilitate other kinds of Care based on resonance.

Some of the specific qualities of the foundational feelings, contagion and lack of obvious object, cause or value, give rise to most of the ideas about 'projective processes' as developed in the psy professions. These are especially important in psychoanalysis and the disciplines related to it, which include group analysis. The 'projective processes' refer a whole range of concepts that describe how feelings are disavowed, disowned and denied by putting them onto and into others. In effect, unconscious projective processes are forms of repression.

Projective processes as forms of communication

Projective processes are used as markers for some psychiatric diagnoses, like borderline personality disorder. In borderline personality disorder it is accepted that excessive use of projective processes causes disturbances internally and in relationships. Projective processes can, though, also be understood as forms of communication where the feelings, in 'beta' form, are projected when the words cannot be found. This is because they can be perceived, felt and analysed between people, as projection, projective identification, transference, countertransference, resonance, scapegoating and introjection.

Others can help find and name feelings when they are difficult to find and express. This is because the feelings are contagious. Because they are contagious, they can be felt empathically too. Because feelings are contagious and can be projected, they can be found, named, identified, analysed and integrated between people. For Foulkes, this constituted therapy. For the group dimension, this is the liberation because the feelings then become available for communication, integration and dialogue. What belongs to me? What belongs to you? How are we doing this together by co-creation? These are some of the understandings that have been produced and theorised in the practice of the psy professions. These are the processes that are happening all the time in everyday social life, consciously and unconsciously, and that are open to facilitative curiosity, which indicates involvement, 'what does this mean for me as an individual?' and detachment, 'What does this mean for me and for you, each of us as one voice in a group or groups?' 'What does this mean for me in relation to the group and what does it mean for you?'

In the group dimension, people are encouraged to understand the feelings as fragments of group processes. In other words, a major question that arises from a feeling, and related to the concept of projective processes, is about its location. Where does it come from? What is the feeling about? Foulkes (1948) called this the 'location of the disturbance' in the group. The feeling is the disturbance. Not all feelings are disturbing, of course. When a feeling is disturbing, difficult or painful, it is especially important to find the root, or location, of the disturbance accurately. It is only when the location of the feelings can be accurately found that the feeling can be expressed, heard and understood as a fraction of a group, or groups, past and present. If relevant, appropriate and effective actions can be taken. It is the search for the location of the disturbance that brings in the other forms of projective processes that Foulkes identified in groups. These other forms of projective processes in group analysis include mirroring, resonance, scapegoating, communication and the idea that each group member speaks on behalf of the whole group. The whole group cannot be known without all the voices being heard, even the silent ones.

In the modern world, where groups are so often separated in time and space but also overlapping, the associations cut across layers of time. Where the strength and definition of the individual is defined by the way that they maintain and integrate their groups inside and outside, the groups most often only exist together inside the individual, who is the group participant node of a specific combination of groups.

There are several important points to be made here. Panksepp's foundational feelings pertain to the feelings that humans share with all mammals. They are in the midbrain. The foundational feelings are only one layer of the human feeling experience that contributes to a sense of a whole self. It is the sense of a whole and integrated self that liberates the feelings of power and strength to be oneself with others. In mammals, the next defining level of the species is when the basic foundational feelings of Seeking, Fear, Rage and Lust, meet and integrate with the social foundational feelings of Care, Panic/Grief and Play. These are present in mammals, but most developed in humans. These social foundational feelings have been identified as the beginning layer of the group dimension.

Layers of self in the group dimension

Humans have other layers. The foundational social feelings interact with the modulations from a cerebral cortex that is much more developed in humans than it is in mammals. It is in this combination of feelings with what humans call thoughts that define human urges, instincts, decisions-making and actions. The decisions and actions, including relationships, that come out of these processes distinguish humans from animals.

The decisions and actions, including relationships, that come out of these layers of feelings and through time also define humans as different from robots. Robots are built to make decisions and act only on cognitive knowledge. Robots admit to not having feelings, even when they are trying to be creative. Thus, although a robot can impersonate a modern human who has been trained in neoliberal capitalism not to be conscious of their layers of feelings or groups, a robot cannot be a human. Nor can a human be a robot. Even when feelings are repressed by projective processes and other defences, they do not go away. They are stored in internal and external compartments, sometimes well away from consciousness but acting always in the unconscious, creating urges and actions that might be difficult to understand, are un-canny or weird. They also become embedded in relationships with people and objects.

Unconscious combinations of cognitive and emotional layers are sometimes expressed in actions. These actions are called 'acting out'. Acting out, like the mumbled symptom 'beta element', is also a form of communication.

Humans always have these layers, whether repressed or not. Trying to act like a robot is deeply disturbing to humans, as evidenced in the 21st-century statistics on mental health. Neoliberalism is creating madness. Consequences include mental health crises, violence, mass shootings, war, crime, corruption and drugs. Humans are being driven mad by the neoliberal denial of society and the neoliberal denial of the importance of feelings, including the importance of feelings in political and economic life, and including the importance of the feelings that come from the basic power inequality of the capitalist and the worker, upon which capitalism is based.

Besides emotional and cognitive layers to human emotional, cognitive and action lives, group analysis has identified other layers that are important in the group dimension. In group analysis, these are expressed as the three layers of the matrix in groups. These group analytic layers are called foundational, personal and dynamic (Kinouani, 2019). Kinouani described these layers as part of her analysis of whiteness and how whiteness has become privileged throughout the layers of human emotional and unconscious life. Projective and destructive opportunities for projection feed into a social formation of difference, particularly of racial difference. In other words, for Kinouani (2019), whiteness created blackness to carry the unwanted and unacceptable, as defined in capitalist and colonial relationships. This dynamic exists on all levels of the group, from the foundational matrix layer, which is both the evolutionary and cultural layer, to the personal matrix layer of the family and then to the dynamic layer of the therapy group matrix.

Intersectionality

In the dynamic layer of the small therapy group, where the hope is that the trauma of racial difference can be heard and understood, it is often silenced. In the silence, some group members are 'othered', creating oppression, privilege and the re-traumatisation of racist experiences. In the small therapy group of group analysis, as well as in everyday face-to-face groups, the discomfort of having to face dynamics that might end in conflict and change is often privileged. This is silencing.

Alternatively, in the small therapy group, experiences of racism can be spoken and heard. There are always risks, with the open possibility of creating conflicts, avoidance and leaving the room. When the conflicts can be held in the room and become part of the conversation, mutual, emotional healing of racism is possible. Although these dynamics have been most developed around the issues of race, they are the same for issues around heteronormative patriarchy and other power, position, privilege and persecution that enter into groups because they are part of the group dimension in other layers.

What Kinouani and other Black and brown writers and group analysts are bringing to consciousness in group analysis is that, once Foulkes let the community into the group, the power and the political also entered. However, it has taken until now for this process to become conscious and accepted as protean. Because of this, the recognition and containment of conflict, often projected into larger groups, anti-groups and out of the small therapy group, needs to be brought back into general group thinking, reflection and into the definition of the role, power and position of the leader or group conductor.

Groups are places of the struggles for power and avoidance of powerlessness that must combat silencing of othering processes, particularly those emotional and political processes hiding behind the Foulkesian mantra of 'Trust the group'. Because of 'trust the group' the group members often turn away from potential conflicts, including those who are potentially silenced by the turning away and fear disturbing the group (Kent, 2021). This is a form of repression, based on projection and introjection as the location of the disturbance in a person or people. The bringing to consciousness of these dynamic relationships includes seeing how silencing and othering is co-created in internal and external relationships. In the modern world, the easiest form of repression is internal and external silencing. In silencing, certain voices are muted or ignored. A disturbing feeling, some voice of the group, might be silenced, disavowed, denied and ignored until evoked by internal and external events. Silence is never the solution (Nayak, 2014).

Kinouani (2019) worked with the idea of the matrix as it is now understood in group analysis. The group analytic idea of the matrix is a structural one. It is surrounded by the boundaries that have facilitated the projection of the more difficult and conflictual feelings and urges into larger and larger groups and anti-groups. The metaphor of the matrix has brought with it useful, therapeutic research and heuristic questions, as well as effective therapy. However, in the world outside the consulting, workshop and training rooms, where the individual is the node of combinations of groups and these groups are always in transformation, Foulkess' concept of the structural matrix is less useful and Elias's concept of figurations is more useful. Figurations emphasise the dynamic nature of group life in all the levels of human moment-to-moment experiencing. Structures only capture moments in time. In reality, processes seldom reproduce themselves exactly through time. Some processes and institutions change more slowly than others and some are not challenged to change. A lack of change might also mean that some processes are stopped by power differentials and by silencing. These ideas link also to Arendt's thoughts about how the consequences of actions are permanent and unpredictable.

How does this feel to the individual human group node in experience-near terms? Ralph Stacey (2003) took up the point of view of how it feels to be this node, yet able to think as part of the complexity of group dynamics and the different layers of self, self-understanding and self-expression. Stacey emphasised the transformational possibilities of change in the here-and-now moment, identified as communication in Foulkes. In interaction, people interpenetrate each other's habits, norms and conditioning through all levels of their groups and relationships, from back to their mothers and through generations of family groups, up to the present and their hopes and fears for the future. Feelings are constantly evoked, along with cognitive modulations, mitigations and urges. Some of these become actions, through words and deeds. When they become actions, they are open, in the moment, to real world responses. It is in the acceptance or denial of these real responses in their accurate momentary understandings, or, very often in their misunderstandings, through the prisms of the layers of self, that emotional and cognitive communications occur. Each time a memory is evoked, for example, it returns to memory, changed by the group and relationship context in which it appeared. If the memory is heard, and the person can hear that it is heard, then the person is no longer left alone with it, for example. This is the emotional healing as contrasted with the cognitive understanding of processes that is also part of therapy.

Thus, in order to understand and communicate a feeling, a complex process of identifying levels and the possibility of different group voices and evocations of responses to action, involvement and detachment are necessary, fully and accurately. Reflective processes are necessary to contain and dialogue over conflicts, particularly those of power and identity. Foulkes's concepts, that grow out of the location of the disturbance, are particularly helpful in this respect. Foulkes put the emphasis on the importance of feeling, thinking and deciphering feelings in the group dimension, even when they are confused as to location. Resonance, for example, invites thinking about how an interaction, understanding or event touches elements of self. Mirroring, a related concept, asks if feelings about another are making self or historic connections. Sometimes, particularly when people come to represent each other's mothers, for example, malignant mirroring can result, where it becomes very difficult for two people to stay in a room together (Zinkin, 1983). Translation is a process defined by Foulkes that entails making links between conscious and unconscious, between past and present, between the symptom and the feeling.

What happens, though, when the large group and the anti-group negative and destructive feelings are not kept out of smaller groups by matrices, boundaries and techniques of leadership? The feelings evoked in the human group nodes of failure of dependency, Rage and Fear, as in Bion's basic assumptions, become salient. De Maré asserts that isolation and the traumatic effects of Panic, Grief and mental pain combine with hatred, Rage and Fear in the large group and are also always present; they are also necessary for dialogue. Dialogue is required for the other forms of communication on all levels. These are not the experience-near concepts that are needed for the courage to stay in the moment-to-moment of difficult feelings in any context. However, the addition of the conscious feeling, the flow and ebb of Panksepp's Seeking feeling, brings with it a consciousness of how important power, and mitigations and modulations of power, become in the group dimension. When with people, or thinking about being with people, individual human group nodes can track the Seeking feeling, along with a recognition of what the ebb and flow of Seeking evokes, both in the past and in the present.

In groups, Seeking is often frustrated by others. If nothing else, this characteristic of groups is what makes them difficult and worthy of thought. Frustrated Seeking leads to Rage, which is without an object. This means that, although the Rage feelings are caused, perhaps most often, by the authorities and the powerful, they can be directed to the closest and more vulnerable person. Pain, which leads very quickly to learning about bad things and Fear, that lasts, is also without an object. Fear is often manifested with no obvious cause. This means that frequently, feelings do not show themselves in the locations in which they were produced. When these negative emotions, such as those described by Bion, de Maré, and the actions of the anti-groups, as identified by Nitsun, are linked to the way that these emotions interrupt and sometimes disable the Seeking feeling of life, power becomes most salient in the attempts to return to Seeking.

The psy professions discuss power, but little has been done to understand power as a kind of social feeling or as a feeling of relationship. In effect, power is produced and destroyed in every single human interaction. When Foulkes, Elias and Panksepp are combined in the group dimension, it has become apparent that power is not a possession or attribute, it is the stuff of human relationships and the interaction of feelings. As in Jane Goodall's chimpanzees and in Richard Lee's experience among the San tribes, power that promotes coherent relationships and power that destroys coherent relationships is at the root of the capacity to interact and dialogue. In groups, power is always being created, destroyed, balanced and mitigated. This is the stuff of creating and destroying equality. In the foundational feelings, power is felt as the creation or destruction of Seeking and is practiced in the emotional level of Play.

At the root of each unique human experience is the mixture of power and powerlessness in the experience of being a baby. As babies in groups, humans are all subjected to absolute powerlessness, dependence and a need for Care. Dependence and failed dependence are the first facts of human life. These dynamics are what Bion produced in his groups by withholding his leadership and creating frustrated Seeking expectations. In the social foundational feelings, Care is a power relationship. The Carer has the power but can choose to use it in the interests of the other, or not, for example. It might often be said that Caring is a reaction to powerlessness in the past. However, powerlessness in the past often contributes to a greed for power that cannot be satisfied. Greed is an example of power that has to be constantly renewed in order to be able to feel the life-giving Seeking. Power, greed and narcissism are all related in the inability to allow satisfaction. Greed and narcissism might be safely regarded as social diseases. Neoliberalism has reified greed and narcissism into power, but they are, at their base, symptoms of profound, emotional lack of power over self. The same is true of contempt. Contempt is a relationship action that cuts someone else down to size. It is also a symptom of powerlessness and a projective process that gives the feeling of being small and helpless to someone else in thought and action. Contempt is a social disease, and often directed at aspects of self in internal human groups.

Although I have been writing in the abstract about the group dimension and the way that human group nodes carry groups around with them, it is only in real human contact, in actual groups, that the best, emotionally corrective moments can occur. These are the moments that are needed to contain and reflect upon power, conflict, projections and introjections in order to promote group coherence, liberation of self with others and recreate the *polis* in politics and economics. These face-to-face moments are not easy and sometimes take time, effort, pain and patience. This is the importance of good experiences in everyday groups of different kinds to create the kind of democracy and democratic dialogue that is needed to escape from the time of monsters and enter the world yet to come, of permanent reform and permanent revolution.

Many everyday groups are manifested in conversations in dyads. Many of these conversations are silenced if one dyadic part of a group conversation is silent or silenced. One of the advantages of thinking in and about groups is that others in the group can feel, think, and help with finding the feelings and their accurate locations, when some of the group voices are disabled. Morris Nitsun, perhaps, best exemplifies the initial thinking about what might be needed for group members in everyday groups to be able to gain the right amount of power, intimacy and trust in order to enable dialogues and provide emotionally corrective experiences for each other and thus for themselves. For Nitsun, a group analyst, this happens in the technique of the conductor. For Nitsun, the key to understanding and containing conflict and acting out in groups is to recognise the manifest and latent destructive aspects of the group.

Nitsun identifies the anti-group as always present in the group, but not always apparent or manifest. He is particularly concerned about hatred and aggression as it appears in the group, as well as directed at the group. This hatred and aggression, Rage and Fear, as coming from failed dependence and from interrupted Seeking, is often about power and authority. This means that the location of the disturbance most likely lies in the power and authority of the conductor, but often is directed at a scapegoat, someone who has a valence for holding the negative feelings of others in the group. For Nitsun, the most important role of the conductor is to be attentive and aware of the anti-group, to be able to help the group to recognise the processes and to share them through empathy and resonance. If the anti-group processes can be experienced and thought about, then the creativity, healing power and liberation of the group can be realised. For Nitsun, the anti-group is a necessary part of the processes of creativity, healing and liberation. The substitution of cohesion for coherence ('We are all the same'), denies the conflict and power issues that lie at the heart of group creativity and possibilities for dialogue. Hatred and Rage are often the most difficult. However, it is important that these are expressed directly because often the kinds of conflicts that are affecting all the group members in different ways are only understandable when emotions can be openly expressed. Sometimes, group members are scapegoated with good things and envied. The group conductor may also only know about the anti-group through their own countertransference responses in the projective processes of the group. Sometimes the group can only remain whole in the mind of the conductor. The conductor must resist any tendencies to split the group in their own mind and take care not to project their feelings back into the group in terms of retaliation or neglect. In terms of acting out, the presence of the anti-group might be indicated by absences, lateness, transgressing group norms and silences. In everyday groups, leaders may not be so aware.

In everyday groups, where the difference between group leaders and group followers is not so obvious, dialogue depends upon each group member combining involvement and detachment to attend to both Care (pro-group) and Panic/Grief (anti-group) dynamics in the moment-to-moment of the group, maintain a sense of wholeness of the group and help to find the conflicts expressed in the here-and-now where they can be spoken, heard and modified. This means that each group member takes some part of the conductor role, that is, to be facilitative as well as to take risks with feelings. In coherent groups, group members can be aware of others and take turns. In everyday groups, the group, including family groups, are continuous with culture. This means that the group is the target of change, but also the force for change. This is where group consciousness needs to begin.

In effect, any kind of polarisation is a symptom of a social illness. Bipolar states of aggregation and massification, as Earl Hopper points out, are non-dialectic and oscillating states of extreme bonding to absence of bonding. Bipolar opposites that cannot be brought into dialogue and create splits and factions can be considered another social illness, based on the presumption of cohesion and the splitting-off difference and conflict. Humans add equality and coherence to mammal tendencies to dominance hierarchies, though the Care, Panic/Grief and Play foundational feelings. In this sense, power relationships are more usefully thought about as homeostatic processes than as structures or even institutions. Power relationships can become easily unbalanced and perhaps more difficult to rebalance. Rebalancing from moment to moment includes an awareness of the coherent voices in the group, including those that might be silenced. Rebalancing power in relationships may very well require finding common ground, trust and intimacy in both economic and political dialogues.

For economic dialogues, it is important to return to Keynes and the question of who decides. I believe that Keynes wrote the General Theory as a treatise for humanisation of the economy. This is why it is so cryptic, as well as brilliant. Humanising the economy will require a de-emphasis on the values of continuous growth, efficiency, productivity and other economic concepts that are only applicable to preserving and honouring the first inequality in capitalism, which is the separation of labour and capital. Labour and capital are both part of dynamic and complex processes that need each other in community dialogues that Keynes identified as 'psychological variables'. Labour and capital do not need to be polarised into class interests if the interests of humanity are recognised as now becoming hegemonic and creating common ground. Workers are now capable of sharing, owning and looking after their own means of production. Socialism and capitalism are no longer relevant polarised concepts if the question of who decides can become part of larger group and community dialogues that are capable of bringing about permanent reform and permanent revolution. These movements can start from the grass roots.

Keynes' ideas about consumption and investment in relatively poorer communities have echoes in the immediate return economies of the hunter-gatherers. Of course, we do not want or need to return to the past. However, it is possible to go into the future with ideas about redistribution, working cooperatively through dialogue, privileging good relationships and, above all, trust. Emotional understanding is also part of the science of economics. Economics is about planning for the future. The psy professions, on the other hand, understand that humans project the past into the future as well as the present. Freud (1919) wrote about how fears of the future are always based on events, relationships and traumas in the past. Keynes wrote about how these psychological tendencies lead to unpredictable outcomes. Keynes also wrote about how the differences between the short-term thinking about the future and the long-term thinking about can lead to very different outcomes. Economics must take on the responsibility for thoughts about generations of future people. The short-term thinking and actions of neoliberalism are killing the planet, and with it, perhaps, all life forms in the universe. This is no longer a choice. It is a necessity.

In the present historical constellation, politics is hegemonic over economics. Money is no longer about production but about extraction and power. In the questions of who decides, political parties are important. Political parties are groups, institutions and organisations that are capable of organising and promoting ways of people to decide together. If the party cannot organise a better democracy for itself, it cannot create one. Consciousness and knowledge of all the group dimension and dynamics that have been mentioned here are crucial to creating the changes needed. This consciousness, which is at base a recognition and renewal of recognition of what it means to be biologically and emotionally human cannot be ignored any longer as if it did not exist. The process of opening up the consciousness of the group that can lead to dialogue depends upon a concerted effort to enter into dialogue and to root out conflicts, silences, operations of silencing and othering that come from conflicts and potential conflicts, etc. Rooting out of conflicts must be faced over dialogues that include racial, gender, cultural and sexual differences. It is not good enough to wait until after the revolution. If people cannot be encouraged to take over their political self-regulation and representation in a better kind of democracy, then we will never be able to leave the time of monsters and enter a world yet to come.

This process, too, involves a decolonisation of minds from neoliberalism and from extractive capitalism. Money can no longer be the only reason to do things. Money is only a fictitious symbol of value. Money is valuable only because it mirrors the goods and values in society. It needs to be treated as such. Heteronormative patriarchy is no longer relevant in the modern world. Women can do just what men can do; the differences are miniscule compared to the importance of being able to work together in equality. The same things holds for race, gender, sexual and ability differences. Having these dialogues depends upon each and every human group node being willing and able to take their turn at tracing the ebbs and flows of Seeking and the other foundational feelings and using them to walk towards conflict and contain it to find the creative solutions in every dialogue. This takes time and patience.

I am coming to the end of this work. However, I do not consider this to be an ending, but a beginning. I hope that all that I have written here has been able to touch my readers with what they already know about themselves and others.

It is no little irony that, as I write this last part of my life's work, I believe that I am dying of lung cancer. My lung cancer may very well be a symbol of the disorganising and destructive effects of neoliberalism to humanity, as it takes me over while I wait for my bodily care and reinforcement from chemotherapy. Will it come soon enough? Although it may not come soon enough for me, I consider this to be just a beginning of seeds of ideas that are starting to become more needed, popular and spreading. I hope that I have been able to express the ideas in the best way and that this expression of these ideas become elaborated in many more works. I would love to continue to part of this process, but I fear that my contribution must end soon. I hope that each of my readers will be able to take away something new and important to grow in their internal and external groups and pursue the renewing effects of liberation.

References

Bion, W. (1961) *Experiences in Groups, and Other Papers*. Hove: Brunner-Routledge.

Foulkes, S. H. (1948) *Introduction to Group-analytic Psychotherapy: Studies in the Social Integration of Individuals and Groups*. London: Maresfield Reprints.

Freud, S. (1919) '"A Child is Being Beaten": A Contribution to the Study of the Origin of Sexual Perversions', in J. Strachey (ed.), *The Standard Edition of the Complete Psychological Works of Sigmund Freud*, Vol. XVII. London: The Hogarth Press and the Institute of Psycho-Analysis.

Kent, J. (2021) 'Scapegoating and the "angry black woman"', *Group Analysis*, 54(3): 354–371.

Kinouani, G. (2019) 'Difference, Whiteness and the group analytic matrix', *Group Analysis*, 53(1): 60–74.

Klein, M. (1986) *The Selected Melanie Klein* (edited by J. Mitchell). Harmondsworth: Peregrine.

Nayak, S. (2014) *Race, Gender and the Activism of Black Feminist Theory: Working with Audre Lorde*. Abingdon and New York: Routledge.

Stacey, R. (2003) *Complexity and Group Process: A Radically Social Understanding of Individuals*. Hove: Brunner Routledge.
Stock Whittaker, D. (2000) *Using Groups to Help People*. London and New York: Routledge and Kegan Paul.
Strachey, J. (1934) 'The nature of the therapeutic action of psycho-analysis', *International Journal of Psycho-Analysis*, 15: 127–159.
Zinkin, L. (1983) 'Malignant Mirroring', *Group Analysis*, 16(2): 113–126.

Index

acetylcholine 116, 122, 128, 149, 150
acting out 184, 188, 189
actions: Arendt on 47, 48–49; producing complexity 48–49; speech and 47
adrenocorticotropic hormone (ACTH) 143
AEA *see* American Enterprise Association
AEI *see* American Enterprise Institute
Affective Neuroscience (Panksepp) 108, 109, 145
aggregation 37, 39–42, 43, 54, 61–62, 76, 177, 189; *see also* massification
American Enterprise Association (AEA) 64
American Enterprise Institute (AEI) 64
American War of Independence 22
amygdala: Fear pathway 122, 123, 126, 129; Play and 150; Rage pathway 128; Seeking pathway 115
animal feelings 110, 111; *see also* foundational feelings
animal laborans 20, 21, 34, 36, 46, 49; idea of 29, 30; labour of 36, 74; as women's work 30, 75, 138
animal spirits 44–45
anonymity 171
anti-group 188–189
anti-labour ideas 64
antisemitism 34, 59
anxiety 121, 123, 137, 143, 147, 173
The Archaeology of the Mind (Panksepp and Biven) 109
Ardipithecus ramidus 86
Arendt, Hannah 8, 20–21; on actions 47, 48–49; on freedom 49, 79–80; happiness for 36; *The Human Condition* 8, 19–20, 79; on labour *vs.* work 46; Marx's socialised man for 28–29; on mere talk *vs.* speech 47; social for 48; on speaking and acting 47; *vita activa* for 20, 29, 36; *see also animal laborans*

art, works of 46, 47
assembly line manufacture 34
Australopithecus afarensis 84, 86–90, 101; bipedalism 87; brain and brain change 87–89, 90; dominance hierarchies 89; as object of feline predators 90; sexual dimorphism 87, 90–91; walking 87
auto-shaping 118, 169, 173
awakening 26

Banking Act of 1935 36, 50
Bank of England 24
basic assumptions 173
bed nucleus of the stria terminalis (BNST) 146
Begun, David 81–82
benzodiazepines (BZs) 123, 147
Beveridge Report of 1942 50
biological sociability 103
Bion, Wilfred 172–173, 174, 175, 176, 177, 178, 181, 186, 187
Biven, Lucy 109–110
Black Death 13–14
Bloomsbury Group 33
BNST *see* bed nucleus of the stria terminalis
Bohm-Bawerk, Eugen von 30
bonding windows 141–143; *see also* Care
bonobos 13, 81, 82, 83, 84–87, 88, 91, 94–96, 97, 119, 129, 136; *see also* chimpanzees
boundaries to human affairs 48
Bowling Green State University in Ohio 109
brain: *Australopithecus afarensis* 87–89, 90; as black box 151; primary process layer 111; secondary process layer 111; septal area 128–129; tertiary process layer 111; *see also* foundational feelings

Index

Brain-Derived Neural Growth Factors (BDNF) 150
BrainMind 112
Bretton Woods Agreement 50, 56, 66, 68
Britain 30–31; capitalism in 13–14; Chartist Movement 24; Combination Acts 22, 23; Factory Acts (1833 and 1834) 23; industrial hegemony 23; money and industry 15–16; Poor Laws 14–15, 16, 17, 22, 23, 30; post-First World War 35; Reform Act 23, 24; workers' organisations 22–23; *see also* Keynes, John Maynard (Keynesian economics); neoliberalism
British Trades Union Congress 30
Burns, Lizzie 26
Burns, Mary 26
Bushmen *see* San

Callaghan, James 69
Capital (Marx) 26–28; response to 30–31
capitalism 2, 11–31; dialectical conflicts 27–28; forces of 21–22; group dimension 21, 28–30; *see also* neoliberalism
care 138–144; birds and 140; bonding windows 141–143; co-creation 140–141; evolution of 155; humans and 138, 139; Lust and 139; mammals and 139, 140; motherhood and 138; neuropeptides 141; Panic/Grief and 140, 145, 146, 147, 153, 167; as power relationship 155, 187; receiving and giving 143; reptiles and 139–140
cerebral asymmetries 94
Chamberlain, Neville 50
charity 74
Chartist Movement 24
Chicago School of Economics 64–65, 66
childcare: changing from gentle to aggressive 164
chimpanzees 12–13, 81, 82, 83, 84–91, 94–96, 97, 101, 109, 129, 136, 162–164, 187; *see also* bonobos
Clause IV 35
collectivism 59
collectivist greed 58
Combination Acts 22, 23
communication 125, 156, 161, 164, 166, 180–182, 186, 187; acting out as 184; alpha elements 181; Fear as 169; group analysis 170; patterns of 175; projective processes 167, 182–183; Rage as 131, 169; as therapy 174–176, 180; unconscious 167, 168
communism 11, 30
consolidation 126–127
consumption 29, 30; automation of labour and 46; employment and 41, 54; gap between income and 39, 41; Hayek's economics 54, 57; Keynesian economics 40–41, 75, 190; Seeking (feeling) and 116, 117, 120, 149, 168
contagion 171; emotional contagion and 119–120; *see also* group mind
contemplation 20
contempt: as relationship action 188; as social disease 188
corticotropin-releasing factor (CRF) 122–123, 143, 146–147, 149
countertransference 156, 168, 189
COVID-19 crisis 70
Cro-Magnons 93

dark laughter 150
Darwin, Charles 111, 113
Dawkins, Richard 101
decolonisation 5, 74, 161, 191; from neoliberalism 2–3, 102–103
de Maré, Patrick 8, 175–177, 178, 186–187
detachment 165–166
dialectic/dialectical thinking 26, 27
dialogue 45, 74–76, 80, 102–103, 135, 157, 170, 175, 176, 189–191; consciousness 100, 164; containing conflict and differences 4, 7, 29; decisions making ability and 114; democracy and 1–2, 20, 21, 43, 79, 112; detachment and 166, 168; double-bind figurations and 166; feelings and 3, 186–187; group analysis and 125; individualism and 3; intellectual 62; internal integration 5–6; Keynesian economics 33, 75–76; for knowledge of thoughts and feeling 100; maximising 164; patriarchal heteronormativity and 136; polarisations as reason for 2; political 139, 143; politics of 74–75, 138; reflective processes and 186; resistance and 164–165; Seeking and 119, 121; sexual division of labour 30; singularities and integrational coherence 152; small

groups 30; thinking and 154–155; *see also* communication
division of labour 96, 137; mammals 137; Marx on 27; sexual 101, 138
dominance hierarchies 84–85, 100, 155; *A. afarensis* 89; male 84; Rage and 129–130
dorsal pre-optic area (dPOA) 146
double-bind figurations 165–166, 175
Dryopithecus 81, 87, 89, 119; brain size 82, 84; dominance hierarchies 84–85; fruit eater 82; groups 83–84; as LCA of great apes 82; suite of characteristics 82–84
dynorphin 146

Early Miocene Epoch 82
economic crises of the 1970s 63–64
The Egalitarians – Human and Chimpanzee (Power) 162
Elias, Norbert 8, 17, 29, 47, 48, 62, 75, 76, 80, 81, 102, 162, 164, 171, 176, 177, 180, 187; civilising process 8; figurations *see* figurations; group processes 80; *Involvement and Detachment* 165; *vita activa* 29; war as self-feeding processes 165
employment: Keynes on 37, 38, 39–40; social psychological variable 39
Engels, Friedrich 28, 32, 34; *The Condition of the Working Class in England* 24, 26; father of 25, 26
English Civil War (1642–1651) 16
English Poor Laws 14–15, 16, 17, 22, 23, 30
evolution 7–8
The Evolution of Thought (Russon and Begun) 81
expectation 39, 43, 44
experience-near concepts 166–167
Experiences in Groups and Other Papers (Bion) 172

Fabian Society 13, 31, 32, 33, 35, 37, 42, 53, 63
facial expressions, universality of 111
Factory Acts (1833 and 1834) 23
Fear 121–127; anxiety 123; chemicals 123; learning and 126; neuropeptides and neurotransmitters 122–123; pain and 122; sympathetic nervous system 123; triggering 182; *see also* Seeking

FEE *see* Foundation for Economic Education
feelings 3, 4, 7, 80; animal 110, 111; art and 47; foundational *see* foundational feelings; of freedom 80 *see also* freedom; importance of 3; individualism and 3; Keynes on 38; Panksepp on 110–114; process layers (of brain) 111; thoughts and 100
female bodies 94–95
female bonding 130
female dominance hierarchies 130
fertility 94–95
figurations 8, 17, 75, 157, 164, 170, 185; defined 162; double-bind 165–166, 175
Ford, Henry 34, 38
Foulkes, S. H. 8, 17, 29, 47, 48, 62, 75, 80, 81, 102, 157, 164, 166, 173–178, 180, 181, 182, 183, 185–186, 187
foundational feelings 7, 109, 110, 111–114; Care *see* Care; communication *see* communication; as conscious 167; as contagious 167; Fear *see* Fear; Lust *see* Lust; modulations 167; Panic/Grief *see* Panic/Grief; Play *see* Play; Rage *see* Rage; Seeking *see* Seeking
Foundation for Economic Education (FEE) 64
free association 175, 178
freedom 14, 58, 62, 80; Arendt on 49, 79–80; choice and 79; concept of 22; feeling of 80; of neoliberalism 79
free enterprise 58–59
free-floating discussion 175, 178
French Revolution 22
Freud, Sigmund 113, 154
Friedman, Milton 64, 66, 67, 68
functionless investor 45

GABA 123, 128, 143, 149
General Theory of Employment, Interest and Money (Keynes) 6, 36
George, Lloyd 35
Germany 11; anticapitalism in 59; antisemitism in 34, 59; fascism in 11, 58; post-Frist World War reparations 35; Revolution of 1918-1919 34; state investment in economy 36
Glass-Steagall Act of 1933 36
glutamate 123, 128, 143, 149

Gombe Stream Research Centre in Tanzania 162
Goodall, Jane 101, 161; *In the Shadow of Man* 161
Gramsci, Antonio 8, 11
grassroots movements 74
Great Britain *see* Britain
greed 117, 119, 120, 132, 169, 170; collectivist 58; Play and 150–151; power and 187–188
Grief *see* Panic/Grief
Griphopithecus 82
group: as basis for thought and action 75–76; belonging to 170; contexts and changes in contexts of 162–165; group analytic 170–171; human evolution and 161; as implied collective 161; individuals and 161; Le Bon on 171; neoliberal individualism destroying 156–157; taken-for-granted 171; unconscious 171
group analysis 8, 170–178; communication *see* communication; dialogue and 125; psychoanalysis and 125, 127, 166, 168
group analytic moment 171–172; *see also* Northfield Experiment
Group Analytic Society (GAS) 8, 177
group mind 171
Group Psychology and the Analysis of the Ego (Freud) 171
group size 176–177; emotional impact of 176; large 176; as silo 176–177; small 176
group space: for personal and social integration 177–178; therapeutic 177

Harrison, Tom 172
Hayek, Friedrich: as anti-Marxist 53; 'Colloque Walter Lippmann' 63; on democracy 58; fears 58, 60; on freedom 62; impersonal forces 59; on liberal socialism 59; on money 57, 58; on monopolies 57, 59–60; on planning 57, 58; *The Road to Serfdom* 6, 55–63; on social welfare 57; on unemployment 60, 61
Hitler, Adolf 34, 36, 55, 171, 174
Holloway, Ralph 88–89
hominins 93–94
Homo clausus 171
Homo erectus 93
Homo ergaster 93

homo faber 20, 21, 30, 34, 35, 36, 46, 47, 75, 138
Homo habilis 93, 94
Homo sapiens 94
hoover-up effect 71
Hopper, Earl 189
The Human Condition (Arendt) 8, 19–20, 79
humanisation of economy 189–190

ideological struggle 11
immediate-return economy 97, 163; *vs.* delayed-return 163
impartial reasoning 17
individualism 3, 45, 56, 60, 70, 73, 112, 119; neoliberal 156–157
industrial hegemony 23
instincts as drives 111
Institute of Group Analysis (IGA) 177
Institute of Public Policy Research (IPPR) 70
International Monetary Fund 50
intersectionality 2, 184–191
investment market 43–44
Invisible College 172, 176
Involvement and Detachment (Elias) 165

Karl Marx and the Close of his System (Bohm-Bawerk) 30
Keynes, John Maynard (Keynesian economics) 6, 7, 33–46; animal spirits for 44–45; Bloomsbury Group 33; booms and busts for 61; demand and supply 39; dialogue and 33, 75–76; *The Economic Consequences of the Peace* 35; education of 33; expectation 39; family background 33; *The General Theory* 36, 76; individualism for 45; macroeconomics 37; Paris Peace Conference 35; profit for 39; revolutionary ideas 35–36; state economics 36, 37; threats to liberal capitalism 62; Victorian morals and 33
Kinouani, G. 184, 185
Klein, Melanie 172
Knight, Chris 95
Kohut, Heinz 166

Labour Party 32, 33, 34, 35, 53, 69
Last Common Ancestor (LCA) 81–82
Last Universal Common Ancestor (LUCA) 81

Index   197

leadership, group 172–173; passive 173
Leakey, Louis 162
Le Bon, Gustave 171
Lee, Richard B. 97, 98–99, 187
Lewin, Kurt 172
life 152–153
Lippmann, Walter 50; *An Inquiry into the Principles of The Good Society* 63
London School of Economics 32, 53
London Stock Exchange 22
lordosis 134, 135, 136
Luhnow, Harold 64, 65, 66
Lust 130, 132–138; brain pathways 133–135; gendered bodies 133–135; group dimension 137–138; sexual behaviour 136–137
Luxemburg, Rosa 34

Main, Tom 174
Mannheim, Karl 173–174
Marshall, Alfred 33
Marx, Jenny 25, 26–27
Marx, Karl 12, 24, 34, 51; adult life 25; Arendt's critique of 28–29; death of 32; Jenny and 25, 26–27; socialised man of 28–29
Marxism: criticism and counter-discourse 30–31
massification 61–62, 177, 189; *see also* aggregation
mass production 34
Matte Blanco, Ignacio 167–168
medial frontal cortex 122
median groups 176
memories 141; consolidation 126–127
MindBrain 112
mirroring 186
mixed sex groups 84, 129, 137–138, 155
money: industry and 15–16; inequality 72–73
monopolies 59–60
Mont Pelerin Society (MPS) 13, 16, 32, 53, 63, 64–65, 66
MPS *see* Mont Pelerin Society

National Health Service (NHS) 50, 56, 61, 67
negative feelings 116, 117
neoliberalism 66–76; behaviourist thinking 151; decolonisation from 2–3, 102–103; devastating effects 70–73; freedom of 79; mental health and 184; as new narrative 79
neuroscience 108–109; psychoanalysis and 109–110
Nitsun, Morris 177, 178, 187, 188–189
Nitzgen, D. 172, 174, 178
noradrenaline 116
norepinephrine 116
Northfield Experiment 171–177

obsessive-compulsive disorders 119
oestrogen 130, 134–135, 140, 141
orgasm 133
oxytocin 128, 130, 137, 140, 141, 142, 143, 146, 149

palaeontology 81
Panic/Grief 113, 114, 121, 139, 140, 170, 183, 189; anxiety 123; Care and 140, 145, 146, 147, 153, 167; as conscious and contagious 167; CRF 146–147; depression and 147; distress vocalisations (DVs) 145–146; mammals and 145–146, 155; modulation 167; pathway 123, 145, 146–147; triggering 182
Panksepp, Jaak 7, 108–114; *Affective Neuroscience* 108, 109, 145; *The Archaeology of the Mind* (with Biven) 109; Biven and 109–110; death of 110; family background 109; foundational feelings *see* foundational feelings
Paris Commune 30, 171
Paris Peace Conference 35
Parker, Ian 159
Pavón-Cuéllar, David 159
periaqueductal grey area (PAG) 121–122, 128, 146; *see also* Fear
Play 117, 147–151; chemicals in 149; defined 148; dreaming and 150; epigenetic changes 150–151; humans and 148–149; mammals and 147, 148; neural pathways 148; rough and tumble noises 147, 148; Seeking and 148, 149–150; sensory systems 149; touch and 148, 149
polarisation as social illness 189
polis 13, 20, 21, 22, 29, 30, 36, 38, 49, 57, 108, 125, 135, 138, 143, 164, 170, 176, 177; demise of 74; grassroots communities remaking 74; history of

75; of large houses 75; as plurality of humans 80; politics and 48, 103; recouping 47
political parties 190
political realm 48
Poor Laws *see* English Poor Laws
posterior parietal cortex (PPC) 89
poverty 2, 36, 40, 61, 69–72, 102, 103; agriculture and 13; capitalist mode of production and 16; division of labour and 27; Factory Acts of 1834 23; freedom and 14; laissez-faire production 19, 24; Poor Laws and 14–15; wealth and 15; welfare state and 67
power 155–156; collectivism and 59; greed and 187–188; rebalancing in relationships 189
Power, Camilla 95
Power, Margaret 101, 162, 163–164, 165
price changes 54
primary process feelings: being conscious 111
primary process layer of brain 111
'Prison Notebooks' (Gramsci) 11
processes 2–3
production, capitalist mode of 12
progesterone 130, 135, 140
projection 155, 156; psychic processes of 156
projective processes 182–183
Prosperity and Justice: A Plan for a New Economy 70
protest 73–74
psychiatry 124–125
psychological crowd 171
psychology 125, 156
psychotherapy 125, 127
psy professions: behaviourists of 151; projective processes 182

racism 34
Rage 121, 127–131; aggressive feelings *vs.* 130; chemicals promoting 128; deprivation leading to 127–129; dominance hierarchies 129–130; healing 130; as overwhelming 131; power and 130; as rapid attack 128; septal area of brain in 128–129; triggering 182; *see also* Seeking
Reform Act 23, 24
reparations: post-First World War 35
reptiles 139–140

resistance 73–74, 164–165
resonance 181, 182, 186, 188
Rickman, John 172, 173, 175
Rivers, W. H. R. 172
The Road to Serfdom (Hayek) 6, 55–63
Robbins, Lionel 53
robots 184
Roosevelt, Franklin D. 36, 53–54
runaway brain 93–94, 112, 126; emotional contagion and 119–120
Russon, Anne 81–82

San 96–99; as egalitarian 97; food sharing 97–98; indirect competition 99; population 97; residential shift 99
schizophrenia 119
Scott-Heron, Gil 105
secondary process layer of brain 111
Seeking 22, 39, 115–121; absence 116, 117–118, 152; addictions and 117, 169; dopamine pathway 116, 118–119; drugs and 117; ebbs and flows 116; emotional contagion of 119; happiness and 120; learning and 117, 118; libido and 117, 125; life preservation and 152–153; losing and restoring 169–170; maintaining awareness of 168–169; making memories 118; as reward 116–117, 121; tracking 168; as value free 170; withdrawal of 121; *see also* Fear; Rage
selective serotonin reuptake inhibitors (SSRI) 123
selfish gene 91
The Selfish Gene (Dawkins) 101
sexual cells 133
sexual interactions 141
sexual jealousy 130
sexual relations 163–164
sexual reproduction 133
Shaw, George Bernard 32
shell shock neurosis 172
singularities 152; complexity and 152, 153
size of group *see* group size
Smith, Adam 13, 16–19, 20, 26, 27, 28, 48, 49, 80; Hayek and 54, 55; invisible hand 28, 29, 54; *The Theory of Moral Sentiments* 16, 17; *The Wealth of Nations* 16, 18–19, 22, 25
socialism 2, 11
speech: action and 47; mere talk *vs.* 47

Stacey, Ralph 186
state intervention 41–43

territoriality 163
tertiary process layer of brain 111
testosterone 128, 130, 134, 135, 141
Thatcher, Margaret 61, 77, 79, 81, 101; election 68, 69; foreign exchange controls and 50; housing policy 69; neoliberalism of 69–70; privatising nationalised industries 72
The Theory of Moral Sentiments (Smith) 16, 17
thinking/thoughts 3, 110; behaviourist 151; dialectic/dialectical 26, 27; dialogue and 154–155
think tanks 63–64; United States (US) 64
totalitarianism 54–55, 59, 61, 62; fear of 60
Totem and Taboo (Freud) 171
trade unions 30
transference 156, 168
translation 186
Treaty of Versailles 35
trickle-down effect 71

unconscious/unconsciousness 111; logics 167–168; Matte Blanco on 167–168; thinking processes and 110
Unemployment Assistance Boards, Britain 36
United States (US): Banking Act of 1935 36, 50; Glass–Steagall Act of 1933 36; Keynesian economists in 50; stock market crash of 1929 35, 36, 49

vasotocin 139–140
ventral tegmental area (VTA) 115, 140, 141, 146
vita activa 20, 29, 36
von Westphalen, Jenny *see* Marx, Jenny

wages 37, 39–40, 71–72
Watt, James 18
The Wealth of Nations (Smith) 16, 18–19, 22, 25
Webb, Beatrice 32
Webb, Sidney 32
Wilson, Edmond O. 101
Wolpoff, M. H. 87, 90–91
women 13, 24, 191; as *animal laborans* 30, 75; Bloomsbury Group 33; changes in bodies 100–101; public works employment 41–42; Reform Act and 23; San and 97; sexual division of labour 97, 101; suffrage 35; work of 19, 20, 21, 138
work 12; Arendt on 46; Keynes on 37–38; of men 19, 20, 138; as production cost and basis of demand 39–40; without adequate pay 71–72; of women 19, 20, 21, 138; mammals 137; Marx on 27; sexual 101, 138; *see also* division of labour
workers/working classes: British 22–23, 30–31; capitalists and 22–23; consumers as well as producers 38; Keynes on 37–38
World Bank 50

zero hours contracts 71

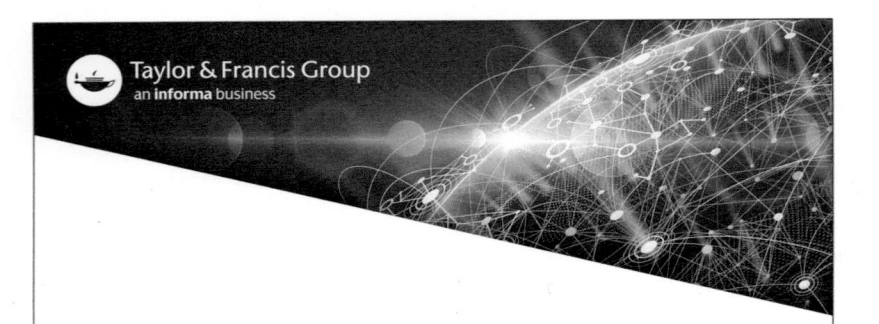